Maharani's Misery

Maharani's Misery

Narratives of a Passage from India to the Caribbean

Verene A. Shepherd

THE UNIVERSITY OF THE WEST INDIES PRESS

Barbados • Jamaica • Trinidad and Tobago

University of the West Indies Press
1A Aqueduct Flats Mona
Kingston 7 Jamaica

06 05   5 4 3 2

CATALOGUING IN PUBLICATION DATA

Shepherd, Verene.
Maharani's misery : narratives of a passage from India to the
Caribbean / Verene A. Shepherd.
p. cm.
Includes bibliographical references and index.

ISBN: 976-640-121-7

1. Maharani (Indentured servant). 2. Women, East Indian – Guyana –
History – 1803–1966. 3. Allanshaw (Schooner). 4. Indentured servants –
Guyana – History. 5. Indentured servants – Guyana –
Trials, litigation, etc. I. Title.

F2391.E2S53 2002   988.102

Cover illustration: The *Allanshaw*, 1874. *Illustrated London News,*
12 November 1881, 472. Print by courtesy of the National Maritime
Museum, Greenwich, London (neg. 58/5569).

Set in Adobe Garamond 11/14 x 27.
Book and cover design by Robert Harris
E-mail: roberth@cwjamaica.com

Printed on acid-free paper.
Printed in Canada.

Dedicated to

Maharani and others who died on the passage from India

*Chandra Kumari, who outsmarted the immigration
officials in Jamaica*

and

*Mrs Beryl Williamsingh, one of the first women on the executive
committee of the once active East Indian Progressive Society,
and the current president of the National Council on
Indian Culture in Jamaica*

CONTENTS

ILLUSTRATIONS

TABLES

CAST OF CHARACTERS

The following are the principal actors in this tragic account. The spelling of names is inconsistent in the various accounts, but in the case of the crew, the spelling in the crew list has been maintained.

A.H. Alexander	Immigration agent general, Guyana
J. Erickson (Allickson)	Able seaman
John (Emmanuel) Anderson	Able seaman
Alexander Bain (Bayne)	Able seaman
G.A. Banbury	Emigration agent, St Helena
Colonel Blunt	Acting governor of St Helena
Charles Bruce	Government secretary, colonial Guyana
Chitamun	Passenger
Mr Clarke	Barrister-at-law for Nourse Limited
William Clintworth (Clansworth, Clentworth)	Cabin boy
George Colthurst (Colthirst)	Second officer/mate
Thomas David (Daly)	Able seaman
Godfrey W. de la Mare	Chief officer/first mate
Dr Finlayson	Georgetown doctor
Golap	Indian nurse in the ship's hospital and herself an emigrant
James T. Grant	Assistant compounder (dispenser)
Dr Robert Grieve	Acting chief medical officer, Immigration Department, colonial Guyana and later acting surgeon general

Dr E.A. Hardwicke	Surgeon-superintendent
Heerdayaram (Hurdayram)	Hospital attendant, dispenser
J.C. Homagee	Law officer of the Crown, St Helena
Robert Ipson	Able seaman accused of raping Maharani
Henry Irving	Governor of colonial Guyana
Henry Kirke	Police magistrate and sheriff of Demerara
Lutchmun	Cabin boy, hospital attendant (return emigrant)
William Lee	Able seaman
William Leslie	Ship's steward
Maharani	The victim
August Makohl	Ship's engineer
Mohadaya (Mahadarie)	Female emigrant (return emigrant)
Molai (Molarie)	Sirdar
Moorti (Murti)	Female emigrant (return emigrant)
Nandhal (Nandoolall)	Chief compounder/dispenser (babu/baboo)
Nathur	Sweeper (topaz/topass)
James Joseph O'Brien	Able seaman
James Oliver (Olliver)	Able seaman (Ipson's alleged co-conspirator)
A. (J.) Peterson	Able seaman
Ramyadd (Ramjead)	Passenger and cook
Ramkhelawan	Sirdar
Rupia	Fellow patient in the ship's hospital with Maharani
Sesahoye (Sisahari, Sisheya)	Cook (return emigrant)
John Smith	Able seaman
Walter R.S. Stokes	Third officer/third mate
G. Soderland (Sutherland)	Able seaman
William Urquhart	Sailmaker
Joseph Warner	Able seaman
Frederick C. Wilson	Captain
E.F. Wright	Inspector of police, colonial Guyana

PREFACE

SINCE THE 1980s SCHOLARS have subjected the experiences of Indians who were affected by what Madhavi Kale has described as "[British] imperial labour reallocation"[1] to the colonial Caribbean, to more rigorous gender analysis, seeking to problematize the idea that under immigration and indentureship, despite broad similarities in the class/caste position of the majority, the status of Indian women and men was not equal. Most of those who have employed gender analysis in their accounts of Indian labour migration have made immigrant women central to their discourse. The focus on Indian women is a reflection of the impact of the historiographical revolution of the 1960s and 1970s which resulted in a pluralization of the discourse on the experiences of subaltern people and the new attempt by academic feminists, in the aftermath of the emergence of "women's history", to target the masculinist project that served to disarticulate the subaltern as woman.

This book seeks to contribute to the ongoing archaeological project of excavating gender-differentiated data on the nineteenth-century movement of Indians to the colonial Caribbean in order to understand better the nature of the indentured Indians' experiences, especially as they undertook the passage from India. More specifically, the book represents a contribution to that genre of historical writing that focuses on the exercise of social power and authority, through the medium of socio-sexual manipulation, by empowered males over less empowered women. Essentially a case study, the book combines documentary evidence with a surrounding narrative interpretation in order to highlight the experiences of the emigrant woman, Maharani, who died subsequent to an alleged raped on board the ship *Allanshaw* that sailed from Calcutta to colonial Guyana in 1885. While the voyage was problem-ridden, with a near "mutiny" by some of the sailors, the circumstances under which Maharani died were primarily responsible for the four investigations held into the voyage of the ship in that year. The one in colonial Guyana lasted nine days and involved some twenty-two witnesses, including some of the emigrants themselves. By making use of the depositions of the emigrants who were asked to testify, the book *attempts* to project the voices of marginalized bonded people, though the negative outcome of the case brings into sharp focus Gayatri Spivak's insightful question, "Can the subaltern speak?"[2] But by 1885 the ideological terrain upon which indentured "labour migration" had been constructed was firmly in place. Representations of racial and gender inequality had already found roots in the colonial setting in both India and the Caribbean.

I should like to record my profound gratitude to those who assisted me as I embarked on the difficult task of compiling this problematic book with its depressing subject matter. First of all, I express great appreciation to my husband, Bramwell, and my sons, Duane and Deane, who supported me in my "temporary exile" to research and complete the first draft of the book. The staff at the Public Record Office, Kew, London, not only fetched documents in their usual timely and efficient manner but were efficient in the reproduction of the numerous pages of documents on this case that I needed. The Public Record Office also gave permission to publish the documents. I thank the University of the West Indies, Mona, for the sabbatical year off which facilitated my research trip to London. I am indebted to the Institute of Commonwealth Studies, London, for the visiting fellowship which gave me much needed facilities for working on the manuscript. I am particularly grateful to the director of the Institute of Commonwealth Studies, Professor Pat Caplan, for her hospitality. Others in London, notably colleagues Professor Mary Turner, Marika Sherwood, Professor Gad Heuman, Ruth Heuman and Dr John Campbell (who also helped me with the photocopy order from the Public Record Office); friends Annette and Philip Brade, Hilrett Owusu and Cherry Brown; and family members Angella Lazarus and Sylvia Martin, gave support and hospitality. I am also indebted to Professor Bridget Brereton of the St Augustine campus of the University of the West Indies, Professor Veronica Gregg of Hunter College and Professor Brij Lal of the Australian National University, who took time out of their busy schedules to read early drafts and provide valuable comments. Maxine Clarke, graduate student at the University of Cambridge, England, and Dr Clem Seecharan of the University of North London gave help with the newspaper search at Colindale and in Guyana, and I am indebted to them. For help with making sense of the medical evidence and the cause of Maharani's death, I thank Dr Kamla Dixon and Dr S. Wynter. Feedback at various conference and seminar fora at the Mona and St Augustine campuses of the University of the West Indies, the Institute of Commonwealth Studies in London and the University of Warwick also proved stimulating and invaluable.

I thank the College of Charleston for having me as scholar-in-residence for the spring semester of 2000 and for providing me with the time, space and other facilities vital for productive work. The assistance given by Professors John Rashford and Jack Parson, by the provost, Dr Conrad Festa, and by the director of women's studies, Professor Jeri Cabot, was really invaluable. I benefited from the kindness of Professor Marvin Dulaney, chair of history, and the administrative and other academic staff of the Department of History at the College of Charleston, in particular Professors Randy Sparks (now at Tulane) and Rosemary Brana-Shute.

I thank Professor Paul Lovejoy (director) and Professor David Trotman (associate director) of the York/UNESCO Nigerian Hinterland Project for appointing me network professor for the academic year 2000–2001, thereby providing me with further time off to complete several writing projects, including this book.

Finally, I thank Valerie Bedward and Grace Jutan for help with typing; Nadine Spence and Ahmed Reid for help with proofreading; Kerry-Ann Morris for help with bibliographical research; and the reviewers for their helpful comments and criticisms.

INTRODUCTION

SINCE THE 1970s, THE historical experiences of women have formed a more essential aspect of accounts of Caribbean history, beginning with the pioneering work of Lucille Mathurin Mair, Kamau Brathwaite and Barry Higman, and continuing in the works of Bridget Brereton, Hilary Beckles, Marrietta Morrissey, Barbara Bush, Verene Shepherd and many others.[1] More importantly, since the 1980s and the slow shift from women's history to gender history, the perspective of gender has assumed a more important role in analyses of Caribbean history. Scholars such as Brereton, Beckles, Rhoda Reddock, Linnette Vassell and Patricia Mohammed have shown that while the excavation of women's experiences is crucial to fill an empirical gap, gender analysis allows such experiences to be better contextualized.[2] This awareness of the necessity of looking at the relational aspect of men's and women's experiences has been reflected in the work on Indians, many of whom were relocated to colonial Caribbean plantations as indentured labourers in the aftermath of the complete abolition of African enslavement. The presence of Indian women in the new labour system in the region altered the epistemological foundations of Caribbean women's history. This was reflected in scholars' efforts to show awareness of the increasing ethnic heterogeneity in the Caribbean by adding ethnicity to the analytical categories of class, colour and gender.

Scholars such as sociologist Reddock, historians Shepherd, Rosemarijn Hoefte, Pieter Emmer and Walton Look Lai, and gender studies specialist Mohammed, building on the pioneering work of Keith Laurence have succeeded in uncovering a wealth of gender-differentiated data on the history of working-class Indians in the colonial Caribbean.[3] More specifically, as most of these scholars have targeted women in their discourse, the results of the new academic enquiry into Indian women's experiences have been instructive. We now know a great deal about women's reasons for emigration, the process of their recruitment, the explanations for the sexual disparity in migration schemes, women's integration as workers in the capitalistic plantation system and their experiences as rebels, mothers and wives on Caribbean plantations. However, the perspectives from which these scholars have analysed the Indian woman's experiences have not been unified.

Two conflicting, even dialectical arguments seem to have emerged. One is that the Indian woman's experience of emigration and indentureship was one of extreme hardship, exploitation and "sexploitation". The other, now closely associated with David Galenson, Emmer and David Northrup, although expressed by Charles Doorly since the early twentieth century, is that emigration was of significant material benefit to those who left India.[4] Emmer, for example, argued that emigration was a vehicle of female emancipation "from an illiberal, inhibiting and very hierarchical social system in India".[5] His view echoed the early sentiments of Doorly, protector of emigrants in the Madras Presidency, who, in a retrospective look at women's emigration in 1915, remarked: "I am convinced that emigration is a blessing to a large number of the women we send, and opens to them a way of escape from lives of misery, poverty and prostitution."[6] The first perspective, which reflects aspects of Joseph Beaumont's and Hugh Tinker's neo-slavery thesis, is most clearly articulated in the work of Reddock, Jeremy Poynting and Jo Beall, but it is also shared at differing levels by other scholars including Brij Lal for Fiji, Hoefte for Suriname, Shepherd for Jamaica, Marina Carter for Mauritius and Moses Seenarine for Guyana.[7] David Trotman's 1984 work on crime, including uxoricide, also highlights the role of Indian women as victims under the indentureship system.[8] The work done by some of these latter scholars reveal that even though the majority of Indian women arrived in the Caribbean as single, independent wage workers intent on bettering their lives (and some succeeded in this regard), wages were low and gender-discriminatory and tasks sex-typed, giving an overall advantage to male workers. Women's childcare responsibilities also affected the time spent at work outside the home, and therefore the level of their wages. These economic facts combined with clear evidence of sexual abuse and other forms of gendered tyranny toward Indian women determined that the overall conclusion of those who fall within the neo-slavery school of thought would differ drastically from Doorly's and Emmer's optimistic "material benefits" thesis. Indeed, after studying the fraudulent, deceptive, abusive and exploitative elements of the indentureship system, Beall argued strongly that Indian women suffered "ultraexploitability", Reddock that their whole experience was one of "freedom denied", and Poynting that they experienced "multiple oppression".[9]

These differing perspectives are reflective of the dichotomizing discourse on slavery and freedom that emerged in the aftermath of the abolition of slavery when the search for an alternative labour force intensified[10] and will no doubt continue to characterize the research problematic for some time. But it is arguable whether an either/or perspective is useful or sustainable in light of the paucity of gender-differentiated data on emigration and indentureship. No realistic refutation of the "material benefits thesis", for example, can be achieved without precise gender-differentiated quantitative data on remittances to India, money and jewellery taken back by repatriates, real estate and savings held in the colonies. The conclusion that emigration and indentureship can be located within the discourse of slavery is equally problematic, not only because no matter how harsh, the experiences of Indian women never approached the brutal conditions endured by African women but also because those who support this perspective have failed to provide the requisite sustained and systematic comparative analysis. Hugh Tinker's path-breaking *A New System of Slavery* does attempt such a comparison but lacks sufficient gender-differentiated data about the Middle Passage of slavers and the transatlantic passages of nineteenth-century emigrant ships. Indeed, the majority of studies that argue that Indian women suffered gender-differentiated exploitation as a result of leaving India, voluntarily or by force, have been located within the context of their recruitment in India, their experiences as workers on colonial plantations, and their encounter with white and Indian masculinity and gendered tyranny on the estates and in the private sphere. Far fewer works have been focused on the voyages from India, yet no definitive conclusion about the similarities between African enslavement and Indian emigration (assuming that a comparison makes sense) can be reached without studying the journeys from India and the abuses on the emigrant ships.

This present book does not attempt to settle the (unnecessarily?) dichotomizing neo-slavery/material benefits debate or to end the polarized discussions over the most appropriate model within which to locate the Indian woman's experiences of emigration and indentureship. Its objective is more modest. It simply provides empirical evidence from the passage from India that should certainly form a part of the ongoing interpretive debate. Its point of entry is at the level of gender-specific exploitation or, more precisely, "sexploitation" on emigrant ships. Even though comparative details on the treatment of enslaved African women on Middle Passage slavers and Indian women on nineteenth-century ships sailing from India to the colonial Caribbean are vital to the somewhat academic neo-slavery debate, empirical evidence of the sexploitation of emigrant women has not been a prominent part of the existing works on Indian emigration.[11]

The reasons for this research trend are unclear and have not really been sufficiently problematized in the historiographical essays on Indian immigration to the Caribbean. The reasons certainly cannot be attributed to lack of evidence of the abuse of Indian women in the documentary sources. The reports of colonial emigration and immigration officials,[12] the records of the Colonial Land and Emigration Commission, and the reports of the surgeons-superintendent on emigrant ships testify to the existence of, and their great concern over, the sexual abuse of Indian women on the passages from India. So great was this concern that regulations were laid down prohibiting "cohabitation" between the women and the crew and among emigrants themselves unless they embarked as couples. It was also obvious from the security measures, restrictive legislation, and the manipulation of both space and human cargo on the ships, that there was concern that such ships should not become spaces of "sexploitation", thus giving ammunition to the anti-slavery and anti-emigration causes.

The rape of enslaved women on Middle Passage slavers had been one of the most brutal manifestations of gendered tyranny during slavery, and pro-immigration forces, concerned with avoiding any charge that Indian emigration was a new system of slavery, attempted to use legislation to prevent similar treatment of emigrant women. But the distance between regulations and practice was equally evident from the records of the nineteenth-century ships. Neither sexual segregation, spatial organization, the maintenance of a hierarchy among sailors and officers, nor the putative separation of the different races (black, white, Indian) on the ships protected Indian women from sexual violence. In addition, differences of culture (for example, caste and religion) could not be as carefully managed, leading to intra-ethnic violence. Moreover, class and ethnic stereotypes and myths about Indian women's sexuality,[13] already developed fully on both sides of the Atlantic by the time of the sailing of the *Allanshaw*, inevitably collided and were evident in the behaviour of those (black and white) charged with the proper treatment and care of the emigrants. Poynting, quoting from a nineteenth-century source, noted that a perception had developed, that the Indian women who regularly boarded emigrant vessels comprised principally "young widows and married and single women who have already gone astray".[14] Some commentators, such as James McNeil and Chimman Lal, also pushed the idea that some who boarded were prostitutes, despite Doorly's and G.A. Grierson's claim that some Indian women agreed to board the ships in order to escape the dreadful alternative of prostitution in India.[15] Ships' surgeons also commented on the abusive treatment that some emigrant women received from their shipboard spouses, explaining that this sometimes stemmed from the contempt with which lower-caste women were viewed by higher-caste men with whom they formed "alliances". What Poynting euphemistically terms "immoral relations"[16] between Indian women and white men on the plantations had not only become widespread by the 1880s, but were often linked to the stereotypical association of working-class and lower-caste women with promiscuity.[17] Such an association had long been made in relation to enslaved black women who were regarded as incapable of being raped as they were allegedly "naturally promiscuous", and pursued sexual "relations" with white males for their own material and social betterment.[18] In fact, as Beckles points out, "rape as a form, or degree, of sexual violence perpetuated against enslaved women by males . . . was not considered a legal offence, and evidence of it does not appear in litigation records".[19] The traditional perspective on the so-called promiscuity of black women not only resided in the contemporary works of noted racists and sexists, such as Thomas Atwood and Edward Long,[20] but also surfaced in the twentieth-century works of such scholars as the African-Jamaican Orlando Patterson. In his *Sociology of Slavery,* Patterson, influenced heavily by the contemporary writings, noted that enslaved women in Jamaica mated promiscuously and sometimes engaged in outright prostitution, that "the family was unthinkable to the vast majority of the population and promiscuity the norm", and that "the nuclear family could hardly exist within the context of slavery".[21] Higman and others have, of course, found far greater incidence of nuclear families among enslaved people in the Caribbean than previously thought.[22]

Part of the explanation for the lack of attention to these issues in the traditional literature on population movement from India to the Caribbean might lie in the general lack of focus on women and gender analysis that characterized the field of migration studies before the 1980s and 1990s and the related reluctance of many (primarily male) scholars to pay attention to what is regarded as the "private lives" of emigrants. In this regard, those who specialize in the field of migration studies have lagged behind slavery scholars who have published numerous works illuminating the sexual violence perpetrated on the bodies of enslaved women in all sections of the Atlantic world.

While part of the reason for the recent attention given to the subject of the rape of enslaved women lies in the discovery of the Thistlewood journals, which unambiguously catalogues one white man's rape of several enslaved women and highlights the intersection of race, class, gender and power in societies that enslaved Africans, other scholars have used other evidence to illustrate the trend.[23] This is evident in the work of Mathurin Mair, Bush and Beckles, among others, who all provide ample proof of the socio-sexual manipulation and exploitation of women by superordinately empowered white male managers of enslaved labourers. Their work reveals the ways in which womanhood was targeted and preyed upon by patriarchal authority and interest. Beckles's essay "Property Rights in Pleasure" provides a chilling reminder of the fact that under colonialism, systemic violence was sanctioned: "New World slavery led to the legal and customary institutionalization of the slave owner's right to unrestricted sexual access to the enslaved woman as an intrinsic and discrete product."[24] Some of the evidence used by these slavery scholars is derived from African-descended people themselves. Robert Wedderburn, son of a planter, James Wedderburn, and an enslaved woman, Rosanna, and thus a direct product, witness and victim of the British-imposed slave system in Jamaica, testified to the sexual exploitation that his mother and other enslaved domestics had to endure. His writings on the "horrors of slavery" (edited by Ian McCalman)[25] are in fact corroborated by Thomas Thistlewood's memoirs. No one will now doubt his claim that it was "a common practice ... for the planters to have lewd intercourse with their slaves", or that "My father's house was full of female slaves, all objects of his lusts; amongst whom he strutted like Solomon in his grand seraglio, or like a bantam cock upon his own dunghill."[26]

The present book thus breaks no new ground in terms of its focus on women's sexploitation but rather falls into an existing genre of historical writing dating back to the eighteenth century. Nevertheless, it refocuses attention on Indian women's exploitation via the post-slavery indentureship system and provides firm empirical data, by way of one woman's personal history, of Indian women's sexploitation. Emigration officials had consistently denied that emigrant women were abused on nineteenth-century ships, and every effort was made to entice women to leave India in order to satisfy the quota agreement stipulated. Women were encouraged to emigrate not only because plantation owners were already familiar with women's productive labour but also because they were concerned that the sexual needs of the majority male workers be satisfied. Recruiting and shipping women, and avoiding any charge that their treatment replicated enslavement, were thus crucial concerns of the system. The documentary evidence provided here, however, demonstrates that Indian women by no means had a smooth "ride" to the colonies but were preyed upon by males of various ethnicities, many of whom waylaid them in the area of the water closet (toilet). Their exploitation was related clearly to their gender, race, class and caste, and, of course, to their status as bonded labourers.

Most of the documentary evidence used in the book comes from the over four hundred pages of correspondence generated by the investigation into the journey of the *Allanshaw*.[27] Briefly, during the early morning hours of 24 July 1885, Maharani, along with 660 other contract labourers, embarked at Calcutta on this sailing ship, owned by James Nourse, bound for colonial Guyana. The ship's captain was F.C. Wilson and the surgeon-superintendent was Dr E.A. Hardwicke. Maharani did not complete her passage to the southern Caribbean; she was among the seventeen who died before the ship reached colonial Guyana. While the causes of death of sixteen of these were ascertained and recorded without question, Maharani's death was the subject of intense controversy, uncertainty and speculation. Dr Hardwicke vacillated between "shock to the nervous system", "inflammation near the womb", "shock from shame" and "peritonitis" as the cause of death, and a few fellow female emigrants attributed her death to "criminal assault" based on what Maharani allegedly told them before she died. Inspector Wright of the Guyana Police Force and Dr Robert Grieve, acting medical officer to the Immigration Department and later surgeon-general, and a member of the Commission of Enquiry ordered by the governor of colonial Guyana, both believed that rape was the cause of her death. Dr Grieve's fellow commissioners, Alexander, Kirke and Clarke, disagreed with him, arguing that the evidence presented was contradictory and inconclusive. Robert Ipson, the twenty-two-year-old black man accused of taking part in the rape, denied the charge, believing that he had been set up. Some of his fellow sailors agreed, especially as the other man accused, the twenty-year-old Englishman James Oliver, was never investigated or charged.

Many questions emerged as I tried to make sense of this case with its conflicting documentary evidence. The most pressing one was: Why had there been so many attempts to investigate this particular case, the last one to be an elaborate Commission of Enquiry in colonial Guyana? It is true that Commissions of Enquiry were central features of the emigration and indentureship systems from their inception, continuing to the eve of their abolition, as evidenced by the 1910 Sanderson Commission and the 1915 investigations of McNeil and Lal. However, none of them had been driven so overwhelmingly by a complaint of sexual abuse despite the frequency of such abuses against emigrant women. While some emigrant men had also been physically and verbally abused on this voyage, and while six seamen had almost staged a "mutiny", as Governor Irving made clear, it was "the death of the woman Maharani which was the originating cause of the enquiry", not the other incidents (though those attracted attention also).[28] Another obvious question, then, was what factors had created the conditions under which, in contrast to the period of African enslavement, litigation was contemplated in cases of alleged rape of bonded labourers? During slavery, despite the prevalence of this violent act against black women, it was not considered a case for litigation and certainly was never even thought to have been possible. Enslavers claimed ownership over the bodies of enslaved women and thus used them at will. Had the racialized ideological justification that "lower-class" women were "naturally promiscuous" and thus "could not be raped" undergone fundamental changes in the post-slavery period? Also, while the attitude of the sexist and racist men in charge of the ship could easily be explained, why was the possibility of rape discounted even by some of the emigrants and subordinate crew familiar with the treatment of lower-caste and lower-class women? Were they afraid of reprisals or of prejudicing their chances of being allowed on future passages, perhaps under some of the same officers, the same captain and surgeon, as Dr Grieve and his colleague, Dr Finlayson, suggested? At the same time, what evidence was needed in the nineteenth century to convict a man of rape? Additionally, other Indian women had been raped on emigrant ships to the colonial Caribbean but had never had their cases so elaborately investigated. So why did Maharani's case receive so much attention? Was it because none of the other rape victims had allegedly died from the effects? Did Maharani receive preferential treatment because she was of high caste, or because she was well known on board and a friend of the very influential return emigrant women on board? Did this case attract special attention because of the growing anti-female emigration sentiment in India at this time? Was the investigation driven by the fact that Ipson, said to be the chief offender, was a black man[29] within the context of a racially charged environment and the push by captains and surgeons to eliminate "coloured" crew members on emigrant ships? Was this investigation a part of the articulated objective of Britain and India to avoid the charge that nineteenth-century labour migration, especially the treatment of women, was slavery revived? Why did Grieve break rank in the context of a colonial world where empowered officials traditionally united against the colonized and where non-elite men, innocent or not, often felt the harsh hand of the law? Did Ipson and Oliver escape conviction because the difficulty of attracting seamen to the Asian Indian labour trade made the captain and surgeon-superintendent wary of scaring off future crew? Did they thus close ranks? Had the administration of "justice" in the post-slavery Caribbean become much fairer than before? Was Ipson really innocent? Did the fear of a labour crisis in colonial Guyana affect the outcome of the case if incidents like this were to bring an end to the system of Asian Indian labour migration? The planter class, faced with a declining sugar industry in 1884–85, was opposed to such a potentially damaging case coming to light and only the resolve of Governor Irving kept it alive.

Perhaps these questions have not been answered satisfactorily, partly on account of evidential gaps. The question of high caste as a reason for the detailed investigation is perhaps the easiest to answer, though. It is true that "Maharani" in Hindi translates literally into "Great Queen" or "Her Majesty" (wife of the Maharaj),[30] but there is no evidence that in this case her high-caste status pushed this investigation. Otherwise the outcome might have been different. Claims of relationships to royalty and high-caste status were some-times taken seriously by emigration officials. At times, such claims resulted in the release of immigrants from indentureship, especially if they could argue fraudulent acquisition and shipment persuasively.[31] But Maharani was not the first high-caste woman ever to sail to the Caribbean as an indentured servant or to have experienced abuse on these ships.

One factor that could have influenced the investigation was the presence of returning emigrants who spoke English and who seemed to have had some influence over the captains and surgeons-superintendent. It appears that the presence of these experienced emigrants was often feared by captains because of their insistence that emigrants' rights be protected, and they were sometimes accused of fomenting resistance. There were several of these experienced emigrants on the *Allanshaw*, including Mohadaya and Moorti,[32] the two female friends of Maharani who had informed the surgeon-superintendent of

Maharani's claim that she had been criminally assaulted. These two seemed to have had quite some influence on board with the high-ranking officials. Returning emigrants on this ship had also, on one occasion, urged the emigrants not to assemble for breakfast as "the quantity of Gram was not sufficient".[33] The surgeon-superintendent justified why returnees often had privileges not shared by "new emigrants": they spoke English, "they are invariably more intelligent, more turbulent and more independent than the new Kulis and they have the greatest power of influencing the others to good or bad behaviour".[34] Consequently, great efforts were made to "keep the return Kulis on the side of authority".[35] This took the form of giving them positions of authority on the ship (cook, nurse, sirdar, and so on) or by communicating with them more freely than with the others. Clearly, Mohadaya and Moorti could make trouble for the captain and surgeon-superintendent, and they ensured that their friend Maharani's case was not swept under the carpet.

As Ipson was black, this was an important factor to be taken into account. Black or "coloured" seamen were not favourites of the white crew, and concerted efforts had been made in the nineteenth century to reduce their employment on Asian Indian emigrant ships. This particular "coloured" man had also reportedly been "troublesome" on the voyage in other ways and it is possible that the high-ranking officials wanted to make an example of him. Both the captain and the surgeon-superintendent had been dissatisfied with Ipson's behaviour, especially the way he questioned the captain's handling of disciplinary matters on the ship. Ipson had influenced about five other men to stage what the captain called a "near mutiny" because they disagreed with the way in which he disciplined a cabin boy who had wounded an emigrant. But an elaborate Commission of Enquiry was not vital to arrest Ipson and his gang for the captain had some police powers on the ship; he could have placed Ipson "in irons".

The need to enforce emigration and immigration regulations and the attempt to counter charges that the voyages from India were exactly like the African Middle Passage cannot be ignored as factors influencing the investigation, especially the one the Colonial Office urged Governor Irving to conduct in colonial Guyana. Concern to avoid such a charge had, indeed, led to the greater frequency of official enquiries and reports after the 1870s, though none of those had been driven specifically on account of a charge of alleged rape. However, in the face of the mounting opposition to the emigration of women who, many women's groups in India claimed, were being "exported" for purposes of prostitution, and in light of the need to appease these anti-emigration forces, officials may have thought it wise to be seen to be doing something to stem abuses, even if encouraging such an investigation did not endear them to the employers of indentured Indians. As rape was a crime when perpetrated on "free" as opposed to "enslaved" women (and here it was clear that indentured women were differentiated from enslaved women) and, as suspects had actually been pointed out and a complaint lodged, action had to be taken.

There is still, of course, the question of what evidence was needed for a conviction? Clearly the investigators were looking for the perpetrator(s), eyewitness accounts, consistent depositions at the official enquiry rather than conflicting ones, medical evidence and some proof that Maharani had resisted the attackers. Merry Wiesner's study of women and gender in early modern Europe notes that while rape was a capital crime in many parts of Europe (including England whose customary laws on rape would have been patterned in the nineteenth-century Caribbean), convictions were more likely "if the victim [could] prove that she had cried out and made attempts to repel the attacker".[36] As the investigators claimed not to have found any of the "convincing evidence" they sought, the case was not settled to the satisfaction of the women who complained and some of the men who testified. Furthermore, at least two of the commissioners believed that Maharani had had consensual sex with those accused of raping her. First, they read something sinister in the fact that Maharani had gone to the water closet by herself, though even Dr Hardwicke admitted that this was not an unheard of occurrence, and that she had not complained to Hardwicke and nearest sirdar about her ordeal. Second, they ignored the testimony of those who said that Maharani was a quiet, well-behaved girl who hardly fraternized. They preferred to believe those who hinted that she "had asked for it", that she was promiscuous and might even had had a special man on board and that she had not raised an alarm or a "hue and cry". So, even though the commissioners found men who fit Maharani's description of her attackers, people who linked Oliver and Ipson to the crime, people who swore that Ipson had told them of his intentions of the act, deponents who swore that Maharani was a well-behaved girl, testimonies that Maharani had been prevented from raising an alarm because the attackers had stuffed her sari into her mouth, loopholes in the ship's log, contradictions between the post-mortem report and emigrants' testimonies, and evidence that crew, officers and emigrants feared an outcome prejudicial to themselves and thus had been reluctant to tell all, most members of the commission ruled against Maharani.

The conclusions in the official report of the Commission of Enquiry thus help to settle the question of why rape was discounted in the end (as such cases are even today). The erroneous ideology that non-elite women were "naturally promiscuous" was still alive and well in the late-nineteenth-century Caribbean, and so was the racist view, held by men such as Kirke, that the Indians were unreliable witnesses. The crew maintained an ideology of racial, caste and gender superiority that clearly determined their lack of regard for the rights of the Indian women on the ship. The fact that persons found guilty of mistreating emigrants could (at least in theory) be dismissed from the service, fined, imprisoned or have their wages and gratuities reduced might also have been a factor shaping the nature of some of the testimonies. It might also have helped to explain both the denials that abuses had characterized the journey, the failure of the ship's surgeon-superintendent and captain to log all acts of misconduct, and the surgeon-superintendent's questionable post-mortem conclusions. That the crew were routinely warned about mistreating emigrants is not in doubt. When the crew was mustered as the *Allanshaw* pulled out of port, for example, they were reminded that they would lose one month's pay for every proven offence they committed against the emigrants. It is not surprising that almost everyone who testified (even the five who had been logged or warned by the captain or surgeon-superintendent about their behaviour towards the emigrants), swore that the crew treated the emigrants well, that the mortality rate was much lower than on other voyages, that no women were sexually abused, and that security was tight and efficient, making it hard for any woman to be sexually assaulted without being seen. Security was not impenetrable, however. Despite the assurances by Wilson, Hardwicke and the sirdars in charge, some of the crew and emigrants testified that, in cold weather, the sirdars often abandoned their posts to seek warmth below deck, and some testified that the night in question was cold. The conflicting narratives of those called to testify were, therefore, another factor complicating the analysis of the case and the provision of answers to all the questions that I posed. Also dooming the case was Chitamun's retraction of his "eyewitness claim" and the pro-planter attitude of the agent general of immigration and the anti-Indian attitude of Kirke, two of the influential members of the Commission of Enquiry in colonial Guyana, who clearly did not wish to impede the flow of cheap labour from India to colonial Guyana.

However, by making as full a use of the testimonies as possible, the book also aims to add to the growing body of works which *attempt* to recover the voice of the subaltern.[37] In general, the voices of indentured men and women were muted in the discourse of migration; normally, the task of writing the history and capturing the lived experiences of the subjects of the migration discourses is impeded by the depersonalizing, alienating system of emigration and indentureship. However, not one but four official enquires were launched into the voyage of the *Allanshaw*. At the Commission of Enquiry convened in colonial Guyana, twenty-two witnesses, not all from the influential elite but including some of the emigrants themselves, gave evidence. Of course, while we can now speak conclusively about Maharani's existence, her own voice was silenced in that she did not live to relate her experiences directly to the various commissioners. But on the other hand, the depositions of other emigrants to whom she had related her ordeal reflect her voice. Nevertheless, what use was made of these voices anyway? As Marina Carter argues in her work on Mauritius, the depositions of the emigrants and immigrants were considered by officials as unacceptable at face value.[38]

An additional methodological problem is that these voices were filtered through the pens of others. The testimonies of those who appeared before the Commissions of Enquiry were transcribed or recorded by official scribes, for example, the secretary to the commission in colonial Guyana (and thus, like "slave narratives" and court records in themselves problematic). Most of the emigrants could not even read the deposition they were asked to sign, marking an "X" instead. Next to direct oral evidence, however, they come the closest to revealing the voices of the bonded labourers. In this regard, the sources on which this book is based should not be viewed as being any less trustworthy than the official documents on which so many books on post-slavery immigration to the colonial Caribbean are based.

The book is arranged into two parts, with part 1 consisting of three chapters. Chapter 1 presents the background to the emigration of Indian women to colonial Guyana and the wider Caribbean as part of the imperial reallocation of bonded labour after the abolition of African enslavement as well as rehearsing the literature on women and migration to the colonial Caribbean. This chapter also sets the context for the journey that Maharani would later undertake in 1885 and explores conditions on board emigrant ships in order to show that the abuse of emigrants (whether sexual or otherwise) was a central characteristic of the journey from India, despite precautionary regulations and despite the denials of the crew on the *Allanshaw*. Chapter 2 provides details of Maharani's illness and death between India and St Helena. Chapter 3 deals with the various Commissions of Enquiry launched after Maharani's death and presents and analyses the evidence of those who were grilled by the police, magistrates, colonial officials and commissioners. This chapter also outlines Dr Grieve's differing perspective on the events that transpired on the *Allanshaw* and the reasons articulated for his departure from the conclusions of the other members of the Commission of Enquiry in colonial Guyana. Chapter 3 also summarizes the conclusions of the government secretary, the colonial governor and the Colonial Office. Part 1 ends with a conclusion which problematizes the final outcome of the case and demonstrates that the sexual abuse of women on emigrant ships did not end with Maharani's ordeal but extended well beyond 1885.

Part 2 consists of the testimonies of the twenty-two witnesses called before the Commission of Enquiry in colonial Guyana. The presentation of the unedited depositions is considered crucial to allow readers a first-hand glimpse into the complexities and contradictions that determined the final ruling. One obvious drawback to part 2, of course, is that with the exception of a few depositions such as Grant's third deposition, the actual questions posed by the commissioners are not included and do not seem to have been recorded. Occasional indications in the margins of the individual commissioner associated with a particular issue provide partial but unreliable hints. But the transcribed depositions will allow readers to make up their own minds about the case and to agree or disagree with my analysis. Above all, the Minutes of Evidence illuminate the systemic violence that was a part of colonialism and indentureship and was later played out on the plantations. It reminds us of what has been left out of the traditional discourses of sex, gender, race and power in the study of Caribbean history.

PART ONE

[1]

INDIAN WOMEN AND LABOUR MIGRATION

Background to Maharani's Passage from India

M AHARANI BOARDED THE *Allanshaw* destined for colonial Guyana in July 1885. By that year, the colonial Caribbean already had a long history of importing contract labourers from India for commodity production on its many, primarily sugar, plantations. The general history of this post-slavery Indian labour reallocation to the colonial Caribbean is well documented by K.O. Laurence, Hugh Tinker, Walton Look Lai, Basdeo Mangru and many others,[1] and will, for the most part, only be rehearsed from secondary sources in this essentially background chapter which aims at locating and contextualizing the voyage of the *Allanshaw* and the experiences of those on board.

Colonial Guyana pioneered the Indian indentureship system in the Caribbean, receiving some 238,909 Indians between 1838 and 1917. This figure represented 55.6 per cent of the total of 429,623 Indian immigrants who arrived in the colonial Caribbean, and only Trinidad, which imported 33.5 per cent of the total number, came close to Guyana's figure.[2] (See Tables 1.1 and 1.2.) As shown in Table 1.1, Indians outnumbered all other ethnic groups of indentured workers in post-slavery Guyana. According to Look Lai, there were three distinct phases of Indian labour migration to colonial Guyana. The first immigrants arrived in May 1838 on the ships *Whitby* and *Hesperus*. These 396 arrivals were known as the "Gladstone Coolies", having been imported on

3

Table 1.1   Immigrants Introduced into Colonial Guyana, Mainly under Indenture, 1834–1917

Source	Period of Immigration	Numbers
India	1838–1917	238,909
Madeira	1835–1881	32,216
Africa	1834–1867	14,060
China	1852–1884	13,533 ·
Europe	1834–1845	381
Other	1835–1865	1,868
Total		300,967

Source: Clem Seecharan, *Tiger in the Stars: The Anatomy of Indian Achievement in British Guiana, 1919–29* (London: Macmillan, 1997), 3, taken from G.W. Roberts and J. Byrne, "Summary Statistics on Indenture and Associated Migration Affecting the West Indies", *Population Studies* 20, pt. 1 (1966): 127.

Table 1.2   Number of Asian Indians Imported to the Caribbean, 1838–1917

Territory	Years	Numbers Imported
British Guiana	1838–1917	238,909
Trinidad	1845–1917	143,939
Suriname	1873–1918	34,024
Guadeloupe	1854–1887	42,595
Jamaica	1845–1916	38,681
Martinique	1848–1884	25,509
St Lucia	1858–1895	4,354
Grenada	1856–1885	3,200
St Vincent	1860–1880	2,472
St Kitts	1860–1861	337
French Guiana	1853–1885(?)	19,296

Sources: K.O. Laurence, *Immigration into the West Indies in the Nineteenth Century* (Barbados: Caribbean Universities Press, 1971); Gisela Eisner, *Jamaica 1830–1930: A Study in Economic Growth* (Manchester: Manchester University Press, 1961), 144; Seecharan, *Tiger in the Stars*, 4; Verene Shepherd, *Transients to Settlers: The Experience of Indians in Jamaica, 1845–1945* (Leeds and Warwick: Peepal Tree Press and University of Warwick, 1994).

the initiative of the sugar planter John Gladstone, who owned the plantations Vreed-en-hoop and Vreedestein. Gladstone himself used 101 of the 396 and the remainder were distributed to other plantations. This first phase was short lived and there were several stops and starts between 1838 and a temporary halt in 1848. Indian immigration did not resume fully until the 1850s, by which time some of its worst abuses had been corrected. In the second phase, 1851–70, Indians were in the majority but not the exclusive immigrants who arrived in the colony. The third phase, 1870–1917, however, was marked by the exclusive importation of Indian contract labourers. In this latter period, immigration to colonial Guyana, as indeed to Jamaica and Trinidad, was regarded as a new form of settler colonization pushed by British imperialist interests. While repatriation continued to be an integral part of the indenture contract, incentives were held out to entice the Indians to make the transition from transients to settlers.[3]

The massive importation of Indians to the colonial Caribbean changed the ethnic composition of the plantation labour force drastically, especially in colonial Guyana and Trinidad. Whereas in 1851 the African-Guyanese domi- nated the plantation labour force, with Indian labourers accounting for just 16 per cent, by 1891 colonial Guyana's sugar plantation economy had come to rely almost exclusively on indentured immigrant labour, with Indians comprising 80.4 per cent of its 90,000 full-time plantation labour force.[4] Up to the end of the Indian indentureship system, however, the African-Caribbean people in colonial Guyana, as in Jamaica and the Windward Islands, whether as part-time or full-time labourers, continued to be essential to certain tasks on the plantations. The abolition of that system of neo-slavery euphemistically called Apprenticeship in 1838, had given the African-Caribbeans a new mobility which was exploited fully. The trend was towards peasant formation and non-plantation occupations; few remained as resident estate labourers if they had a choice. Despite coercive planter tactics and other obstacles, a vibrant peasantry evolved in competition with the estates for labour.[5]

As was the case with the shipping of African captives, the relocation of Indians to colonial Guyana and the wider Caribbean was characterized by a sexual disparity, especially during the early years of the scheme. There were only fourteen women among the 1838 Gladstone arrivals and this situation improved only gradually. By 1856, 38.2 per cent of the 5,004 imported to colonial Guyana were females, well above the average of 16 per cent shipped from Calcutta to all colonies in that year. The records of the Colonial Land

and Emigration Commission show that in 1857, female numbers reached a high of 69.6 per cent, decreasing thereafter to between 27.2 per cent and 47.7 per cent from 1858 to 1866.[6]

The sexual disparity was not confined to colonial Guyana. Only 11 per cent of the 261 immigrants imported to Jamaica on the first Indian emigrant ship, the *Blundell,* comprised women. If girls are added, the female percentage increases to 15 per cent. In 1863 the *Alnwick Castle* to Trinidad carried only 14.6 per cent females out of its 460 emigrants and the *Golden City*, of the same year, 13.4 per cent.[7] The excess of males over females among Indian emigrants was also noted in Suriname where slavery was abolished in 1863 and immigration began in 1873. The 1872 treaty between the Dutch Parliament and Britain respecting emigration from India stipulated that a 50:100 female to male ratio was to be maintained.[8] This was later lowered to 40:100 as it was for the British-colonized territories as recruiters could not meet the higher quota. This unfavourable female to male ratio, frequently below quota, led the British government to seek a workable solution by imposing standard ratios. These ratios fluctuated between the 1850s and the 1860s, being at various times 25 females for every 100 males and 50:100. The female to male ratio finally settled at 40:100 for most importing territories but despatching the requisite proportion of females for the colonies was a perennial problem for all concerned, as illustrated in the tables below.

Failure to fulfil the ratio requirements often delayed the departure of the ships out of the ports of Calcutta and Madras, but the social implications of a severe shortage of women, such as the high rates of uxoricide in the Caribbean, caused all concerned in the labour migration process to make the effort to come as close to the ratio as possible. As a concession against unforeseen recruiting difficulties, agents were allowed to send off a ship without the stipulated quota provided the deficiency was made up by the close of the following emigration season.[9]

Recruiting agents continued after the 1860s to experience difficulties in attracting women to colonial Guyana and the other importing countries in the Caribbean. Not only were many women reluctant to leave friends and family in India but the system of child betrothal left few unattached women for emigration. Additionally, Indian men were reluctant to subject their wives, daughters and other female relatives to a long and potentially perilous sea voyage. Not all Caribbean planters were supportive of the emigration of "lower-caste" women, categorizing them erroneously as prostitutes. Some,

Table 1.3   Percentage of Females Imported to Colonial Guyana, 1856–1866

Year	Men	Women	Boys	Girls	Infants[b]	Total	% of Females
1856	–	–	–	–	–	5,004	38.2
1857	–	–	–	–	–	3,487	69.6
1858	–	–	–	–	–	7,566	47.7
1859	–	–	–	–	–	9,186	42.6
1860[a]	2,410	1,097	181	151	127	3,966	32.5
1861	2,180	817	340 ch.	–	97	3,434	27.3[c]
1862	2,352	601	94	77	92	3,216	21.7
1863	1,509	374	48	31	52	2,014	20.6
1864	1,745	427	101	64	89	2,426	21.0
1865	3,071	845	297	161	282	4,656	23.0
1866	1,265	442	89	65	59	1,920	27.2

Source: CO 386, Letter books of the Colonial Land and Emigration Commission.
[a]incomplete returns
[b]not differentiated by sex, therefore excluded from the calculations
[c]% of women, not females. Children not differentiated by sex
– = not stated

influenced by the post-slavery Victorian ideologies which were being imposed on the Caribbean and ignoring the long experience of productive female labour during the period of enslavement, tried to hide this prejudicial sentiment by arguing that women did not make as good agricultural labourers as men, or that women should function in the private sphere. The restraints on the emigration of women who had large numbers of children with them also complicated the emigration process with respect to filling the female to male ratio. The view was that ships which took on board large numbers of children were likely to experience an outbreak of epidemic diseases such as measles and that the death rate was likely to be high in such cases. For example, the death rate on the *Merchantman* and the *Maidstone* sailing to colonial Guyana in the 1856–57 emigration season was 31.17 per cent and 24.53 per cent respectively. The complaint that the death rate tended to be higher and to increase in direct proportion to the numbers of women, children and infants on board was disputed by emigration officials who provided the quantitative analysis for 1850–58 (see Table 1.5).

Table 1.4   Percentage of Females on Emigrant Ships to Colonial Guyana, 1867–1868

Year	Ship	Men	Women	Boys	Girls	Infants	% of Females
1867	Lincelles	200	102	31	16	8	33.8
	Indus	247	128	32	19	8	34.5
	Janet	230	198	40	24	11	45.1
	Cowan Clarence	261	128	27	19	9	33.8
	Oasis	241	92	23	12	7	28.3
	Orient	267	80	15	11	11	24.3
	Trevalyan	259	110	9	5	5	30.0
	Jason	291	92	11	4	7	24.1
1868	Ganges	307	88	7	3	5	22.5
	Clarence	369	73	10	7	5	17.4
	Adamant	269	60	16	7	5	19.0
	Harkaway	164	35	2	6	5	19.8
	India	249	85	19	6	13	25.3
	Howrah	298	97	18	4	16	24.2
	Trevalyan	271	90	16	15	15	26.8
	Winchester	297	103	27	8	18	25.5
	Himalaya	258	106	31	7	25	28.1

Source: CO 386, Letter books of the Colonial Land and Emigration Commission.

Unacceptably high death rates would have given anti-emigration forces more ammunition with which to continue their opposition to a system of labour reallocation which, while not like the African Middle Passage in all respects, resembled it closely in many, leading Joseph Beaumont and Hugh Tinker to characterize Indian immigration and indentureship as the new slavery or a "new system of slavery" respectively.[10] The "opposing voices" in Look Lai's terms or the "critics of indenture" in Mangru's, using arguments based on mortality, cost, treatment and so on, could already be heard from 1838 in colonial Guyana. Indeed, the earliest opposition was over the extreme cases of poor treatment meted out to some of the immigrants who were among the "Gladstone Experiment" batch. Opposition continued in colonial Guyana, as it did in Jamaica and Trinidad, over the entire period of the trade, from the

Table 1.5   Proportion of Women and Children Embarked on Ships from Calcutta
to the West Indies, 1850–1858, with Per Cent Mortality

Year	Women to Men (proportion)	Children/infants to adults (proportion)	% mortality on whole no. embarked
1850–1851	9.09	5.11	3.61
1851–1852	16.93	10.89	4.45
1852–1853	23.96	16.53	5.60
1853–1854	14.36	7.84	3.30
1854–1855	18.34	7.48	2.75
1855–1856	35.72	10.82	5.75
1856–1857	35.27	14.67	17.26
1857–1858[a]	66.48	29.08	9.10

Source: CO 386/91, T.W.C. Murdoch and Frederic Rogers to Herman Merivale,
11 August 1858.
[a]Figures for Salsette of 1858 excluded.

Anti-Slavery Society and other groups such as the missionaries, the coloured
middle class and the African-Caribbean freed people objecting to the scheme
on the basis of cost, implications for freed peoples' employment and wages,
and humanitarian concerns. There was also opposition in India over the
suspicion that Indian women were being exported for the purposes of prostitution. This opposition later fuelled the female arm of the anti-emigration
lobby in India in the late nineteenth and early twentieth centuries.[11]

In an effort to increase the numbers of women available for emigration,
some of the restrictions on female emigration were gradually relaxed, but the
sexual disparity was never eliminated, though the records indicate that a great
effort was made to conform to the ratios set after 1860. For example, the female
to male ratio on the St Kilda to colonial Guyana in 1871 was 57.8:100. The
ratio never fell below 40:100 on the ships which sailed for that territory in
1872, with this allowable ratio also being maintained during 1873.[12]

Several incentives were given to recruiters in India in an effort to conform
to the quotas set. The most widespread was the payment of higher rates of
commission on every female recruited. For Suriname, recruiters were paid 25
rupees for each male recruited but 35 rupees for each female. In the nineteenth

century, the rates for the British-colonized Caribbean territories were 45 rupees for males and 55 rupees for females. By 1915, as opposition to emigration grew and the supply became scarce, recruiting rates escalated to 60 rupees for each man and as much as 100 rupees for each woman. The rate for boys aged twelve to sixteen was half that of adult males. No incentives were paid for the recruitment of boys below the age of twelve, but the full female rate was applied to girls over ten and 20 rupees were paid for girls under the age of ten.[13] This gender disparity, even among children, was due to the enormous need to increase the numbers of females shipped. There were charges that the payment of high commission rates, especially during times of extreme scarcity of prospective female emigrants, created the conditions under which kidnapping flourished. By the early 1870s, kidnapping had reportedly become prevalent in recruiting districts of Allahabad and the north-west provinces. The news-paper, the *Pioneer of India,* carried a report in 1871 about an attempted kidnapping of an Indian woman in Allahabad by four peons, Gohree, Baldeo, Raoti and Rumzan. The woman was to be sent to Jamaica. The men were convicted and sentenced to prison terms ranging from six to twelve months.[14]

There were charges of fraudulent behaviour in other aspects of the recruiting process. For example, planters exhibited a preference for married women, so recruiters, unable to fulfil this request to the extent required by the planters, manufactured couples for emigration. Admittedly, some of these alliances formed at the depots were consensual and once declared, all were accepted. The extent of the phenomenon of depot marriages is indicated by the returns contained in the protector of immigrants' annual reports. On the ship *Silhet,* which arrived in Guyana in 1883, thirteen depot marriages were registered. The numbers were at times higher, for example, in the same year forty-three marriages were registered on the *Berar* and forty-four on the *Bann.* But, as Brij Lal has observed, the number of married couples recruited in the normal process was higher than "depot marriages", and the phenomenon of depot marriages has often been exaggerated.[15]

It was not unheard of for men and women to change their minds, and their partners, once on board or upon arrival in the Caribbean. For example, on the ship *Rohilla,* the agent general's report dated 24 March 1883 indicated that "the Nepalese woman, Moti, refused to acknowledge Amirbur [?] as her husband who is apparently an inhabitant of the plains. This couple was accordingly not registered as man and wife."[16] On the ship *Foyle,* which arrived in Guyana in 1886, Asserum requested that she be located on a different plantation from Aladin, her "depot husband", as she had changed her mind about wishing to live with him. Indeed, she seemed to have made this decision on the voyage itself, benefiting from his protection on board, but never sleeping with him.[17]

The castes from which the women originated continued to be a matter of concern to the planter class, which evinced a preference for higher-caste women. According to Mangru, the women who boarded emigrant ships for colonial Guyana comprised young widows and married or single women who had severed ties of relationships in India. He also claims that higher-caste women tended to be available for emigration in times of economic hardships in their villages.[18]

Preference was expressed for young, healthy labourers. Planters requested young women in the age range of twenty to thirty except where they emigrated as a part of a family unit, in which case some age flexibility was allowed. The minimum age for girls to be recruited independently of a family was sixteen. In reality, recruiters often misrepresented the ages of the recruits, at times putting quite old people (with grey hair dyed black to disguise this) on board the ships. Such fraud was usually detected halfway through the journey.

The imbalance in the female to male ratio was initially reflected in the settler population being 11:100 in Guyana in 1851. Settlement in the colony at the end of indenture, increased importation and natural increase improved the ratio by the 1850s. The female to male ratio was 62:100 in 1858, 58:100 in 1891 and 73:100 by 1914. From a high of 61:100 in 1900, the ratio among the Indian immigrant population in Trinidad dropped to 42:100 in 1905 and 40:100 in 1914.[19] In Jamaica the imbalance continued up to 1921, reaching 49:100 by 1943. (See Table 1.7.) The male dominance continued in most importing countries up to 1946, not balancing out until the 1960s.

Women were recruited or captured from roughly the same geographical areas as men, though, as was the case under slavery, many were obtained far from their own villages, with the result that their area of origin was often wrongly represented. In the first phase of Indian labour migration, they were recruited from among those described as "hill people", from the Dhangar ethnic group from the Chota Nagpur division of the Bengal Presidency. Some originated among the poor elements of the cities of Calcutta and Madras and among the "untouchables" in the districts surrounding Madras. Some recruits or captives also came from the north-western regions and had been driven into the cities by famine in Upper India. Although some "tribal" people, including

Table 1.6   Percentage of Females on Emigrant Ships to Trinidad, 1863–1872

Year	Ship	Men	Women	Boys	Girls	Infants	Total	% of Females
1863	Alnwick Castle	381	61	10	6	2	460	14.6
	Assaye	223	52	8	1	5	289	18.7
	Athlete	258	64	9	7	10	348	21.0
	Brechin Castle	180	71	17	11	8	287	29.4
	Golden City	388	56	7	5	3	459	13.4
1864	Alnwick Castle	339	83	15	13	7	457	21.3
	Spitfire	353	104	29	10	21	517	23.0
1865	Sydenham	307	79	15	19	4	424	23.3
	Atalanta	333	92	25	15	22	487	23.0
	Newcastle	403	79	19	17	20	538	18.5
	Carleton	297	97	48	37	14	493	26.4
	Empress	295	116	48	31	24	514	27.3
	Roxboro Castle	286	93	26	16	7	428	26.0
1866	Salisbury	258	127	28	22	10	445	34.3
1867	Alnwick Castle	233	166	30	32	17	478	43.0
	Sevilla	194	77	13	16	14	314	31.0
	Liverpool	329	159	22	13	9	532	33.0
	Ellenboro	195	136	14	9	6	360	41.0
1868	Sevilla	190	89	4	8	5	296	33.3
	Ancilla ·	243	68	8	3	5	327	22.0
	Malabar	330	82	12	4	7	435	20.1
1869	Poonah	217	116	22	12	20	387	35.0
	Arima	200	67	19	15	12	313	26.4
	Sevilla	163	80	26	25	19	313	35.7
	Ancilla	169	80	34	24	17	324	34.0
	Flying Foam	249	139	35	27	26	476	37.0
	Braumaris Castle	192	142	73	54	43	504	43.0
	Wiltshire	217	210	77	56	57	617	48.0
1870	Atalanta	188	118	42	23	26	397	38.0
	Cochin	288	120	35	16	23	482	30.0
	Java	279	124	28	24	20	475	32.5
	Hougomont	204	99	13	14	9	339	34.2
1871	Brechin Castle	274	110	19	17	12	432	30.2
	Indus	266	74	10	14	10	374	24.2
	Atalanta	275	81	9	9	7	381	24.1
	Syria	249	119	25	11	14	418	32.2
	Ganges	235	112	17	10	11	385	32.6
1872	Indus	250	104	20	16	23	413	31.0
	Woodburn	331	132	49	38	27	577	31.0
	Rajah of Cochin	218	111	44	26	14	413	34.3
	Delharrie	241	154	48	36	37	516	40.0

Source: CO 386/99, Colonial Land and Emigration Commission.

Table 1.7   The Asian Indian Population in Jamaica, 1871–1921

Census Year	Male	Female	Total	% of Females
1871	5,339	2,454	7,793	31.5
1881	6,941	4,075	11,016	37.0
1891	6,338	4,467	10,805	41.3
1911	9,928	7,452	17,380	43.0
1921	10,203	8,407	18,610	45.2

Source: Jamaican censuses, 1871–1921.

santals ("tribal" people from the Chota Nagpur Plateau of the Bengal Presidency), continued to arrive in the Caribbean up to the 1860s, the main recruiting/captive areas by the late nineteenth century had shifted farther westwards as recruiters sought to combat the competition of the Assam tea gardens for workers from among the Dhangars and as planters demanded recruits who were not as subject to high mortality on the ships and plantations. By the 1870s major recruiting areas were the districts in the north-west Indian provinces of Orissa, the Punjab and Rajputana, and the various districts in the United Provinces of Bihar and Oudh. About 86 per cent of those recruited for colonial Guyana came from among the Bhojpuri–Hindi-speaking United Provinces. Only a minority were recruited from the Southern Madras Presidency from among both the Tamil-speaking and Telugu-speaking districts.

At times the percentage despatched to colonial Guyana from specific catchment areas varied from year to year depending on local happenings. For example, some participants in the so-called Sepoy Mutiny of 1857 were shipped to the colonial Caribbean. Look Lai notes that in the 1883–84 season, semi-famine in Bengal and Bihar caused recruits from these areas to be higher than usual among the emigrants.[20] Recruits from these areas exceeded those from the United Provinces in the 1884–85 seasons and in the last nine months of 1885, the year in which the *Allanshaw* sailed. In general, however, the majority came from the United Provinces after the late nineteenth century. Raymond Smith concluded in a 1959 study that between 1865 and 1917, the year Indian labour migration ended, 70.3 per cent of the recruits to colonial Guyana came from the United Provinces and 15.3 per cent from Bihar, with a minority from other areas. Look Lai confirms the pattern further, stating that in 1898 a full 83 per cent of the 3,450 destined for Guyana from Calcutta came from the United Provinces.[21] The female recruits or captives came from the same cross-section of religious and caste groupings as men, with lower Hindu castes predominating over high-caste Hindus and Muslims.

After being recruited or captured, both males and females, accompanied by *chaprasis* (messengers or orderlies), were taken to the depots in the area of first recruitment then transported by train to final embarkation depots either in Calcutta or in Madras. There were about ten Emigration Agencies serving the various colonies individually or in combination in Calcutta in the 1880s, but only three to four depots: the Mauritius depot at Bhowanipur, the Demerara depot at Garden Reach and others at Ballygunj and Chitpur. Each was staffed by an Emigration Agent, doctors, clerks, watchmen and sweepers. These depots, all built on the same pattern, were not in the healthiest of spots, with grave implications for the health of those accommodated in them. They were surrounded by a high wall to prevent uncontrolled movement in and out and contained a number of barracks with bungalows for the staff. Accommodation was sufficient to provide for two shiploads at any time in the larger depots.[22] Emigrants spent on average one to three weeks waiting to be shipped, although in extreme cases they could wait up to three months. On arrival at the depots, each recruit was told to bathe and issued with a change of clothing while the old clothes were washed and returned.

Since the process by which Indians were obtained for transportation was dogged by fraud, attempts were made by the various emigration officials to ensure that emigrants had voluntarily signed up for emigration. Despite the improvements and efforts to tighten control over the process, fraud and deception were never completely eliminated. Many recruits found themselves on ships bound for places they had not opted to go to or on journeys longer than they had been led to believe. Such fraud at times led to what emigration officials liked to style "mutiny".[23] For example, there was a reported case of mutiny by emigrants on the ship *Clasmerden* from Calcutta to Guyana in 1862. The ship was forced to stop at Pernambuco in Brazil. The emigrants revolted because they claimed that they had been misled about the length of the voyage.[24] Interestingly enough, some of those involved in this so-called mutiny had also been involved in the Sepoy Mutiny of 1857 and had been shipped out to the Caribbean, presumably to rid India of such "rebels". "Mutinies" were not confined to Indian emigrants. Chinese emigrants on the *Pride of the*

Ganges bound for Guyana in 1865–66 rebelled over inadequate rations. Some of the emigrants who arrived in Trinidad in 1857 complained that Trinidad had not been their choice of destination; they had been led to believe that they were going to Guyana. These may have been encouraged to embark on a ship that was ready to sail, the ship for Guyana not yet being filled.

At the embarkation depots, emigrants were given several medical examinations, by the native doctor and the government-appointed European doctor, to ensure that they were fit to undertake the long journey to the Caribbean. The women were not given as detailed an examination as the men for two reasons: first, officials wanted few obstacles in the way of female emigration and opted for a cursory examination, and second, for cultural reasons, the detailed examination of women by male doctors was unacceptable to the women and the men, especially husbands. By the early twentieth century, agitation had increased for female doctors to be appointed to the depot to examine the women. Part of the preparations included administering the appropriate vaccinations and allowing the recruits to sign their indenture contracts. The emigrants were also issued with clothes for the journey: a pair of woollen trousers, jacket, shoes and a cap for males, and for females, a sari, two flannel jackets, one woollen petticoat, a pair of worsted stockings and shoes. With the exception of the sari, these clothes were not those of the typical rural Indian. In response to complaints about inadequate clothing before the 1860s, calls were made in 1867 for an additional petticoat to be issued to the women.

Once the emigrant was certified as fit for agricultural labour and embarkation, an emigration certificate was signed to that effect for each one by the surgeon-superintendent and the depot surgeon, and countersigned by the protector of emigrants at the port of embarkation and the emigration agent for Guyana. This certificate, duly signed and countersigned, was delivered to each emigrant. It contained the emigrant's name, father's name (Pargas[?] in the case of Maharani),[25] age, caste, height, name of next of kin, marital status and name of partner, if applicable, distinguishing marks, and place of origin in India. Each emigrant also had a "tin ticket" or identification disk placed around the neck or arm, and an embarkation number. These details have allowed many descendants to trace their immigrant ancestors.

Once all the preparations were made, the emigrants were put on board the ships for their voyage to the Caribbean. The typical batch of women would have comprised a mixture of single, independent women who emigrated

voluntarily to be involved in commodity production on Caribbean plantations; those who had been kidnapped or otherwise forced into emigration by
depressed financial circumstances linked to the impact of British economic
policies on the textile industry in India; those deserted by husbands and who
were seeking a new life in a new country; a few (like the women Moorti and
Mohadaya on the *Allanshaw*) who had previously been indentured in Natal,
Mauritius, Fiji or the Caribbean, and who had opted for return and reinden-
tureship; wives and dependents accompanying husbands or other relatives; and
those (such as Chandra Kumari, who in 1891 embarked on the ship *Erne* for
Jamaica with her boyfriend, Tek Bahadur) who were simply out for a new
adventure. Chandra was at first located on the Belvedere Estate in Jamaica but
refused to do any work. She claimed that she was the daughter of the king of
Nepal and that she wished to be released from indenture. Under Jamaican Law
23 of 1879, her indenture was cancelled. Further research into the matter
revealed that she was not "royalty" as she had claimed. The protector of
immigrants was told by Mr Wylie who did the background check in India that
Kumari "was either a runaway slave girl from one of the nobles' establishments
in Nepal or a courtezan who has gone off with Tek Bahadur".[26] Charles Doorly,
the protector of emigrants at the Madras agency, added as factors of emigration,
"domestic unhappiness caused by quarrels with their husband's relatives or
with the other wives; widowhood and all its attendant miseries".[27]

The Ships: Spaces of (S)exploitation?

Recruits were transported from Calcutta (as were those from Madras) in ships
specially selected to participate in the Indian labour migration scheme. They
were also placed under the care of crew members who were instructed in their
responsibilities towards those in their care. A primary concern of those who
decided on the ships to be used and the crew to be hired was the necessity of
avoiding any charge that Indian emigration was a new system of slavery. As
the way in which a society treats its women is considered a measure of
"civilization", and since the condition of African women on the Middle Passage
and on the plantations had featured so highly in the anti-slavery campaigns of
the late eighteenth and early nineteenth centuries, emigration officials were
particularly concerned that the regulations concerning the treatment and care
of Indian women on emigrant ships should be observed. This section of the
chapter outlines the major regulations and explores the extent to which

Figure 1.1 The *Allanshaw*, 1874 (*Illustrated London News*, 12 November 1881, 472)

emigrant ships were efficient transporters of labourers or simply "large spaces of (s)exploitation".

Regulations for Emigrant Ships: Managing Space and Human Cargo

Specific standards relating to size, space, crew, diet and medical stores were laid down for ships accepted to participate in the Indian labour migration scheme. In general, the ships were larger in tonnage than those used in the transatlantic trade in enslaved Africans. Indeed, Herbert S. Klein records that between 1782 and 1788, the size of ships engaged in transporting enslaved Africans to Jamaica averaged just 172 tons. The average size increased to 236 tons between 1791 and 1799 and 294 tons between 1800 and 1808. The average number of captives carried per ship in these same periods was 396, 328 and 289, respectively. The Parliamentary Slave Trade Regulating Acts of 1788 and 1799 had reduced the number of captives per ton ratio as a way of reducing the overcrowding and high mortality on slavers, because in order to compensate for inevitable deaths, slavers had been packed way over their capacity. After

1799, the regulations provided for one captive per ton as opposed to the previous 2.6 per ton. The tonnage of ships also rose after 1788, though few ever approximated the size of the emigrant ships.[28] The emigrant ship *Whitby* to colonial Guyana in 1838 was among the smallest ships used in the trade in Indian contract labourers, being just 350 tons. By the 1850s, a larger class of ships was being used. Some, like the *Ganges* owned by James Nourse, were 839 tons. The Nourse Line became the principal carrier to the Caribbean, although Sandbach, Tinne and Company was also involved. From the 1880s, ships increased in size to 1,600 tons or larger; but smaller ships were not eliminated, the *Salsette* which sailed from India to Trinidad in 1858 being 579 tons.[29] Between 1884 and 1888 Nourse brought seven iron ships into service, including the 1,674 tons *Allanshaw* (built in 1874 by Renfrew, W. Simons and Company and registered at Lloyds of London).[30] Steamships made the voyage in less time. For example, the first steam ship to Guyana, the *Enmore*, took just 49 days.[31] The journey on sailing ships, like the *Allanshaw*, could take up to three months, sometimes longer. The *Silhet* took 96 days to reach Jamaica in 1878 and the *Lightning* 112 days, while the *Salsette's* journey lasted 108 days.[32] Despite their longer sailing time, sailing ships were never totally replaced, and in 1895 there were still twenty-two of them in service. Slavers from West Africa had taken four to six weeks on average. Though some ships passed through the Suez Canal, the usual route, such as the one made by the *Allanshaw*, was around the Cape of Good Hope.

Ships had to be well ventilated and, from the 1860s, were required to be supplied with lifeboats, fire appliances and other rescue equipment. No firearms or flammable materials were allowed on board. Emigrant ships had to carry an adequate number of officers (referred to as "mates" on merchant ships such as those in the Indian labour trade), crew and deckhands. The personnel usually consisted of the captain, who was in overall control of the ship and supervised the officers and crew; the surgeon-superintendent who had responsibility for the "passengers" or emigrants; three officers, each with special responsibilities (for example, the third officer was also the boatswain); and the crew comprising ordinary sailors, "able(-bodied) seamen", deckhands and workers with special skills (some drawn from among the emigrants), such as cooks, sweepers (usually called a "topaz" or "topass"), nurses, hospital attendants, and dispensers/compounders. Respected men, usually second-time emigrants, drawn from among the Indians, were designated "sirdars" or leaders, and assigned to supervise the emigrants in a ratio of 1:25.

Once the ship had embarked all its "passengers", the officers and crew were mustered on the quarterdeck and reminded by the captain of their duties and responsibilities on the voyage. Failure to carry out assigned duties to the satisfaction of the captain and surgeon-superintendent could result in loss or reduction of gratuities and even jeopardize future employment on emigrant ships. This could have affected the statements given by those called to give evidence before the Commission of Enquiry in colonial Guyana after the voyage of the *Allanshaw*. In the special case of the Indian labour trade, even captains and surgeons-superintendent could lose future employment on emigrant ships if investigations found them negligent in their duties.

The ship's surgeon-superintendent was crucial to the voyage and great effort was made to select competent and experienced ones. As Mangru observed, the rate of mortality among the emigrants depended considerably on the care, competence and character of the surgeons-superintendent employed. The positive correlation between competent surgeons and low mortality on some ships did not escape the attention of emigration officials.[33] Despite the acceptance among all involved that the role of the surgeon-superintendent was essential to the success of the Indian labour migration scheme and that the best qualified ones were to be selected, the surgeons-superintendent were inevitably a mixed group of competent and not-so-competent men. Some of them had a wealth of experience in the Australian service, some were former army doctors, and others were inexperienced men employed in the Indian medical service and Indian gaols. As was the case with the ships' doctors under slavery, not many qualified surgeons wanted to participate in this "disagreeable trade". Falconbridge, in discussing the surgeons on slavers, observed: "It may not be improper here to remark that the surgeons employed in the Guinea trade, are generally driven to engage in so disagreeable an employ by the confined state of their finance."[34] Strained finances might have been a major reason for the surgeons-superintendent to join emigrant ships, though their salaries were far from attractive. Indeed, the low remuneration may have been one factor militating against the ability of emigration officials to secure more competent surgeons. Surgeons-superintendent received a gratuity per head on those landed alive with an increase in proportion to the number of voyages undertaken. A surgeon-superintendent such as Hardwicke on the *Allanshaw* would have received a higher rate of gratuity than some others as he had undertaken about nine voyages in this service.[35] This per capita pay was lower than that paid to those transporting emigrants to Australia; consequently, the better ones gravitated towards the Australian service. Those on the emigrant ships were guaranteed a free return passage to India or England, but they were not entitled to a pension, free outfits or continued employment in the service. Besides gratuities, surgeons proceeding to the Cape of Good Hope or Australia were given fixed sums of £40 and £60 respectively, claimable within a specified period, in lieu of return passage.

The continued difficulty of attracting competent surgeons resulted in an increase in their pay by the late 1860s when it went up from 8 shillings a head landed alive to 10 shillings for the first voyage, 11 shillings for the second, as long as the surgeon's conduct was deemed satisfactory, and 12 shillings for subsequent voyages. Still, a veteran in the Australian service could earn up to 20 shillings (£1) a head.[36] The Emigration Act XLVI of 1860 also stipulated the appointment of European surgeons or Indians who had received collegiate training in the European system of medicine (though the lack of respect accorded Indian surgeons on board the ship made them less likely to join an emigrant ship). The nationality and skill requirements were not always easy to meet, and thus were not always observed when prospective surgeons were scarce. Where the European surgeon was not fluent in the language of the emigrants, an interpreter was provided. At the same time, Act XIII of 1864 laid down in greater detail the duties of the surgeon, which started before the ship departed the port of Calcutta or Madras. Both surgeon and compounder were to be appointed at least ten days before the ship was scheduled to sail. The surgeon was to visit the depot daily, or at least five or six times, to examine the emigrants individually, inspect the ship's ventilation, hospital, privies, water and distilling apparatus, and report any defects or deficiencies. However, the surgeon was never given the ultimate responsibility of deciding on the fitness of emigrants to embark. There were continual complaints from the surgeons, especially when mortality had been exceptionally high on a particular voyage, that many who embarked should never have been put on board by the emigration agents.

On the voyage the surgeons-superintendent were required to attend to the medical care of the emigrants on board the ship, making sure to detect and treat illnesses before they assumed epidemic proportions. They were to "keep up spirits" of the emigrants by encouraging them to sing and dance, and supervise the cooking and serving of food. Because of the difficulty of attracting competent surgeons to the Indian labour migration trade, infractions of the rules laid down for their conduct were often overlooked; still, there were cases, however infrequent, of withholding of gratuities and outright dismissal. Some carried out their duties diligently, others did not.

Up to the 1850s males and females had been separated on board without any attention to family, but this was later modified. The strict spatial separation by gender had been maintained on the grounds of "decency" and to reduce the spread of sexually transmitted diseases by limiting, or trying to prevent, sexual contact. It was the negatives of this arrangement which dictated later modifications. The negatives stressed were that families and couples were separated and that there was an increased likelihood of sexual harassment of women by sailors. Indian men, the supporters of modification argued, were necessary to protect Indian wives on board. Consequently, by the 1860s single men and women were separated but couples were kept together. Single women were placed aft (the rear of the ship), married couples and children were amidship, and single men were placed in the forward part of the ship.

Regulations were laid down regarding clothes and diet, the space allocated to each emigrant and the sleeping arrangements. The food supplies provided for Indians conformed to caste and religious preferences. By the 1870s, meat (mostly fresh mutton) had been introduced into the diet on board instead of dried fish which had previously been the choice. Dried fish was still recommended for the first few weeks of the voyage when unstable sea conditions made cooking difficult, but fresh meat was to be cooked thereafter. Increased portions of rice, flour, ghee and dhal were implemented in 1871. The cook was usually drawn from among the highest Hindu castes on board in an effort to avoid caste-conflicts, but such conflicts could not be avoided completely. Furthermore, the choice of Hindu cooks (and, at times, what they chose to serve) offended Muslims, usually a minority on emigrant ships. Twenty Muslims on the *Jura* bound for Guyana in 1891 reportedly refused to eat because the sheep had been killed by a Hindu. The food was thrown overboard. On arrival of the ship *Grecian* in Georgetown in 1893, the agent general of immigration reported that three Muslims had been placed in irons on the voyage on 17 September 1892 for inciting the other immigrants not to eat the food issued to them because the meat was pig and beef not fit for Mohammedans.[37] Of course, the objection might have been related more to the fact that the meat was not *halal* (prepared as prescribed by Muslim law) than because of the ethnicity of those who prepared it.

The use of space on emigrant ships was regulated as a result of the concern about avoiding the overcrowding and high mortality so much associated with slavers in the African Middle Passage. In 1842, the numbers of migrants allowed on board were related to the size (tonnage) of the ships, one emigrant to two tons. By 1845 this was abandoned in favour of the cubic measurement of seventy square feet or twelve "superficial" feet for each emigrant. The colonial land and emigration commissioners were insistent that sufficient space should be allocated to allow for "respiration and motion" and that such space should be such that a "full grown man" of about an average height of five foot, six inches "might lie down, supposing no system of berthing [on-ship beds or bunks] be adopted [and] move about without much inconvenience".[38] Despite the opposition from some quarters, Act XIII of 1864 reduced this to ten superficial feet for each adult. Increased numbers could be carried by this reduction. This allotment again caused overcrowding and inadequate ventilation, and so was reversed by the Colonial Land and Emigration Commission to the 1845 space for adults. The allocation of ten superficial feet was retained for children. No upward limit of numbers was actually stipulated, but preference was shown for larger vessels with better ventilation and space for recreational facilities than smaller vessels. There had been an attempt to stipulate that emigrant ships should not carry more than 300 to 350 contract labourers on board, but this had been abandoned in 1860 on the grounds that not only did it increase the cost of passage but it restricted the emigration agent's selection to small ships which could not be as well fitted out or ventilated for comfort as large ships.

Initially, the emigrants slept on mats on the deck of their quarters. In 1866 a recommendation was put forward by Dr Pearse, surgeon-superintendent on the *Oasis,* for raised wooden platforms instead of mats. This was in an effort to improve health and reduce the mortality on ships, but it is unclear if this recommendation was effected on all ships involved in the indentured labour trade.

Regulations Concerning the Care of the Emigrants

Strict rules regulated the conduct of the sailors towards the emigrants. For example, when the forty-six men were mustered on board as the *Allanshaw* started its journey, they were reminded that "any member of the crew found amongst the emigrants talking to, or interfering with, or molesting them in any way, will be fined one month's pay each offence", and Robert Ipson seemed to have been reminded about this constantly by Captain Wilson and Dr

Hardwicke.[39] Fraternizing between the crew and Indian women was especially forbidden. The hatchways were guarded, especially that section leading down to the single women's quarters. Men were forbidden to enter this section of the ship, and this applied to both fellow emigrants and crew, whose quarters were usually in the forecastle, next to the prow. Some surgeons ensured that the decks below were well lit, especially the female section, to prevent what they termed "promiscuous intercourse".

The strict legislation regarding protecting women from the crew and single male emigrants makes it clear that there was a real fear that emigrant women were always in danger of sexual assault. Indeed, Seenarine recently concluded that "the entire 'coolie ship' was an unsafe place for single females, as well as married women, as they were frequent targets of sexual attacks".[40]

Regulations required that adequate food be provided for the emigrants. The sirdar received and distributed daily rations, helped to supervise the cooking and sanitary arrangements in addition to his other role of assisting in the maintenance of discipline and promoting the emigrants' general welfare. Emigrants were normally fed twice per day and the emigrants usually took their meals on deck as long as the weather was good. Breakfast was served by nine o'clock and the evening meal between five and six o'clock.

The emigrants were encouraged to be on deck as much as possible and to entertain themselves by dancing, singing and playing games. Adult men and women were provided with chillum pipes and women were provided with combs and other supplies for their comfort.

Every attention was supposed to be given to the health of those on board, particularly with a view to maintaining as low a death rate as possible. Emigrant ships were fitted out with water closets, separate ones for men, women and the crew by 1885. This not only prevented their quarters from being smelly from excrement but also reduced the spread of diseases on account of a filthy environment. Emigrants were encouraged to bathe at least once a week, to keep active and to oil themselves with coconut oil weekly. After the near disastrous 1856–57 emigration season in which the death rate on ships from Calcutta to the Caribbean ranged from 6 per cent on the *Wellesley* to 31 per cent on the *Merchantman*, an average of 17.27 per cent, regulations were improved with a positive impact on the death rates which had fallen to 3 per cent by the 1862–63 season. Apart from enormously high death rates when accidents happened – as in 1858 when 120 out of 324 emigrants on the *Salsette* to Trinidad died en route, when in 1865 the *Fusilier* was wrecked at Natal with

Table 1.8   Mortality at Sea: Voyages to Colonial Guyana, 1871–1890

Year	%	Year	%
1871	1.60	1881	2.68
1872	4.74	1882	1.46
1873	5.56	1883	0.64
1874	5.58	1884	2.04
1875	1.12	1885	2.50
1876	1.08	1886	1.41
1877	1.52	1887	1.59
1878	3.30	1888	1.82
1879	1.55	1889	1.50
1880	1.34	1890	1.41

Source: D.W.D. Comins, *Note on Emigration . . . to Guyana, 1893*, in Hugh Tinker, *A New System of Slavery: The Export of Indian Labourers Overseas* (London: Oxford University Press, 1974), 165.

a total loss of life of 246 (including those who died from fever on the voyage to Natal), and when the *Eagle Speed* was wrecked at the mouth of the Mutlah River with 300 lives lost – in general, by 1885 the mortality rate was much lower. It was 3.26 per cent on the *Jorawur* which landed in Guyana in December 1884 and under 3 per cent on the *Allanshaw* of 1885. The mortality rate was lower on ships sailing from Madras (an average 0.9 per cent in the 1850s) than on those which sailed from Calcutta. Among the improvements were better medical examination and selection of prospective recruits at the emigration depot in India, improved ventilation, separate compartments for the sick, recruitment of experienced surgeons capable of dealing with diseases and illnesses on board, improved water, and better diet on board. By the time the *Allanshaw* sailed, the average mortality was 2.50 per cent on ships to colonial Guyana, and it was to become even lower by 1890, as shown in Table 1.8.

Despite the strict regulations governing the treatment of emigrants on board ships to colonial Guyana and other importing territories, such rules were flouted constantly and flagrantly. In 1862, for example, charges were brought against the surgeon-superintendent of the *Persia*, Mr Chapman, for cruelty to the emigrants on board.[41] In 1863 those on the *Clasmerden* who had staged the so-called mutiny complained that the surgeon, A.N. Watts, had been drunk for most of the voyage and had not carried out his duties satisfactorily. His gratuity was eventually reduced as punishment from 10 shillings to 2 shillings per emigrant landed alive.[42] On the *Jorawur* of 1884 complaints of indiscipline, lack of authority and drunkenness on the part of the captain were made. There were complaints on several voyages that the food was inadequate, that potato, milk and pumpkin spoiled on the way, and that food designated for the emigrants was at times siphoned off for the crew. There were also reports that the water taken on board was contaminated and that emigrants were physically punished by the crew. On the voyage of the *Main* to Guyana in 1888, several crew members breached the rules proscribing physical punishment of emigrants and proceeded to shackle and handcuff those they regarded as having committed offences. Whereas African men were routinely shackled and handcuffed on the Middle Passage slavers, regulations surrounding Indian emigration were that emigrants were to be put in irons only in extreme cases of indiscipline, and only the captain could do this. But the interpretation of what constituted "extreme indiscipline" was often suspect. Putting emigrants in irons was also allowed if they threatened to jump overboard to commit suicide (as several high-caste Indians had done on the *Foyle* of 1887, following the example of Podrath Singh, because they claimed to have been "polluted" by being touched by a low-caste sirdar),[43] or if they were deemed insane. The eight men and five women who had been handcuffed on the *Main* complained to the agent general of immigration upon arrival in Guyana that they thought the punishment had not fit the so-called crimes. One of the women had been handcuffed, for example, for lighting her *haka* (chillum pipe) and smoking in between decks.[44]

Despite the insistence of the emigrants on the *Allanshaw* that they had been well treated on the voyage (see chapter 3), that journey had not been incident-free. The logbooks kept by the surgeon-superintendent and captain were full of incidents in which the crew abused the emigrants. For example, the "coloured boatswain" had struck Auntoo on the shoulder with a rope; Juggessar and his wife had been verbally abused and threatened by Robert Ipson; Ipson had abused others, including the cook and "Kalu/Kaloo no. 289" whom he had pushed and kicked on 30 September. This led Kalu to say to two of his compatriots, Janki and Bhadaya (interpreted for Ipson by a sailor, Templeton), that Ipson might have been one of those who had raped the young woman,

Maharani; Nandhal had been struck with a rope by the engineer; Palukdhan
had been struck by the sailor John Smith; O'Brien had deliberately thrown a
six-pound tin of mutton at the Indian women on deck; Beharie's thumb had
been cut by the cabin boy William Clintworth who was subsequently punished, leading to a near mutiny by the crew; and several sailors had been accused
of annoying the hospital inmates "when they came aft to muster at 8 p.m. [on
23 August] by making ugly noises with their mouths at the doors and
windows".[45]

The regulations against fraternizing between crew and female emigrants and
proscribing sexual relationships between crew and Indian women were also
flouted constantly. If the ships' records and immigration reports are to be
believed, the sexual exploitation of women in this period did not reflect only
white but also black and Indian masculinity in action, and there *is* proof that
the emigrant ships hired non-European crew, many of whom were black.
Indeed, there were at least six black sailors on the *Allanshaw*. Black men
(African, Caribbean and US citizens) had a long history of maritime occupations, a fact that is not often recognized. But as W. Jeffrey Bolster recently
recorded, the stereotypical view that "blacks aboard ships sailed as commodities
rather than seamen"[46] needs to be overturned. He adds that even before the
abolition of slavery, individual enslaved men routinely drew on maritime work
to take charge of their lives or to communicate with distant blacks: "free and
enslaved black sailors established a visible presence in every North Atlantic
seaport and plantation roadstead between 1740 and 1865".[47] This was as true
for US blacks as for African-Caribbeans. A post–War of Independence shipping boom in the United States created jobs for enslaved and freed African-
American men, and since "seafaring in the age of sail remained a contemptible
occupation for white men, characterized by a lack of personal independence
and reliance on paltry wages", according to Bolster, it became an occupation
of opportunity for black men.[48] Shipboard work for blacks became less
significant after the abolition of slavery in the United States when white men
increasingly dominated this occupation, so many African-American seamen
sought jobs with the English shipping companies. This helps to explain the
presence of "Yankee sailors" (a description applied to Ipson who had served in
the American navy) aboard nineteenth-century Indian emigrant ships. Indeed,
apart from Ipson (from the Danish Caribbean), the *Allanshaw*'s crew list made
it clear that British maritime commerce hired seamen from countries outside
the British Empire, including Brazil, Germany and Finland. It has already been

noted that Indians, some passengers themselves, were also hired as crew. A few positions, like that of sirdars, were held by high-caste Indian men and a few cases have surfaced in the manuscript sources of these sirdars molesting women on board. Sweepers and cooks also tended to be Indians.

Race was never irrelevant aboard ships. As Bolster observes: "Black men understood that among sailors, race worked in an ambiguous and sometimes contradictory fashion." So, in general, while seafaring was a way of escaping the discrimination in post-slavery societies and facilitate upward social mobility, certain roles on the ships were assigned to blacks on racial grounds. On the Indian emigrant ships, while black men never held the lowliest positions, which seemed to have been reserved for subaltern Indian men for cultural reasons (for example, Indians would never agree to black men cooking their food), they tended more to be rank-and-file seamen rather than officers for the most part. But even as seamen, they held some position of authority over the bonded labourers on board. Still, while black men may have felt superior to their "culturally alien" "human cargo", they were keenly aware of the racial hierarchy *vis-à-vis* European crew.[49] Bolster records that black men often suffered disproportionately the capricious nature of shipboard punishments and, I daresay, discipline. Despite collective work and an easy familiarity between non-European sailors and their white shipmates, social identities were still conditioned significantly by race, and many white seamen just did not like non-white or black seamen.[50] Ipson's claim that he had been singled out for particular attention by the *Allanshaw's* officers might therefore not be unbelievable; neither might be his claim that some of the Indian emigrants deliberately lied about his involvement. For it is undeniable that inter-racial prejudices coloured inter-ethnic relations on board nineteenth-century Indian emigrant ships.

However, although there was no love lost between European and non-European, especially African and Caribbean, crew, as is indicated by the frequent outbreaks of conflicts between them, and the equally frequent requests by the surgeons-superintendent of the ships that black crew members be replaced by Europeans, it would seem that the actions of both groups towards Indian women reveal that indentureship, like enslavement, manifested signs of gendered tyranny on the part of those who exercised, and abused, their power over the emigrants they were exclusively employed to protect. Although the duty of the seamen and officers was to see to the health and comfort of the emigrants aboard the ships engaged in the trade in contract labourers, they often held out rights as "privileges" in order to force compliance among the women. Above all, the actions of black and white men towards Indian emigrant women on the ships destined for the Caribbean demonstrated that the roots of the racist and ethnic tensions which later characterized the host societies in which Indians settled, were deeply embedded in the voyage from India and did not suddenly emerge in the region. As settlers, both Indians and African-Caribbeans harboured mutual feelings of contempt and superiority towards one another; such feelings, no doubt, had already found expression on the passage from India. Thus Donald Wood's view that Indians "encountered Negroid peoples for the first time in their lives when they landed in Port-of-Spain"[51] is not completely accurate. The whites on board, both officers and rank-and-file sailors, harboured a certain contempt for Indians as a race, perhaps a racial attitude towards non-whites inherited from enslavement and strengthened by British imperialism in India, and the emigrants as a class. One surgeon-superintendent, Dr R. Whitelaw, noted in his diary of 1882 that "there is a great tendency among officers, apprentices and men (if European) to consider the coolies [sic] a people who may be pushed about, abused and annoyed at will".[52] Even Ipson articulated clearly that he did not know what all the fuss on the *Allanshaw* over the emigrants' welfare was about: he "had been in emigrant ships before and with as many as 800 on board and never saw such a damned fuss as these was made on board of this ship about them".[53] Their views about lower-caste women were clearly seen in their treatment of female emigrants on the voyages and came out strongly in the evidence given at several official enquiries launched over the period of indentured labour migration when complaints about sexual assault and other misconduct of the crew could not go unnoticed or pushed under the mat. The rather "democratic" spread of the practice among the men in charge of the ships, as this section will demonstrate empirically, reflected a certain amount of acceptance of it.

    True or not, the complaints about the abuse of emigrant women by black men were seen in the reports of emigration officials and ships' surgeons. Indeed, one argument used by the surgeons who called for the reduction in the number of black men employed as crew on Indian emigrant ships, or their total elimination, was the usual ethnic stereotype that they had an "incorrigible addictedness to sexual intercourse". This view was articulated strongly by the surgeon-superintendent of the *Moy* which landed in Jamaica in June 1891 and whose crew apparently consisted mostly of black men. He wrote in his report:

the greatest difficulty was experienced during the voyage in preventing intercourse between the [black crew] and the female passengers. I concur in thinking that on account of their generally incorrigible addictedness to sexual intercourse, negroes [sic], if so employed, should be in a minority on a cooly [sic] emigrant ship.[54]

Individual black men were implicated on several occasions, before and after the case on the *Allanshaw*. The Agent General of Immigration, in summarizing all the data relating to the voyage of the *Avon* to Guyana in 1892–93 for transmission to the Colonial Office, reported that it had come to his attention that Steed, an African crew member "had so often been cautioned against interfering with or molesting the immigrants that the surgeon-superintendent, on arrival at St Helena requested the Inspector of Emigrants to have [him] removed from the ship". The inspector of emigrants refused to take this drastic action on the basis that no actual assault had taken place and so no legal charge could be brought against Steed.[55] Although some surgeons-superintendent complained that black men were more likely than white men to molest women on board emigrant ships and used this argument to justify their call for a white only or predominantly white crew, a higher proportion of the complaints about the sexual abuse of emigrant women by officers and crew on emigrant ships to the Caribbean was directed at European men. The surgeons themselves were infrequently implicated, based on complaints made by the emigrants on arrival at their destination. My research has uncovered more evidence of "sexploitation" on the ships destined for Guyana than on those destined for other Caribbean territories. This may be a reflection of the uneven nature of the contents of the reports submitted by emigration officials and surgeons. It could also be explained by the fact that far more reports exist for Guyana which outpaced any other receiving territory in the region, and was the destination of numerous ships from Calcutta and Madras.[56]

The major sources of evidence are enclosed with the correspondence between the emigration agents and the land and emigration commissioners for the period 1854–60 and with the correspondence between the colonial governors and the Colonial Office officials. It was customary for all reports of the surgeons and agents general of immigration/emigration (protector of immigrants/emigrants in some territories) to be forwarded to the Colonial Office and these have proven to be a wealth of information on the issue of the abuse of women. The reports of the agents-general of immigration in colonial Guyana are replete with complaints of "misconduct" on the part of the surgeons-superintendent, captains and crew, for immigrants were usually encouraged to lodge such complaints on arrival in the colony. Such complaints were made against Dr Wilkinson on the *Bucephalus*, Dr Galbraith on the *Devonshire*, Mr Simmonds on the *Royal George* and Dr Cook on the *Assaye* – all to Guyana. The captain of the *Thetis* was said to have indicated that he had no intention of interfering when the Indian women and the sailors on the ship engaged in sex, and the surgeon-superintendent of the *Canning* of 1860 lost a part of his gratuity because he was accused of getting three women drunk so that they could not testify against him. On that same ship, two sailors had "violently assaulted" women to have sex with them, yet no-one found out who the individuals were so that they could be punished.[57] The crew on the *Dovercastle* to Guyana in 1871 was accused of "misconduct" towards the women on board. The land and emigration commissioners complained that as long as the water closets were placed where they were [in the fore of the ship] "these things will happen". Murdoch of the Colonial Land and Emigration Commission, in a letter to R.H. McCade, indicated further that "we have always maintained the impropriety of so placing them, notwithstanding the opposition for several years of the Indian Authorities".[58] There were complaints that the drunken captain of the *Jorawur* of 1884 and the crew and the steward of the *Grecian* of 1885 molested the women.

Dr Atkins, surgeon-superintendent on the ship *Silhet* to Guyana in 1882, was said to have formed a relationship with the female emigrant Janky despite the fact that Deemohammed, a sirdar, had staked his claim to her previously. Predictably, Atkins was absolved of any "illicit intercourse" with Janky during the voyage and was later allowed to marry her, a highly unusual occurrence for the nineteenth century. On arrival in Guyana, Atkins requested the cancellation of Janky's indenture on payment of the required sum. After this was agreed, but before the final permission to marry was granted, a contract was drawn up "securing to the wife control over the sum of £250 deposited on her behalf by the husband with the Acting Administrator General, to be applied for the benefit of the said wife as he and his successors should think proper". The sum was invested with the receiver-general. Janky was given a letter addressed to Messrs W. and H. Brand of 109 Fenchurch Street in London, who were agents of the Department of the Administrator General. This letter instructed them to give Janky any advice she needed in the event of her husband's absence or death.[59] They were married in Georgetown, Guyana, by the minister of the St Andrew's Church, and Atkins was directed to present himself to the emigration agent on arrival in London, where he proceeded to take Janky.

Such complaints about the surgeon, captain and other crew on emigrant ships were not confined to Guyana but applied to Jamaica and Trinidad as well. An early case to come to light on a voyage to Jamaica involved Dr Prince, surgeon-superintendent of the *Ravenscraig* of 1861. In addition to having been accused of excessive drunkenness on the voyage, Prince was said to have committed "criminal assaults" on some of the Indian women "under circumstances of an extremely aggravated nature".[60] As the alleged offences were committed before the Atlantic crossing and, as was usual in such cases, the ship stopped at St Helena, the governor there ruled that there was sufficient evidence against Prince. He ordered that Prince be sent to Jamaica under arrest and relieved of his duties. On Prince's arrival in Jamaica, however, the police magistrates and other officials released him on the basis that there was not enough evidence to convict him. They paid him his salary and gratuities as set out in his contract. The police magistrate and his supporters felt that even if such intercourse had taken place between Prince and the women on board, "it is clear that it must have been with their consent".[61] How they came to this conclusion is unclear, but it was not unusual for lower-caste women from India, as African women enslaved in the Americas had been, to be regarded as loose and promiscuous and incapable of being raped.

The reports of voyages to Trinidad also contained complaints about illicit intercourse between crew and emigrant women. Complaints were made in this regard about the *Nerbuddah* of 1885. Complaints also originated among emigrants to Mauritius and one Dr R. Brown was actually dismissed from the Mauritius service after four voyages when he was reported for drunkenness and pulling off the clothes of female emigrants.

It should also be pointed out that Indian women also suffered abuses at the hands of Indian men on board as domestic violence was not unheard of in instances where people tried to live as couples and families on board. On the *Artist* to Guyana in 1874, there was "a murderous assault on a woman by her husband", who was subsequently "put in irons to be dealt with upon landing".[62] While on the journey of the *Silhet* to Guyana in 1883, the male emigrant Gazee and his wife had an argument. She complained, and the third mate hit Gazee and threatened him with further action if he continued to ill-treat his wife. The surgeon-superintendent's report indicated that Gazee seemed to have believed that he had "a prescriptive right" to ill-use his wife.[63] Perhaps Gazee's attitude was reflective of the caste and gender hierarchy which were organizing principles of the Brahminical social order and which resulted in the subordination of women.

A male emigrant on the *John Davie* in 1885 reportedly tried to rape a young girl. He was beaten, even though corporal punishment was not supposed to be carried out on emigrant ships. The captain and surgeon-superintendent, however, felt justified in breaking the regulation in view of the gravity of the offence. The man was given six lashes "with a moderately hard rope on the buttocks".[64]

The protector of immigrants in Trinidad reported that a woman, Bhagwandie, a passenger on the *Nerbuddah* of 1885, had jumped overboard "after she had been assaulted by a man . . . who appears to have slept with her several nights during the voyage". It turned out that this man was Indian, a sirdar, who had also stabbed her in her side with a bayonet. He was arrested on arrival.[65] Several Indian sirdars and Lascars were also accused of molesting Indian women on this voyage.

The foregoing examples should indicate that the sexual abuse that Maharani claimed to have experienced on the *Allanshaw* before its arrival in Guyana in 1885 was not implausible. Emigrant ships were not only transporters of contract labourers to colonial plantations, they were also "spaces of (s)exploitation". This should be borne in mind when analysing the findings of the Commission of Enquiry held to investigate Maharani's death. Also to be borne in mind is the racism at work on nineteenth-century emigrant ships which targeted black men for exposure far more than European men and Indian men, even though the latter were clearly not blameless in the "sexploitation" of Indian women.

[2]

JOURNEY
INTERRUPTED

Maharani's Death on the Allanshaw

V ERY FEW PERSONAL DETAILS about Maharani have
surfaced, except that she was emigrant number 353 on the *Allanshaw,* the
"daughter of 'Pargas' ", and probably between sixteen and twenty years old.[1]
Additionally, her name suggests that she was of a higher caste than the majority
of Hindu emigrants on board. Biographical details are sketchy because her
certificate of indenture, emigration pass and form of agreement (see examples
in Figures 2.1, 2.2 and 2.3), which would have provided details of her age,
height, village or district of origin in India, police post in India, distinguishing
marks, her next of kin, and so on, have not so far been located despite searches
in the United Kingsdom, India and Guyana. It is easier to locate such
documents for those who landed alive than for those who died and were buried
at sea. Her emigration number and the name of her father were revealed in the
various enquiries held in the aftermath of her death, and other bits of
information were supplied by others on board the *Allanshaw.*

Maharani had no relatives on board the ship and so fitted the profile of the
majority of Indian women shipped to the Caribbean; that is, she was a young,
independent, single female. Whether she was forced to embark or opted to
emigrate voluntarily is not known, but the possibility that she was kidnapped
cannot be discounted. On the other hand, she could have made the conscious
decision to emigrate to the Caribbean to work and better her economic status.
Many people on the *Allanshaw* knew Maharani. Fifteen of those who testified

Ship: **DINAPORE**
25 Garden Reach, Calcutta, the 19th Nov. 1873

Name   Oree

Father's Name   Bhowanidin

Age   21

Caste   Bania

Height   5ft 7½ ins.

Name of Next of Kin   Bro' Rambocus

If married, to whom   ....

Zillah   Barabunky

Pergunnah   Sunnoighat

Village   Tekaitnugur

Bodily marks   Scar outside of shin

We certify that the man above described (whom I have engaged as
labourer on the part of the Government of British Guiana where he has
expressed his willingness to proceed to work for Hire), has appeared before me and that I have explained to him all matters concerning his duties
as an emigrant, according to Section 38, of Indian Emigration Act VII of
1871.

COUNTERSIGNED

....

Protector of Emigrants at Calcutta   Emigration Agent for British
                                            Guiana

Figure 2.1   Typical emigrant's embarkation certificate, colonial Guyana

Source: Basdeo Mangru, *Benevolent Neutrality: Indian Government Policy and Labour Migration to British Guiana 1854–1884* (London: Hansib, 1987), 242.

COLONIAL EMIGRATION FORM No. 44.

WOMAN'S
EMIGRATION PASS.

HEALTH CLASS.

Depôt No. *404*

For Ship

No. *951*

PROCEEDING TO JAMAICA.

Jamaica Government Emigration Agency.
21, GARDEN REACH,

CALCUTTA, the _____ *26/5* ____ 190*5*

PARTICULARS OF REGISTRATION	Place,	*Raipur.*
	Date,	*3. 4. 05*
	No. in Register,	*48.*

NAME, ... *Jeera.*

Father's Name, ... *Fakilal.*

Age, ... *25*

Caste, ... *Kurmi.*

Name of Next-of-kin, ... *Hira Ram   Brother.*

If married, name of Husband, ...

District, ... *Raipur.*

Thana, ... *Saraipara.*

Village, or Town & Mahalla, ... *Kesli*

Bodily Marks, ... *Scar on right side of back.*

Occupation in India, ... *Labour.*

Height, ... *4* Feet *11/2* Inches.

CERTIFIED that we have examined and passed the above-named Woman as fit to emigrate; that she is free from all bodily and mental disease; and that she has been vaccinated since engaging to emigrate.

DATED

The _____ 190

_____
Depôt Surgeon.

_____
Surgeon Superintendent

CERTIFIED that the Woman above described has appeared before me and has been engaged by me on behalf of the Government of JAMAICA as willing to proceed to that country to work for hire; and that I have explained to her all matters concerning her engagement and duties. This has also been done at the time of registration by the Registering Officer appointed by the Indian Government.

DATED

The *8. 4.* 190*5*

_____
Government Emigration Agent for JAMAICA.

PERMITTED to proceed as in a fit state of health to undertake the voyage to JAMAICA.

DATED

The *2. 6.* 190*5*

_____
Protector of Emigrants.

J. N. Banerjee & Son, Printers, Calcutta.—300—1-1905.

Figure 2.2   Typical woman's emigration pass

at the enquiry in colonial Guyana stated clearly that they either knew or remembered her. Almost everyone who testified described Maharani as having been well behaved, even shy, and always in the company of the women and children on board. Hardly anyone on board ship accused her of constantly being in the company of men. She died several days after she confided to some of her female compatriots that she had been "criminally assaulted" by two crew members. She described them in detail, leading to suspicions first against Robert Ipson. Extracts from the medical history of the voyage also indicate that James Oliver from Bath, England, might have been the second man who raped Maharani, but no action seems to have been taken against him and, indeed, his name was mentioned in only one document.[2] Three people stated that they had even heard that at least three men were involved.

The information which surfaced in the aftermath of Maharani's death indicates that her ordeal started eleven weeks out of India, two hundred miles from the Cape of Good Hope, before the ship had undertaken the transatlantic crossing. As far as can be ascertained from the documents, on the morning of 24 September 1885, she was found lying on the deck suffering from fever and complaining of a pain in her arm. Dr Hardwicke described his discovery to the Commission of Enquiry in colonial Guyana as follows:

> One day while sitting on the poop, I noticed the woman Maharani lying on the poop under a blanket. I was not aware at first who it was and took no notice of it, as this was not an unusual occurrence. After an hour or so I saw her still remaining there, and I heard her call out to one of the girls to bring her some water. I then asked one of the girls who it was and what was the matter. They told me it was Maharani and that she was sick. I got up and went over to her and uncovered her. I asked her what was the matter. At the same time I felt her pulse and she told me that she had hurt her arm by falling on it and that it was very painful. I examined her arm and found nothing the matter with it, apparently, but she had a quick pulse, and on asking her she owned that she had a fever.[3]

At this point, Hardwicke did not consider Maharani sufficiently ill to warrant hospitalization, and so sent her down to the ship's dispensary to get some liniment and medicine. He also took the precaution to ask Nandhal (called the "babu"), the chief compounder, if he had, in fact, seen Maharani. When he said "no", the doctor sent him "down in the between decks to bring her up", and he gave her some medicine. She was then sent back to her quarters below deck. The next morning, 25 September, Nandhal was

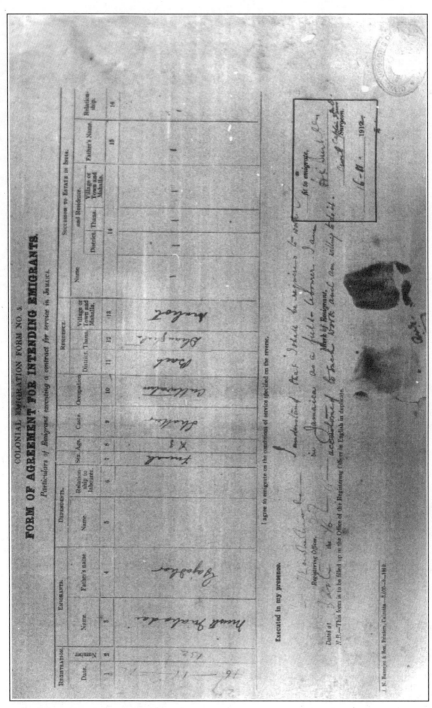

Figure 2.3   Typical form of agreement for intending emigrants

told that Maharani had been heard crying all night, so he took her from her sleeping quarters and at about six o'clock in the morning and confined her to the area on the ship designated as the hospital. While in the hospital, she complained, in addition, of pain in her head and abdomen, and this was confirmed by Mohadaya, Golap and Heerdayaram. She was allegedly examined twice by the nurse, Golap, and by the surgeon-superintendent, who indicated that the pain and tension continued all day. Dr Hardwicke entered in his casebook of 26 September that he considered Maharani's case "somewhat mysterious", but he observed that she was "very reticent and would give no information" that would have helped to clarify what was wrong with her. On the morning of 27 September 1885, after yet another (early morning) examination by Hardwicke, Maharani was described as having been "very much exhausted, pulse small, quick and thready". By half past ten in the morning, she was dead.

Maharani's case was considered "perplexing" and serious enough to warrant, first, an investigation by Dr Hardwicke; second, a further investigation by the governor of St Helena; third, an attempt to prosecute Ipson by the inspector of police in Guyana when the ship arrived in port; and fourth, the appointment of a Commission of Enquiry by the governor of Guyana, Sir Henry Irving, who was obviously dissatisfied with the outcome of the police case.

Dr Hardwicke's enquiry was undertaken after about half an hour after Maharani's death. Two returning emigrant women, Moorti and Mohadaya, who had first gone to see their friend on the Friday after she was hospitalized, informed him that Maharani confided in them that her illness was due to her having been "criminally assaulted" by two sailors.[4] Hardwicke, after consultation with Captain Wilson, decided to conduct a post-mortem examination of the body at two o'clock in the afternoon on 27 September in the presence of the compounder and the assistant compounder to discover medical proof of the allegations (which, at first, he seemed inclined to believe). Indeed, initially, Hardwicke claimed that the result of the post-mortem "appeared to be more or less confirmatory of the rumour [of rape]", but this was not eventually reflected in the evidence he gave before the Commission of Enquiry or in his official medical report. Among other things, the surgeon's official report of the post-mortem revealed that Maharani was well nourished, was not pregnant and had no venereal disease, despite the rumours of the spread of gonorrhea. Hardwicke also found that the girl's bowels were distended. He claimed that there was no external sign of violence on the body except for some post-mortem "darkening on the darsium [dorsum?]", and there was no inflammation or laceration of the vagina. He did admit later on that as the incident had taken place several days before Maharani's death and therefore the post-mortem, physical signs of violence could have disappeared or faded.[5] He recorded further that there was some "purulent matter at the entrance to the vagina", but that otherwise there was no abnormal appearance there. While he found no hymen, he claimed that there was nothing to lead to the supposition that this membrane had recently existed (which would have given some credence to the claim of rape).

In the end, Hardwicke entered in his casebook that the death was caused "principally from shock to the nervous system", as he did not find convincing physical evidence of forcible sexual intercourse or other signs of violence on the body to attribute death to "criminal assault". Clearly, the definition of rape that the doctor used included only "violent sexual assault" and not lack of consensual sex. He later elaborated on the impact of "shock to the nervous system", saying: "In a European, I would expect the shock to be severe at first and become less severe as time passed; but I ascribe the shock in this case [which persisted even five to six days after the alleged incident], to a considerable extent to mental depression as the result of shame."[6] He did not say explicitly that the reason for this "shame" was the mental effects of sexual assault, but this was implied, complicating his views even more. He also said that without the additional non-medical information of the women, he might not have concluded that death was the result of shock. He might have concluded that she had peritonitis, though he would still have found his diagnosis unsatisfactory as a cause of death as he really saw no sign of "general peritonitis". Hardwicke failed to explain what medical evidence led him to conclude that Maharani's death was due to "shock", but maintained that a person could die from shame and mental depression. When pressed to give a cause of death at the hearing against Ipson in the City Police Court in colonial Guyana, however, Hardwicke conceded that Maharani died from "internal inflammation and shock to the nervous system". He added that "the inflammation might have been caused by a blow or by a serious assault or by someone attempting to outrage her".[7]

After another consultation with Captain Wilson, Hardwicke also decided to conduct an enquiry. They both agreed that "the best course to pursue, in the absence of direct [medical] evidence, would be to quietly collect all the evidence that could be obtained by enquiry and observation, and not to take any further steps until the authorities at St Helena had been communicated with".[8]

The captain yielded to Hardwicke's wisdom on the issue. According to him, even after hearing about the incident, "I did not take any steps at the time. I left it to the Surgeon." Even though the crew was his responsibility and even though he had heard that "a man was suspected", he did not confront this man. His rationale was: "I consulted with the doctor and he considered it better to get up the evidence first."[9] The surgeon proceeded to do just that between 27 September and 17 October 1885.

Hardwicke interviewed sixteen people on the ship in the course of this "quiet investigation": Mohadaya; Moorti; Rupia (a fellow patient); Nathur, the hospital topaz; Heerdayaram, the hospital attendant; Nandhal; James T. Grant, the Guyanese national who was assistant compounder (dispenser); W. Stokes, the third officer; G.W. de la Mare, the chief officer (first mate); Prirum and Molai, the sirdars on watch that night; G. Colthurst, the second officer; Captain Wilson; crew member Thomas David; and two returning male emigrants, Sesahoye and Ramyadd. The glaring omissions were, of course, Ipson, who was identified as having been the chief suspect, and his fellow sailor Oliver, neither of whom was subjected to a physical or oral examination. Hardwicke also seems not to have officially interviewed Golap. Unlike the Minutes of Evidence taken in colonial Guyana and written down verbatim by an official scribe, those taken on the ship were written in reported speech, indicating that Hardwicke summarized the statements. Hardwicke, of course, would not have had the benefit of an official scribe.

Mohadaya was the first to be interviewed, followed by Moorti. Mohadaya reported that when she first went to see her in the hospital, Maharani complained of a "great pain in her belly". She had told them that around ten o'clock on the night of Wednesday 23 September, when she went to the water closet, she was violently seized by two sailors and "criminally assaulted". The two men allegedly pulled her out of the water closet, gagged her with her *kapra* (sari), dragged her to the fore end of the hospital, and ravished her, taking turns, one holding her mouth with her sari while the other assaulted her. Mohadaya's later testimony was as follows:

> I came in the ship [*Allanshaw*] with Maharani. I have been in the colony before. I knew Maharani well. I did not sleep with her. I am married. My husband is in India. I know Moorti. She is married, but her husband was not with her. She slept near Maharani. I do not remember when Maharani became sick. One day she told me

she had a pain in her hand. The doctor took her to the Hospital. I saw her in the Hospital. She did not call me, I went myself to see her. She said she was very sick, that two sailors had connexion with her and that she was ashamed to tell me. I asked her if she had any pain in her belly. This was on a Friday. She did not tell me on what day the men had connexion with her. She said two sailors dragged her from the closet and had connexion with her on the deck. She said it was at night time. She did not say how many days this was before. I did not ask her. She described one sailor as having a red shirt and tattoo marks on the breast. I did not hear any of any other sailors having connexion with the women or see them talking to the women. Maharani told me not to tell and that when she got better she would tell the babu. She only complained of the little pain in her belly. She was not very sick. After she died, the same day, I was speaking with Moorti and we told the doctor. Maharani was young; about my size. She did not tell me that she struggled with the men or cried out. She said that she could not cry out because the sailor put cloth in her mouth. She did not say the sailor hurt her very much. I never saw Maharani go up to the closet alone. Or any other woman. The women generally go in twos and threes.[10]

Moorti gave much the same evidence as Mohadaya, though hers was more succinct:

> I came in the ship *Allanshaw*. I knew Maharani. I went to see her one Friday evening. She was in hospital. I asked her what was the matter. She said that two sailors dragged her from the closet and had connexion with her. She did not say that she had a pain in her belly. I did not ask her whether she cried out. She did not say anything to me about crying out. Maharani told me nothing more.[11]

Questions were later to be raised about why Maharani had gone to the water closet by herself on this occasion. However, although it was more usual for the women to go in groups to the water closet, located some six feet from the hospital on this ship, it was not completely unknown for some to go by themselves as Maharani, described by Dr Hardwicke as having "a very good character as a modest, retiring girl", had done.

Maharani did not seem to know the identity of the men who attacked her, for she called no names and said she could not identify them. But her pre-death "testimony" was certainly helpful in their eventual identification. For she described them in detail. One was said to have been "a tallish stout man tattooed on his breast and had on a red shirt".[12] This alone might not have led to fingers being pointed at Ipson as other seamen had tattoos and possessed red shirts. But she went on to say that man with the tattoo was the same man who had abused the emigrant Juggessar's wife earlier on the trip.[13] Unless she, Moorti or Mohadaya was lying, this pointed squarely to Ipson. Apparently on 29 August, Ipson had verbally abused and threatened Juggessar, emigrant number 384, and insulted his wife. The other, she reportedly claimed, was "a short, stout man with a round face". No explanation has been found as to why this implicated Oliver. Ipson was, of course, angry when he heard the rumour that he was a suspected rapist, hitting the person from whom he heard this and indicating his anger in no uncertain terms to the captain and surgeon-super-intendent.[14] Yet he later denied that he had known ahead of arrival in St Helena that he was a suspect. Perhaps he referred to the fact that he had not been informed officially by the captain or surgeon-superintendent, both of whom wanted to prevent further unruly behaviour among the sailors.

According to Mohadaya, Maharani had said that if she recovered she would go to the doctor and tell him all the circumstances. Moorti reported that she was curious as to why Maharani had not cried out to the sirdars on watch, but she also reported that when asked this, Maharani's response was: "How was I to call [out] with my mouth shut up with the cloth?" Although she had told Mohadaya that she would report the incident if she recovered, she seemed less sure when Moorti asked her about this, stating that she was "too much ashamed to tell". When Moorti went to see her again the next day, this time in the presence of Grant, she denied the story, but then (perhaps after Grant had left) repeated it to her once more.

Rupia, who had been in the hospital with her sick child when Maharani was brought in and placed in the bunk beside her, reported that she had also overhead the conversation between Maharani, Moorti and Mohadaya (al-though they thought she had been asleep). She said that Nathur (the hospital topaz) and Heerdayaram (the attendant), both of whom had heard the story, urged Maharani to "tell the babu". When examined, Nathur admitted that he had overheard some of the conversation, and certainly enough to know what had transpired. But he did not tell the babu about what he had heard because he was "ashamed to tell such a [private] thing".[15] Heerdayaram, however, had reported the incident to Grant, who in turn passed on the information to Nandhal and two of the officers. Grant also asked Moorti to go with him to the hospital and stand in front of him so that Maharani could not see him, and encourage her to repeat the story so that he could hear it for himself. It was then that Maharani denied the incident, only reaffirming it after Grant had left. Nandhal had not bothered to discuss the matter with Dr Hardwicke as he had heard that Maharani had denied the story subsequent to having first told it; in any case, he had not believed it himself.

Walter Stokes, the third officer, Godfrey de la Mare, the chief officer, and George Colthurst, the second officer, all admitted that they had heard the story from Grant and the hospital attendant. The sirdars both denied having heard anything unusual that night. When examined, the captain affirmed that there was a full moon on the night in question, that it was a fine night with little wind, and defended the security of the ship, stating that "any disturbance on deck would have been easily heard". The officer on watch that night, the acting boatswain who walked the quarterdeck, and the sirdars on watch all said that they had heard no noise on the night in question. They said it had been a fine night with a good moon and little wind and no clue that any criminal behaviour had been taking place.[16]

When questioned about what they knew about the case, the two return emigrants Sesahoye and Ramyadd both said that Ipson had said in their presence that he had had a woman in Calcutta and that before he got to Guyana he would have to f—— one of the women. They had also seen him looking at the emigrant women on board. Thomas David gave the most damning testimony, stating on 17 October that Ipson had not only admitted to him that he had had sex with one of the women on board but had also showed him his badly and recently chafed penis as proof.

At the end of his investigation, Dr Hardwicke ruled that, as Maharani had indicated, the evidence pointed strongly to Ipson, though he himself still found the medical evidence too "slender" to accuse him of the act. Thus he did not arrest Ipson, claiming that he had no power to do so. He chose to report the incident to the officials at St Helena and leave it up to them to investigate further and take action. St Helena was a normal revictualling spot for transatlantic ships and in the nineteenth century played the dual role of point of investigation and action, if necessary, when crimes and misdemeanours were committed even before emigrant ships began the transatlantic crossing. There is no evidence that Hardwicke tried to find the other perpetrator fitting the description given by Maharani to her friends.

The investigation undertaken by Dr Hardwicke was later criticized by the Commission of Enquiry appointed in Guyana, as well as by some of those who gave evidence, as having been too cursory. Most felt that his post-mortem conclusions were unsatisfactory. The assistant compounder, Grant, claimed that Dr Hardwicke did not record all the information which witnesses supplied and made scant use of them anyway. Furthermore, he relied too heavily on the evidence of the officers and called only one witness from among the crew who would have had more information, and he had left more detailed enquiry to the governor of St Helena rather than mining the crime scene when fresh. The Commission of Enquiry in colonial Guyana did not seem particularly critical of the decision to allow the authorities in St Helena to conduct further investigation. It was the first port of call after India, and the British authorities there had police power. Additionally, in the event that they had decided that one or more persons was criminally responsible, they would have taken such a person (or persons) off the ship instead of allowing them to proceed to colonial Guyana. Finally, the commissioners felt that "an enquiry held immediately after the event would be much more likely to lead to a satisfactory result than one instituted at a later period".[17]

The next chapter will explore the actions taken at St Helena and in colonial Guyana on the arrival of the ship.

[3]

INVESTIGATING THE COMPLAINT OF "CRIMINAL ASSAULT"

O N THE ARRIVAL OF THE *Allanshaw* at St Helena on Friday 9 October 1885, the colonial secretary, G.A. Banbury, in his capacity as emigration agent, boarded the ship to inspect the emigrants and to receive the reports of Captain Wilson and Dr Hardwicke.[1] He inspected the ship, which he found "satisfactory in every regard", and was assured that Hardwicke and the officers had used every precaution to "protect the Coolies from the seamen".[2] He also inspected the logbooks and casebooks kept by Wilson and Hardwicke respectively, and he was apprised of all the events that had transpired between Calcutta and St Helena. The emigrants made no complaint against Captain Wilson and Dr Hardwicke, nor did they mention any of the abuses they had suffered at the hands of the crew as indicated in the ship's logbook. There is also no indication that Banbury commented on those abuses. Hardwicke told him about the women's charge against Ipson (though not Oliver) based on what Maharani had confided before her death, and of his own actions in the case. Banbury at once communicated with Colonel Blunt, the acting governor of St Helena, as well as with J.C. Homagee, the law officer of the Crown there (the Crown prosecutor). All three, in fact, reportedly listened carefully to the outline of the case as presented by Wilson and Hardwicke. Homagee decided that the evidence of Moorti, Mohadaya, Rupia and others was not sufficient to charge Ipson with rape leading to Maharani's death or to delay the ship for more detailed investigation. His advice was that, instead, further investigation could be carried out when the ship arrived in colonial Guyana if it were deemed necessary.[3] This advice, endorsed by the Colonial Office, was contrary to the views of Wilson, Banbury and Hardwicke, as they wished Ipson to be ordered placed in confinement or under some form of restraint.

The *Allanshaw* docked in Georgetown harbour, colonial Guyana, on 6 November 1885 with 370 men, 178 women, 30 boys, 33 girls and 41 infants – a total of 652 immigrants – after what Hardwicke admitted had been a long passage (102 days).[4] The immigration agent general, A.H. Alexander, was at once informed of the death of Maharani and the suspicions against Robert Ipson. Again, Oliver's name was not mentioned. On Captain Wilson's recommendation, Alexander immediately ordered that Ipson be arrested on suspected manslaughter and turned him over to the police,[5] who proceeded to gather evidence and prepare the case for prosecution. In arresting Ipson, Wright, an inspector of police, stated that he charged Ipson because he "unlawfully and feloniously did kill and slay one Maharani – against the Peace of our Sovereign Lady the Queen, Her Crown and Dignity".[6] Wright gathered evidence from Wilson, Hardwicke, Ramyadd, Sesahoye, the cabin boy William Clintworth, Thomas David, Emmanuel Anderson and James Joseph O'Brien.

The case against Ipson began on Friday 6 November 1885 and lasted just over a week.[7] It was tried in the City Police Court in Georgetown before His Worship Henry Kirke, an experienced magistrate and sheriff of Demerara.[8] The theory of the prosecution, led by Wright, was based on the statement said to have been made by Maharani herself about having been violently seized, gagged and raped. He also used Ramyadd's testimony that Ipson had said to him: "Before we reach Demerara, I must f—— one of these girls," to which Ramyadd had replied: "If the woman's husband catch you, they will beat you and the other coolies will beat you." Ipson allegedly responded: "Coolie too weak to beat me and Captain and Doctor can do me nothing." Thomas David also testified that Ipson told him four or five days before Maharani died that he "had had a f—— with a coolie woman". When David expressed disbelief, Ipson allegedly "took out his penis and showed me. He said his penis was chafed as he had to force the woman. She was too small for him. I looked at his penis. It was chafed. It was in a most ridiculous state."[9]

David refuted Ipson's claim that he had only had sex with a woman in St Helena, though Bain testified that the women not only came on board the ship at St Helena but that some sailors had gone ashore. Indeed, a total of three women had come on the ship at St Helena but the penis incident was said to have occurred before the ship arrived in that island, said David. William Clintworth, confirmed aspects of David's deposition, stating that Ipson had similarly told him that he had had sex with Maharani "at night on the starboard side of the Hospital".[10] But Clintworth admitted that he did not really take Ipson seriously as he was always "swaggering about". The sailor Emmanuel Anderson had also been shown Ipson's bruised penis, though the victim of Ipson's attack had not been named. From what he saw, "on the forehead all the skin was bruised off and was swollen".[11] Ipson had also allegedly boasted to the sailor James O'Brien about what he had done though, again, he had not named the woman. Hardwicke testified that Maharani had died from "internal inflammation and shock to the nervous system" and that such inflammation could have been caused by a blow, by serious assault, or "by someone attempting to outrage her".[12]

Despite all of these testimonies, the evidence was deemed to be inconclusive, much of it hearsay, and Henry Kirke acquitted Ipson, citing insufficient direct evidence.[13] His view was that "the case for the prosecution was founded on the supposition that the defendant had outraged the woman and [the] evidence [presented] went rather to contradict than support that supposition". On the basis of Hardwicke's testimony, Kirke ruled that "if the deceased had been ill-treated by accused as the evidence of the witness alleged, one would expect to find corresponding injuries on the deceased",[14] but no such injuries had been found. As none of the witnesses had presented direct evidence to convince him that rape had been perpetrated, Kirke felt confident about his decision to throw out the case and not send it forward for trial by a jury. Inspector Wright could do very little about Kirke's decision and could not provide the kind of evidence that the latter wanted. Maharani had not made any formal complaint to any of the ship's officials, the doctor examined the body too late to find signs of physical injury or forcible entry and the accused sailors had not been examined for physical evidence. Ipson was, however, reapprehended on a charge of disobeying "the lawful command of the captain of the *Allanshaw* on the 15th October" and for stealing twenty yards of canvas valued at $6.48 belonging to James Nurse, another crew member.[15] Ipson was sentenced to four weeks in prison for the charge of disobeying the captain and three weeks' imprisonment or a fine of $6.00 for stealing the canvas.[16] Five other "refractory seamen" – J. Smith, J. Erickson, G. Soderland, Alexander Bain and J. Peterson

– had already been accused of this offence. Erickson was acquitted but the other four were each sentenced to one month's imprisonment. Smith, who had also assaulted Captain Wilson, was sentenced to a further ten weeks in prison. Along with Bain, Smith got yet another month's term on a third charge of disobeying Wilson on 5 September 1885. Ipson's case had been deferred but he was charged and sentenced and fined subsequently.[17]

The governor of colonial Guyana, Henry Irving, nevertheless, seemingly unconvinced by Kirke's ruling, ordered a more detailed examination and, on the advice of the Colonial Office, appointed a Commission of Enquiry. His rationale was that "there still remained grounds for a suspicion that the death of this woman had been caused by one or more men having had connexion with her, and that Robert Ipson had been prominently concerned in it". The Commission of Enquiry was chaired by Alexander and consisted, in addition, of Dr Robert Grieve, acting medical officer to the immigration department (and later acting surgeon-general), and Kirke, who had already dismissed the case against Ipson, and Mr Clarke, Nourse's attorney. The commissioners met for nine days (27, 30 November; 2, 4, 5, 7–9, 12 December), and examined twenty-two witnesses (recalling Wilson and Grant more than once) including Hardwicke; Wilson; Golap; Urquhart; Heerdayaram; Grant; several of the forty-one sailors, including Ipson, and officers; a select number of male and female fellow emigrants, including Moorti and Mohadaya; and a Georgetown medical doctor, Alexander Finlayson, with whom Grant had had a conversation considered relevant to the investigation. The chairman turned down a request from the attorneys for James Nourse, owner of the *Allanshaw,* that Captain Wilson be allowed to be present during the examination of all the witnesses but had no objection to Clarke being present. Those called to testify had their statements taken under oath and written down by the secretary to the commission. Those who were literate in English signed their statements to indicate that they were correct; those who were not (mostly the first-time emigrants) had the statement read to them and signed with an "X".

The commissioners directed their attention to six specific areas of enquiry that went beyond the case of Maharani's death itself. As a result, while it was clearly Maharani's death that had driven the investigation, a great deal of information was revealed on all aspects of this passage from India, testifying to the many abuses committed on emigrant ships, including the sexual abuse of emigrant women, which was one of the worst manifestations. The areas of enquiry were (1) Maharani's death; (2) the conduct of the surgeon-superintendent; (3) the conduct of the captain; (4) the conduct of the officers; (5) the conduct of the crew; and (6) the causes of mortality on the voyage (sixteen passengers having died from cerebro-spinal illness, syphilis and other ailments).

The first witness to be called on day one of the hearings was Hardwicke. His voyage on the *Allanshaw* was his ninth in the capacity of surgeon-superintendent. He outlined the details of Maharani's illness and death, the subsequent rumours about her sexual abuse by members of the crew, his own actions on the voyage, in particular his instructions to Golap, the conduct of the post-mortem and on-ship enquiry, and his conclusions. His testimony about these matters varied little from that discussed in the previous chapter. He was also asked to comment on the crew, the captain and officers, and the general condition and treatment of the emigrants on board. He stressed that "the conduct of the captain during the voyage was entirely satisfactory", and that Wilson did everything in his power "to protect the emigrants, to keep the men from the women and to assist me in every way". He also emphasized, truthfully, that the mortality rate was much lower than on other voyages and ships.

Hardwicke believed that the "general behaviour of the crew towards the women was good", not because they were of good character but perhaps because he had been "more particular" than on other voyages in this regard because "I saw suspicious signs at the beginning of the voyage and was afraid the men might go for the women". Perhaps because of this vigilance, this had been the only case of "indecent assault" on the voyage. He claimed to have been particularly suspicious of "a few – among others the man Ipson". In fact, he said that the crew on this voyage was not as satisfactory as on other voyages and six of them had behaved badly, bordering on "mutiny" at one stage of the journey. Many of them had obviously found the regulations too strict. Hardwicke also defended the conduct of the officers.[18] He emphasized that he did not think, given the security arrangements on the ship, that Maharani could have been pulled out of the closet without an alarm being raised. At the same time, he admitted that in times of cold weather, the sirdars went below deck. Therefore, it was possible that there had been a lapse in security the very night Maharani decided to go to the water closet by herself instead of with other women, the more usual practice. Yet Hardwicke, like Grant, Wilson and Stokes, appeared reluctant to portray Maharani as a "loose woman", especially as, in his view, she was a shy, retiring girl of good character. He reiterated his view that she could conceivably have been raped and not show more physical signs of injury though, based on the allegations, he had expected to find more medical proof at the post-mortem.

Captain Wilson was called next. He testified that he had known Maharani and had heard the circumstances surrounding her death from several quarters. He also provided specifics on the location of the ship on the day she died:

> I am Captain of the ship Allanshaw. I knew a girl named Maharani. I know she died on 27th September, Latitude 35"34S, and Longitude 19"27E, about 150 miles from land.[19] The first I heard about the case was from Dr Hardwicke and that was on the day of her death. He told me that he had heard from Mohadaya that she had been ravished by one of the crew.[20]

He confirmed much of what Hardwicke had said regarding the security arrangements of the ship. According to him,

> Coolie Sirdars are stationed at the Hatchways. The fore hatches are closed with grating; the main and after hatches have Sirdars stationed at them. The petty officer walks up and down on the upper deck between the closets and the break of the poop. The Officer on the poop could not see clear along the main deck. The sirdars, are, I believe, relieved every three hours. The Baboo sees them posted. As a rule I go round the main deck about 10 o'clock or 11 to see that all is right. I have known the sirdars go down below to the foot of the ladder in cold weather. It was cold at that time to them. . . . I never saw a woman coming up singly at night to the closet. They always come up in twos or threes.[21]

Wilson's admission that the night in question was cold (and the coordinates of the ship would confirm this) conflicted with entries in his logbook, for in the logbook he recorded that it was a fine night with light winds. Did being under oath force him to be more truthful? Still, this new possibility of a lapse in security arrangements on cold nights, leading to the inability of anyone to hear any alarm that might have been raised by Maharani, seems not have been taken into serious consideration by the commissioners.

Predictably, Wilson defended the officers and crew, disagreeing with Hardwicke's opinion that they represented an unsatisfactory lot, with the exception of Ipson and Smith. Again, his official logbook painted a different picture, with clear indications of other examples of unruly behaviour and assaults on the emigrants by other members of the crew. Like Hardwicke, he was puzzled by what he considered the unusual practice of a woman going to the water closet by herself at night, especially a woman of Maharani's character: "I noticed this girl as a very quiet modest girl. I think she would be the last one a man would have taken any liberty with",[22] and "I had no suspicion while Maharani was alive that any of the crew had anything to do with her."[23] Yet, while it seemed out of character for Maharani to have had consensual sex with the sailors, and while her shy, retiring nature would have made the possibility of rape more believable, Wilson stopped short of articulating this view. Instead, he stressed, like Hardwicke, that if the incident had occurred as described, someone was bound to have heard and raised an alarm. For example, according to him: "There is generally someone sleeping in the Hospital" (near where the incident allegedly happened). Pressed by questions from the commissioners, he admitted: "It is possible that two men could have seized the girl, thrown her down and ravished her without being heard", yet he continued in the next sentence: "Any outcry would have been heard."[24] He eventually admitted: "If she had been suddenly seized and gagged there would have been no outcry." Wilson seemed inclined to believe that if Maharani had been sexually abused, as had been charged, the most likely culprit was Ipson, and supported those who testified negatively about him. Wilson's testimony also clarified a question I raised in the introduction regarding prior cases. According to him – and this is crucial for explaining why this investigation seemed unusual – "I have never experienced before, a voyage at the end of which such charges had to be made as in the case of this voyage."[25]

On days two to nine, depositions were taken from the sailors, officers and emigrants. Whereas Hardwicke and Wilson were asked to comment on all aspects of the voyage, the other deponents were only asked questions relating to Maharani's case and the conduct of the captain, surgeon, officers and crew.

These interviews again reinforced the fact that several people had heard about the incident from Maharani herself: Heerdayaram, Nathur, Golap, Rupia, Moorti and Mohadaya. They, in turn, had passed on the story to Grant and others; however, according to Urquhart, the sailmaker, who gave evidence on day two, the name of the perpetrator had been kept quiet and few knew who had been suspected until they arrived in colonial Guyana, though several drew their own conclusions.[26] Ipson had also told his own version of the story to some of his fellow sailors though he had not identified the woman. But regardless of the source of the information, there was remarkable similarity in how the story of the incident itself was told by these second-hand narrators. For example, most compared well with Mohadaya's quite detailed testimony (see chapter 2), especially her statement that, according to Maharani, "two sailors dragged her from the closet and had connexion with her on the deck. She said it was at night time. She did not say how many days this was before. . . . She described one sailor as having a red shirt and tatoo marks on the breast. I did not hear any of any other sailors having connexion with the women or see them talking to the women."

Predictably, Moorti and Heerdayaram[27] (who had overheard the conversation and had passed it on to Grant) gave much the same evidence as Mohadaya, and so did Grant who had not heard the story directly from the victim. He stated:

> I went in the Dispensary and the Hospital Attendant Heerdayaram told me he had heard Maharani telling Moorti in his presence that two sailors had laid hold of her some nights before on her way from the closet. One had taken her "Kapra" [sari] and held her by the mouth to prevent her making a noise while the other lifted her away (he did not say where) and that both in turn had connexion with her. One he described Maharani said had a red shirt: the other was not described.[28]

Both Golap and Heerdayaram confirmed some of the medical details, but Golap also pointed to some errors in the account given by Hardwicke and Heerdayaram of the medical examination. She did not, for example, examine the victim's "private parts" even after hearing the rumours of sexual assault, and she refuted any claims that she had received instructions to do so. Hardwicke may have issued such instructions but they had not been passed on to her. Hardwicke testified: "After she [Maharani] came into the Hospital she was attended by the female nurse. She made no complaint to the female nurse, but after she was admitted to Hospital I told the Baboo [Nandhal] to get the nurse to examine her private parts. The Baboo told me she had done so and found nothing wrong."[29] Golap, however, testified as follows:

> I was a nurse on board the ship *Allanshaw*. I remember Maharani. She was sick in hospital. The Baboo told me to rub oil on her belly. No-one told me to examine her private parts and I did not do it. I never told the Baboo I had done so. I rubbed oil on her belly. Maharani did not tell me anything about the cause of her illness. I do not know what was the cause of death. There was a good deal of pain in her belly. I think she died from this. I never heard that any of the sailors had connexion with the women. I slept below. The women go up to the closet six or seven at a time. I never saw one alone go up. If I wanted to go up I would take five or six with me.[30]

Grant confirmed most of Golap's account, but denied her claim that she had not been instructed to examine Maharani's "private parts". While he was unsure if Hardwicke was the one who had issued the order, he claimed that he had heard Nandhal tell Golap to do so and that Golap had confirmed that she had. He also supported Hardwicke's view that Maharani did not at first appear to have been very ill, neither was it clear that she had been raped, yet Heerdayaram stated that in hospital, Maharani was groaning and did not take her food. According to Grant:

> I saw a good deal of Maharani while in Hospital. She did not look very low at first. She spoke to me freely and did not look like a woman very deeply ashamed. She did not scream from pain in her stomach. Her legs were not drawn up. . . . She was not crying when she came into the hospital [though he had heard that she had been crying the night before]. Her intellect was quite clear. Before her death we could form no opinion as to the nature of the disease she was suffering from. I did not connect the story of the assault with the cause of her death.[31]

Like Captain Wilson, Grant admitted: "[I]t was hard for me to believe the story [of her assault] as she was one of the women who stayed in the after part of the ship and never had anything to say to the sailors."[32] Also, like Wilson, he found it difficult to believe the rumours as not only did the sirdars keep a tight watch but also the sailors did not molest the women on board. His view of tight security was shared by others like Urquhart. In fact, so sceptical had he been of the rumours that he made an effort to hear the story from Maharani herself, using a duplicitous method. To satisfy his own doubt, and as it appeared that only the women had heard the account directly from Maharani, Grant explained:

> [I] sent for Moorti; took her into the hospital, stood behind the patient as she lay in the bunk so that she could not see me; and told Moorti to question her as to what was the matter. Moorti asked her, but at first received no reply. She kept on asking her and Maharani got at once into a rage, denied having made any statement as to her having been violated by the sailors and further accused Moorti of having spread a report that she had been having connexion with sailors and was ill in hospital with gonorrhea in consequence. . . . That the only thing wrong with her was that she had had a fall on the poop a few days previous.[33]

Moorti was reportedly upset that Maharani had made her look like a liar. Grant in fact believed that this was why Moorti said that she did not believe Maharani's story. On the contrary, Grant felt that she did believe her friend and that the women's account should have been taken more seriously by Hardwicke, especially as Ipson had actually been said to be the attacker.

Most of the emigrants interviewed felt that Wilson and Hardwicke had done a good job on the voyage and that they had been treated well overall. Most, including the women, denied knowledge of any general "consorting" between officers and the emigrant women, and admitted that they had never seen Maharani go to the water closet at nights by herself. Women did go alone, but rarely. That was not the norm. Moorti, rather unsisterly, seemed sceptical about Maharani's story, stating: "I do not believe what she said. I did not hear of any sailors troubling any of the Coolie women. None of them [had ever] asked me to go with them."[34]

Only one person, Chitamun, reportedly saw the incident himself. Lutchmun, a second-time emigrant who joined the ship as a hospital attendant but later became the steward's cabin boy and was also Moorti's shipboard "husband", gave evidence that Chitamun, a passenger on the ship, told him that he watched the whole incident for three-quarters of an hour and that the crime had been committed by two white and one black sailor, looking like an African-Guyanese,[35] who had "taken an Indian woman to the forecastle and had sexually assaulted her". Chitamun had not told him who the men were nor who the woman was, except to identify the nationality of the "nigger" involved, but he had told him that the woman had shouted and asked them to stop. This contradicted earlier statements in the ship's logbook that only two men were implicated. Lutchmun himself had been accused of fetching women, including Maharani, from below deck for the steward, and that he had seen her and other women playing with the crew. He denied this, though admitted that Mohadaya always "skylarked with the doctor and others, dancing, playing tom tom and throwing coloured powder on their faces",[36] but both he and the steward, William Leslie, to whom Lutchmun had related the story, denied such accusations. Leslie further emphasized that he had never behaved improperly with the emigrant women, never gave them sweets, and never heard that other sailors, officers, captain or surgeon had molested the women or treated some preferentially as had been charged.[37] Lutchmun, however, insisted that when Chitamun later learned that the woman was Maharani, he visited her in the hospital where he noticed that "her mouth was swollen, her belly was swollen; and she could not speak". This would have indicated an act of physical violence which was not noted in the doctor's report. Lutchmun said he did not report what he had heard to anyone in authority at the time and no one had asked him anything; however, on arrival in colonial Guyana, he had spoken about it with Lee and

Captain Wilson, who said he would give his name to the immigration agent general to be a witness.[38]

When it was his turn to give evidence, Chitamun admitted that he had spoken to Lutchmun about some of the incidents as he described them, but denied having actually witnessed an act of sexual assault by Ipson. He did admit that about two nights before Maharani died when he had gone with a sick male emigrant, Baboolall, to the closet, he had seen one man, "a sailor, holding a coolie woman's hand. He was carrying her in his arms. He took her into a place where the sailors live".[39] The woman was about the size and appearance of Maharani, he said. But, according to him: "I did not hear the woman calling out. She was not struggling . . .",[40] a statement that heavily influenced the conclusions of the commissioners. He also said something else which, if true, tied Ipson squarely at the scene: he was "the same man who beat the captain and who was handcuffed when the ship came into port. I know the man. I am quite certain as to the man."[41] Chitamun also said that as he was taking Baboolall back, one of the sirdars, Ramkhelawan, came up to him and asked him whether or not he had seen a sailor carrying a woman. He made no comment except to say: "You are a sirdar, you are watching. I brought a sickman to the closet." The sirdar then went to the forecastle door and listened.[42] Ramkhelawan, however, denied having had a conversation either with Chitamun or Lutchmun about Maharani; he could not recall having gone to look for a missing woman or knocking at the door of the forecastle. All he recalled seeing was a sailor boy dressed in a woman's clothes. This boy had on a sari and a piece of cloth on his head. Whether it was a black or white boy, he did not know. But whoever it was had no right being on deck at that time. He only remembered asking Chitamun if the person was a boy or a girl.[43]

William Lee, a native of Montserrat, identified himself as an able seaman with nine years' experience at sea. He had joined the ship in London for the round trip. Lee gave testimony which, like Chitamun's, linked Ipson directly to the incident. While he denied any general knowledge of consorting between officers, crew and emigrant women, especially as the sailors hardly came in contact with the part of the ship where the women stayed, he testified that he had knowledge only of one case:

> I was relieved from the wheel one evening at 12 o'clock and was coming forward, walking on the port side. On the fore part of the water closet, when I got opposite, I heard a bawling, very low, [and] groaning. I stopped at the capstan and went up and heard the woman say, "Salam, salam, he is too big." These were the words used.

I don't know what she meant. I went up and saw this man Robert Ipson with his hands on her shoulder; it was the same woman who died. The woman was standing up and so was he, at the fore part of the water closet. I said to him, "if you follow these women you will get yourself in trouble". I said nothing more to him till next morning and I went to the forecastle, and took my coat off and went to our closet on the portside. I came back and went to my bunk and saw nothing more. I left him standing with the woman just as I found him. When I came back from the closet I found him in the forecastle. The woman was taken ill the next day.[44]

Lee, however, went on to say that he did not see any actual sexual contact, stating: "I did not see him doing anything to the woman."[45] While he later learned that two men had assaulted Maharani, he insisted that he had seen only Ipson. But it is clear that Lee, despite the fact that he saw no actual sexual contact, suspected that Ipson had done something to Maharani, for when he saw Ipson the next morning, he said to him: "You are going to a very bad place, Demerara, to interfere with these people." According to him, Ipson replied: "[D]amn her to Hell, she is big enough to bear it."[46] Lee said further that, to his surprise, even after she died, no one asked him anything, and he did not volunteer any information even after hearing the rumours about Ipson. Above all, he did not think that she had been forced as she had claimed. Even though he did not think much of Ipson who he described as a "rough and unruly young man", he felt Maharani must have given her consent.[47] He did admit that he found the handling of the whole matter strange, for he had been on other emigrant ships where even if someone was accused of troubling a child, all of the crew would be called up and questioned. He later confided to Grant that "if all hands had been called aft at the time, the doctor would not have got away so easily; because I did not think the doctor made sufficient enquiry at the time. If he had, I would have spoken out."[48] He also hinted that Ipson should have been given a medical examination, for he had heard that Ipson had "shown his private parts", which were "mashed up, cut up", afterwards to two crew members, David and Anderson. William Clintworth later admitted that Ipson had told him and a few other men: "Last night, I had a coolie woman." Whether Ipson was lying or not, he could not say.[49] Despite his views on the matter, when the police commissioner came on board at Georgetown to arrest Ipson and asked him if he knew anything about the case, he said "no". He defended his actions on the basis of the late stage at which Ipson was questioned and his reluctance "to get anyone in trouble".

The sailors all denied that they or their fellows had been involved; if the crime had in fact been committed, the perpetrator should be sought among the officers, not among the sailors. Most felt the voyage had gone well and the emigrants had been well treated, with only a few incidents of indiscipline involving Ipson and his gang. Not one mentioned the cases of abuse of emigrants entered in the captain's logbook. Only Ipson and Grant testified that they had any first-hand or second-hand knowledge about sexual encounters or social relationships between emigrant women and the officers and the surgeon-superintendent, charges that were vehemently denied by the latter.[50]

William Urquhart, for example, testified that although there had been some acts of indiscipline on the ship by sailors, mainly Ipson and Smith, in general the crew had behaved acceptably: "if I were told that the crew said they went among the women, regularly, I would not believe it. The crew have been told more frequently this time to keep from the women than on either of my other two voyages." Interestingly, Urquhart was one of the few who actually used the word "rape" to describe what he heard had taken place. When examined on day two of the enquiry, he said, among other things: "I heard after her death that there had been a rape committed", although, "I did not hear at any time who did it. It was kept quiet until we came here [Guyana]." But he also did not think that "a woman could have been dragged out of the closet and ravished by two men if the Sirdars had been in the watch and doing their duty".[51] Whether or not they were doing their duty on that particular night he did not say, simply confirming what he knew the arrangements usually were:

> The boatswain kept watch on the main deck between the main mast and the mizzen mast. There is no one between the main and foremast. The watch on deck remain forward and are not allowed to come aft unless for duty. An outrage such as that described could hardly have taken place on a moonlight night without attracting the notice of the boatswain.[52]

There was, of course, controversy over whether the night in question had been moonlit or not, and he did concede that all of this was assuming that the boatswain was on the correct side of the ship, for "If the boatswain was on the weatherside it might have happened on the leeside." Furthermore, "Two of the watch could easily leave and go aft without being missed." Evidently, the security of the ship was not all that impenetrable; several persons testified that the sirdars not only left their posts on cold nights but could be bribed to look the other way. The sirdars held a key position on emigrant ships, being placed in a position of guarding the approaches to the women's quarters. Clearly, those who wished to gain access to the women had to befriend them.

Robert Ipson testified at this enquiry, unlike the situation at Hardwicke's on-board enquiry when he had not been interviewed. He said that he was born in Santa Cruz[53] and served some time in the American navy.[54] He was employed at Calcutta, unlike some of the other crew members who joined the ship in London. His journey on the *Allanshaw* was his first appointment on an Indian emigrant ship. He had heard about Maharani's illness from a fellow sailor, Warner. He claimed to have been told by the head topaz on board that the officers at times bribed some of the sirdars with tobacco so that they could get women to their cabins or to the sail locker in the middle of the night. Ipson testified further that even though he could not deny that Maharani had been assaulted, he doubted very much that such an assault was carried out by the sailors. If anything, he believed the crime to have been probably committed by the officers, a view he said was shared by the head topaz. His view was that the attempt to pin the blame on the sailors was the result of collusion between the surgeon-superintendent and the captain, both of whom had things to hide. He further testified:

> I myself have seen larking between the Officers and the coolie women, the Captain, the doctor, the first mate, 3rd mate and Steward. I have seen extra diet given to the women by the Captain, doctor, mate and Steward, soft tack, butter, cheese, sugar and cooked food. I have also seen them get fresh water and soap to wash their clothes. This was done to about half a dozen fancy women. I do not know their names.[55]

"The Captain," he continued, "used to get out of his armchair and let one of them sit down in it." He charged that the captain and the doctor shoved their hands between the women's legs. He denied having had anything to do with Maharani, particularly as he already knew from what Lutchmun had told him that she was "the mate's woman". Above all, he denied having anything to do with Maharani's death. He said:

> All I know about it is that I was in the forecastle one day eating dinner and a man named Warner, who is always on the poop assisting the sailmaker, came to us in the forecastle and said, "Well, no matter we're a rough crowd, but I believe everyone has the principle of a bloody man."[56]

Being the nearest to this man, he asked him what he meant, "so he told me he heard the doctor, the Baboo and the Captain were speaking on the poop that there was a girl in the Hospital sick and they thought some of the sailors must have been getting foul of her".[57] He subsequently heard more people with the story but, like his fellow sailors, believed that if any such incident had happened, it had not been committed by the ordinary crew but by those in higher positions who used emigrant women on board for sexual fun. Indeed, he claimed that a return emigrant on board, Lutchmun, who was fluent in English, had told him confidentially that Maharani had had "connexion" with the steward of the ship a week before she died. Lutchmun had denied this. Ipson added that three weeks before the ship's arrival at St Helena, this same Lutchmun told him that, from conversations he had overheard, there was a conspiracy afoot between Wilson and Hardwicke "to charge the sailors with the death of Maharani".[58] He claimed ignorance of any knowledge that he was a suspect in the case until the night before the ship arrived in Georgetown. This latter statement conflicts with the report in the ship's log that Ipson, on hearing that he had been implicated in Maharani's assault and death, dragged the man from whom he heard this to Wilson and Hardwicke, and threatened to hit anyone who linked him to the incident.

Asked about Maharani's claim about the red shirt worn by the offender, he admitted that he owned six red shirts and one white shirt. However, these shirts were never examined he said, and no one had said anything to him officially about the case or the investigation. He felt he was being made a scapegoat for someone else's actions because he was not liked by Hardwicke and some of the officers and crew, like Lee who had linked him to the crime, and often got into squabbles with the captain and officers. He did admit that he had had sex on the voyage, though it was with a woman on shore at St Helena. Others had testified that Ipson had not gone on shore in St Helena.

He admitted that he knew Maharani but even if he wanted to he could not have touched her because "I never had a chance. She was always at the mate's door or on the poop" (though that was not where he reportedly was seen with her).[59] Ipson also added that the likelihood of the sailors getting access to the women was slim because of the security on the ship; the boatswain was on the quarterdeck, the sirdars at the hatches and the mate and apprentices on each side of the poop.

When recalled for the second time, James Grant confirmed assertions that the voyage was unsatisfactory as far as the behaviour of the sailors was concerned. He denied saying that the mate had been familiar with Maharani, that Mohadaya was kept by the captain and surgeon, or that he personally had witnessed partiality to some women. He had, however, seen the officers laughing and talking with some of the women and had heard other women say that the steward (not the mate) had a woman and that Mohadaya got special treatment, that she was "mistress of the ship", but perhaps they were jealous.[60] But his last voluntary deposition on 12 December suggested that Hardwicke had given a few women cigarettes and cigars, and he allowed a few to take their meals on the poop – actions that did not please the other women. He had also heard that Mohadaya had been locked up in the chart room with Hardwicke; at first he had dismissed these as rumours, but later he actually saw Mohadaya exit the chart room and Moorti dragged in, and when she came out she was crying. He could neither say what went on in the room nor if Hardwicke was only skylarking with them or "doing anything of an immoral nature". He denied that he had been threatened about what he might say at the enquiry, as some had claimed, and reminded the commissioners that it was he who had volunteered a third statement.

Grant admitted that he had not told all initially, out of fear that he might meet Hardwicke again and get into trouble, and that he would like to continue in his job as compounder on an emigrant ship. But he had been advised by Finlayson[61] and others in colonial Guyana to tell all. This third statement reinforced the many abuses on these ships and the constant infractions of the immigration rules (though he seemed less forceful about the charges of consorting with women by captain and surgeon). But, according to Grant, "If a Compounder performed his duty faithfully on board these ships he would be at loggerheads with everybody on board."[62]

The officers and those Indians given positions of authority on the ship – the sirdars; Walter Stokes; Joseph Warner, a native of Antigua; William Leslie, the steward; Alexander Bain; G.W. de la Mare; and even Ipson's partner in crime, Smith – all denied that any of the incidents Ipson and Grant said had taken place actually occurred, to their knowledge, especially as the discipline on emigrant ships was strict, as far as the contacts between the crew and the women were concerned. Smith, who was later gaoled for indiscipline on the voyage, thought it was unfair for the blame to be pinned on the crew, especially as he had never seen any consorting between them and the women. But neither did he agree that the officers should be blamed as he had never seen any undue familiarity between them and the women, though he had heard rumours.[63] Stokes said that when he heard the story of Maharani's ordeal, he was not inclined to believe it as such strict watch was kept of the women, and while acknowledging that Ipson was a troublesome man, he did not pronounce on his guilt or innocence.[64] De la Mare, the chief officer (or first mate), admitted having heard a rumour that someone had "split [raped] the Coolie" but had heard no name linked to the incident. He did say that Ipson was logged once for "pushing against a Coolie woman and knocking her down",[65] but he had heard no general complaint about the crew or officers in regard to the women on board. It was not made clear if this was Juggessar's wife, whom Ipson had allegedly assaulted before, or if it was the same woman Hardwicke told Wilson about. This woman, with a child in her arms, had been almost knocked to the deck by Ipson; when she spoke to him about it, he had reportedly told her to go and "f—— herself and get out of the way". When the woman's husband spoke to Ipson, he similarly abused him verbally.[66] Like the engineer, August Makohl (who seemed peeved that those aft got privileges denied the ordinary sailors and who described Ipson as a "rough, childish man"),[67] he swore that he had never seen any "undue familiarity between the Captain, the doctor and officers and coolie women", that he did not think that there was "any truth in the assertion that the culprit should be looked for among the officers and not the crew", and that he never saw "any improper familiarity between the officers and the coolie women". He had no idea why Mohadaya and Moorti had brought the complaint of "criminal assault" to Hardwicke. He did admit hearing Mohadaya described as the "mistress of the ship" and seeing her along with her sister and mother on the poop having their meals regularly; while this was unusual, he attached no "impropriety" to it. Return emigrants, according to him, "were generally more decent than the others" and obviously had privileges on the voyage that first-time emigrants did not have. They were better dressed than the others (though when asked he said that he could not say if they were better looking than the other women), spoke English, and there was nothing "reprehensible, in my opinion, about allowing them on the poop".[68] Nothing in his testimony linked Ipson or anyone else to Maharani's death. He did know who Maharani was, much more so than other crew members. He stated:

> I remember Maharani. She used generally to sit by my door on the poop. My door opens on the main deck. The 2nd mate and I had the same cabin. There was no particular reason why Maharani should have sat at my door. She sat there the whole voyage till her death. Other women sat there with her.[69]

But he denied having taken "any liberty" with Maharani or any other woman. He went further: "I take a solemn oath that this woman Maharani never entered my cabin at all" even though she liked to sit outside his door with the other women.

De la Mare further testified, contrary to Captain Wilson, that the night on which Maharani was allegedly raped was foggy, not moonlit or "fine", and that despite the security measures, she could have been attacked without attracting attention. He also said that Lee had told him that he had heard a scuffling on that same night in the vicinity of the water closet and that a woman had definitely been involved.

Alexander Bain, able seaman, similarly denied any knowledge of consorting between crew or officers and emigrant women, though he hinted at familiarity between the women, Wilson and Hardwicke. He gave evidence that he remembered Maharani clearly as she was always around with Moorti and Mohadaya, but that

> I never saw any of the crew talking or laughing with the coolie women. I never heard
> in the forecastle of any of them having had anything to do with them. A couple of
> times when I was at the wheel I have seen the doctor take one of the girls into the
> Chartroom. I cannot remember if it was the same girl each time. . . . I have seen the
> captain talking to them, but not playing with them. . . . The chartroom is a small
> wooden house on the poop. When the doctor took a girl in there they stayed about
> a couple of minutes. I never saw the doctor playing roughly with the women. I have
> never seen the doctor doing more than making fun with them, giving them cigars.
> . . . I never saw any of the Officers speaking to Maharani.[70]

He also denied having ever seen Lutchmun take women to the officers, nor had he ever seen the steward take women to his cabin. He had never seen Ipson among the women and was surprised when he learned that he had been linked to the incident. He and others believed that Ipson was suspected because "the Captain was down on him. The Captain was down on him because he was always fooling round the deck and was connected with the row about the boy."[71] Finally, he did not believe that Maharani could have been "ravaged" without being seen or heard or that Ipson had shown him his "private parts with evidence of injury". He said something else that was quite interesting: that he had never before seen so much fuss made after a voyage or so many complaints lodged, with five men having been gaoled for misconduct.[72]

Joseph Warner similarly denied any first-hand knowledge of improper conduct between officers, crew and Indian women. He believed that the women had been kindly treated, always being allowed to "play their tom toms and dance on the poop". He testified that he had never seen Wilson and Hardwicke giving sweets to the women, but admitted that he had heard rumours of consorting between officers and emigrant women. However, he attributed the rumours to maliciousness, owing to the strictness of the crew. He admitted that he himself, who had been at sea some thirty-two years, did not like the decreased mobility and strict discipline on emigrant ships, but refused to implicate Ipson in the incident.[73]

Predictably, both Wilson (when recalled on the sixth day) and Hardwicke denied the accusations against them, stressing that they had never had any immoral connections with Indian women on board their ships. Captain Wilson emphatically denied having sexual contact with any of the women and said that he certainly had done no such thing as putting his hands "between their legs, or tickled them", as one witness had accused. According to him, "The most I have ever done was, if they were lying on the hen coop, to slap them on their bottom to make them get out of the way" – by no means a dignified method of keeping "order". He denied that Maharani had sat in front of the mate's door more than any other woman. Several women were in the habit of going to the same place each day. Indeed, he neither suspected Ipson or any other crew member of having troubled Maharani. Once again, he defended the security arrangements on his ship and stressed that the women knew what precautions to take when visiting the water closets.

Hardwicke, upset by claims made against him, especially by Grant, first defended his post-mortem conclusions, stressing that nothing internal or external on Maharani's body made him feel that rape was involved. He had seen nothing wrong with her arm, even though she had complained of pain there. He accused Grant of making untrue and vindictive statements against him in particular about improper actions and preferential treatment, though returnees did have a few extra liberties. While Grant had carried out his duties efficiently, his manner had not always been appropriate and he had had to speak to him about his conduct several times on the trip. He accused Grant of having had sexual contact with the women though it is curious that he had not logged Grant nor recorded any of his displeasure with him. Hardwicke admitted that Mohadaya had visited the chart room, but only while he was taking statements in the on-ship enquiry, and he always had the door wide open, with the captain present on most occasions.[75] Despite his statement that Grant did his job efficiently, Hardwicke later refused his request for a good recommendation (so that he could be re-employed).

In the end, except for the sailors gaoled for insubordination and defiance of the captain's orders (which we only learn incidentally from the documents but which was detailed in several Guyanese newspapers), no other charges were made against the crew, commanders or officers. Above all, the charge of rape was thrown out. There seemed to have been some belief among the investigators that Ipson had sex with Maharani, but this had been with her consent, it was argued. The cause of her death thus remained a mystery and she was left with the shame of promiscuity. There was only some mild censure of the captain and the surgeon-superintendent for allowing things to get out of control on the voyage.

The chairman of the commission, in his summary of the evidence presented, concluded that "a great amount of the evidence is mere hearsay, and quite inadmissible in a Court of Justice". Despite the testimony of the women to whom Maharani had spoken, and the testimony of those who accused the captain and surgeon-superintendent of not always acting appropriately, or even of always maintaining discipline among the crew, the chairman ruled that "the treatment of the Coolies by the surgeon, captain and officers, seems to have been excellent" and deemed statements to the contrary as "perfectly untrue". Alexander and Kirke felt that the captain and surgeon-superintendent had done all that they could to prevent the abuse of women on the voyage, as was their duty. They acknowledged that there were a few incidents of indiscipline among the crew that the captain seemed not to have been able to control, but did not blame the captain totally for such incidents. In further defence of the surgeon-superintendent, the commissioners' report stated that the women he alleged to have treated preferentially (allowing them to take their meals on the poop, for example) were returning emigrants who spoke English, so that it was natural for the surgeon to have wanted to converse with them. They refused to categorize the surgeon's alleged behaviour with these women as "skylarking" as Ipson and others had charged, claiming that what they called skylarking was really just the surgeon's attempt to encourage "fun" among the emigrants.

The commissioners stressed that the duty of the surgeon-superintendent was not only to see to the health and comfort of the passengers but also to see that they had fun and were kept entertained. But, they ruled in Hardwicke's and Wilson's defence, "It is impossible for East Indians to see any familiarity between persons of the opposite sex without inferring criminal intercourse, as in their own country no woman who wishes to preserve her self-respect can speak to a man who is not a member of the family."[76]

The charge that the surgeon-superintendent had women improperly in the chart room was deemed "ludicrous". Alexander claimed that Hardwicke used this room as a writing room, and that from its location, it could not be used for any "immoral purpose". Furthermore, according to him, both Wilson and Hardwicke had testified that they found no fault with the conduct of the officers and certainly had no evidence that any of them had molested the female passengers. There may have been some instances of indiscipline on the part of the officers and some conflicts among the crew, the engineer, for example, having struck a male emigrant; however, such acts were said not to have involved abusing the women. They identified Ipson, described as a "clever Yankee sailor of the worst type", as having been the most guilty of acts of insubordination. These admissions were not considered serious enough by the Commission of Enquiry for them to take any punitive action.

The conclusion that the surgeon-superintendent, officers and captain were above reproach and not culpable was not surprising. Only infrequently were those accused of committing offences on emigrant ships convicted; even then, crew members were more likely than officers to be the ones fined, censured or imprisoned. In this particular case, while some of the sailors were *suspected* of having had something to do with Maharani's misery, the evidence was said to have been insufficient to convict any individual. The commissioners concluded that the result of their investigation

> has been merely to confirm the opinion expressed by the Police Magistrate when he dismissed the charge, viz., that there was no evidence that Robert Ipson had used any force against the deceased, or that there had been a scuffle, or that any body had held her to enable the defendant to commit such an assault; that even the appearance of the woman after death, repudiated the idea that she had been criminally assaulted by any man.[77]

They continued:

> We consider that an assault such as that originally attributed to Robert Ipson could hardly have taken place without an alarm being raised and detection following, especially on a clear moonlight night such as that on which the outrage was said to have been perpetrated; and, further, that it could not have been committed without causing some external and internal injuries of a serious nature on the body of the deceased.[78]

Finally, they said:

> We are, therefore, induced to believe, in accordance with the testimony given by
> Chitamun, that Maharani was carried to the forecastle, probably by Robert Ipson,
> without struggling or attempting to cry out, and that while there, he and others of
> the crew had connexion with her, if not with full at least with forced consent on her
> part, the latter being more probable.[79]

Complaints from previous voyages that the surgeon-superintendent and
officers had sexually abused or, in a few cases, formed permanent relationships
with women on the ships in their charge, or generally failed to carry out their
assigned duties, seemed not to have persuaded even Alexander and Kirke that
some of the rumours on the *Allanshaw* were plausible.

"I Beg to Differ": Dr Robert Grieve's Rebellion

A surprising bifurcation appeared and divided members of the commission.
The report submitted by Chairman Alexander did not have the blessing of the
only qualified medical person on the commission, Dr Robert Grieve. Indeed,
Grieve's views departed so radically from those of his fellow commissioners
that he refused to sign what was deemed the "final" report. Instead, he
submitted his own independent report to the governor in January 1886, stating
that he was "unable to fully concur in the report of the majority of the
Commission" because "I believe that the present enquiry, held at considerable
length and with all obtainable thoroughness, conclusively proves that there
were occurrences on board the *Allanshaw* on this voyage, disgraceful in their
character and serious in their consequences."

He stressed that witnesses had been extremely reluctant to come forward
and reveal all that they knew about life on board the *Allanshaw,* yet they had
stepped forward at great personal risk. So that even if, to protect themselves,
"all be not told", he believed that there was still "sufficient said to justify the
belief that on the whole voyage from Calcutta to Demerara, things were not
as they ought to have been".[80] Grieve singled out Grant to reinforce his view
that some witnesses felt that it was risky to tell all they knew, for the other
commissioners had seemed inclined to dismiss Grant's evidence as contradictory and untrustworthy. But Grieve declared that he found Grant's evidence
no less reliable or trustworthy than that given by other witnesses. On the
contrary, he believed that "the voluntary statement that he made seemed to

me to be the truth, perhaps not the whole truth". If anything, he felt convinced that Grant was holding back information for fear that "if he told anything reflecting upon the conduct of the Surgeon-Superintendent it would prejudice his chance of employment under the Immigration Authorities".[81]

Consequently, Grieve was convinced that "for these incidents, which do not appear to me to have been unavoidable, the responsibility must rest somewhere", especially as everyone, from captain and surgeon-superintendent downward had testified that the journey of the *Allanshaw* had by no means been a satisfactory one, and that several incidents of misconduct had occurred, "rape causing murder, . . . mutinous conduct, . . . assault on the Captain . . . disorderly behaviour and theft".[82] While not dealing in detail with all of the cases of misconduct he cited, nor restating all the evidence of the witnesses who had already been called, Grieve opted to "assume the position of a juryman, who besides hearing the words of the witnesses has the advantage of seeing their demeanour whilst giving evidence".[83]

To help to prove his case and justify his conclusions, Grieve turned his attention to some salient areas, first to the relationship between some of the crew and the officers. The crew had been clearly dissatisfied and some had been inclined to be mutinous. The officers behaved in an insolent and overbearing manner to the crew. A fight had even erupted between the second officer and one of the crew, and this fight was carried on "in the midst of a crowd of Coolies, men and officers".[84] This, in Grieve's view, was a clear indication of a lax captain who had not shown sufficient firmness in dealing with the first indications of an "unruly disposition on the part of his crew".[85] Furthermore, the crew seemed to have had cause to complain and to tend towards a mutinous attitude. For one, they had not been provided with enough food and this ought not to have happened. Grieve also felt that those crew members who were taken on board at Calcutta were "of inferior character to the others" (presumably those sent out from England), and that this had added to the difficulty of maintaining proper discipline. He implied that the selection of crew members should have been attended with more care but, perhaps, ignored the fact that the remuneration on ships employed in the Indian labour migration scheme was so unattractive that it made it difficult to attract crewmen of the highest character and ability since the more competent opted for the Australian trade.[86]

Grieve also addressed the worrying issue that had surfaced of the high mortality on board the ship from syphilis and "cerebro-spinal affection". He seemed less inclined to blame this on poor treatment of the emigrants and poor medical treatment on the part of the surgeon-superintendent. Indeed, he did not seem to think that there had been a greater prevalence of syphilis on board the *Allanshaw* than on other ships in the trade. He also did not think that it was spread by any large-scale sexual contact between crew and emigrants as there was evidence that at least one emigrant had embarked with it. Blame for this would then lie with the depot medical officers. He ascribed the outbreak of cerebro-spinal illness to the "the accidental consumption of diseased grain".[87] Hardwicke did not escape some blame, though. Grieve pointed out that it was worth considering whether greater care ought not to be taken to prevent outbreaks of diseases on board emigrant ships. Since the surgeon-superintendent was in charge of more than direct medical care, some of this blame would have to be placed on him.

Grieve was less merciful toward Hardwicke when he turned his attention to what he considered the more serious matter of Maharani's death. As far as he was concerned, "of the various incidents connected with this voyage of the *Allanshaw,* that of the death of the Coolie woman, Maharani, under the circumstances in which it happened, is the most painful".[88] Not surprisingly, therefore, he levelled more direct accusation at the surgeon-superintendent over his handling of Maharani's death and the medical and inquisitorial procedures which followed the tragedy. He did not share Alexander's and Kirke's view that "improper conduct" had not occurred between emigrant women and the crew on board the ship. Rather, "It is evident that in respect of the relationship between the men and women on board, there was a considerable amount of feeling" and that there were "rumours in the ship of undue intimacy between some of the officers and the Coolie women".[89] He reminded Governor Irving that Hardwicke, in his evidence, said that he saw early indications of a desire on the part of some of the crew to "go for the women". Some of the crew, had, in fact, been extremely disappointed that the separation of the sexes on the ship had been strictly enforced and they had showed their annoyance. This had been at the root of some of the unruliness displayed by the crew. To annoy the crew even more, while they were "rigidly restrained from speaking to a woman", the same regulation had not been applied to the officers. Indeed, far from being restrained,

> there is evidence which places beyond doubt that familiar horse-play, in which the Surgeon-Superintendent shared, took place amongst the Coolie women on the poop. The Surgeon-Superintendent seems to have forgotten that the only way of

maintaining strict discipline amongst subordinates is by the higher authorities showing an example of implicit obedience to it.[90]

In Robert Grieve's opinion, therefore, even if the grosser charges made by some of the witnesses against Hardwicke, such as allowing some of the women access to the chart room and having them sit in his lap, were untrue, "there is enough proved to lead to the belief that his conduct was indiscreet, and liable to the construction which was put upon it. Besides, such conduct was likely to lessen that reliance upon his impartiality and justice which it is so desirable for one occupying his position to attain."[91]

His most damning condemnation of Dr Hardwicke, though, was in connection with his handling of the post-mortem and the enquiry into Maharani's death. His first problem with this was that the medical facts had not been recorded properly, and second, that the cause of death had not been truthfully entered by the surgeon-superintendent. He stated:

As far as can be seen from the medical history of the case, and the changes found in the body after death, neither of which it may be remarked are recorded as completely or clearly as could have been wished, there seems to be no doubt that her death was caused by inflammatory action in or near the womb.[92]

The question he then posed was, "To what was this inflammation due?" His answer was as follows:

Going through the evidence carefully, the conclusion clearly must be that it arose from sexual excitement. The presumption is in favour of the former, and the probability is that the account given by the witness Chitamun, of having seen a woman, about the size and appearance of Maharani, taken up by a man and carried into the forecastle, is substantially correct. It may be safely assumed that Maharani was the woman, and that whatever passed in the forecastle was the exciting cause of the disease which proved fatal.[93]

While accepting Hardwicke's evidence that he saw no sign of forcible entry, Grieve nevertheless felt that "the appearance after death . . . are such as might be expected if the person had been abused by a number of men". However, he claimed: "The opportunity of clearing up any mystery surrounding Maharani's death was lost, when the enquiry into the matter at the time was closed before thoroughly probing it." He believed that, in the haste to incriminate Ipson, the surgeon-superintendent had missed the opportunity to benefit from the freshness of the evidence that these same witnesses called by the commission could have given him, had he called them closer to the time the tragedy happened. Grieve was thus unequivocal in his conclusion that "the death of Maharani was due to her being sexually abused by a number of the crew".

Since the evidence also pointed to gross indiscipline among the crew, lax control by the officers, captain and surgeon-superintendent who were in charge, incompetence and fraudulent conduct by the surgeon-superintendent, and a clear inclination of the crew and officers to fraternize with the emigrant women, Grieve found it hard to accept that no one should be found responsible for the tragedy and other incidents on the *Allanshaw*. Certainly, in Grieve's opinion:

> For the want of discipline I think the responsibility is personal and does not rest in any default of the regulations under which the service is conducted. Therefore, I hold that for the deficiencies found in the maintenance of discipline, the Surgeon-Superintendent and the Captain are both worthy of censure. They are also to be blamed for the imperfect manner in which the enquiry into the cause of Maharani's death was made.

Given the fact that Robert Grieve was the only trained medical officer on the commission, it is strange that his considered professional opinion on the issue did not hold more weight, for the conclusions of Alexander and Kirke were taken more seriously, as the government secretary's and colonial governor's views on the matter revealed.

To understand the contrasting views of the members of the commission, one needs to understand the socio-economic climate of the time in colonial Guyana, the deep divisions that existed among the officials and the planter class in the colony, and the attitude of Alexander and Kirke, in particular, towards Asian Indian immigration and Asian Indians in general. While Governor Irving and Dr Grieve were seen as fairly progressive officials, Alexander was considered to be pro-planter and Kirke both pro-planter and unambiguously racist and anti-Indian. Alan Adamson's analysis sheds some light on this unusual colonial situation in which the united front that normally existed between planters and colonial officials manning the administration was broken. It is clear that Maharani's ordeal on the voyage of the *Allanshaw* and the ensuing investigation in colonial Guyana took place at a rather "fortunate" time for the indentureds. It coincided with the governorship of Sir Henry Irving (1882–87) who had become suspicious of the way the immigration laws were being administered. He had the benefit of the findings of the 1870 Commission of Enquiry into the conditions of indentured Indians sparked by the criticisms of magistrates such as George William des Voeux (who was thereafter transferred to St Lucia). Irving had even laid a series of charges against the agent general of immigration, Alexander, accusing him, among other things, of neglecting his duty as protector of the Indians and pandering to the planters.[95] The governor had introduced a new ordinance that placed the district medical officers under the direction of the surgeon general instead of the Immigration Office, antagonizing Alexander but empowering Grieve. The intended result was that any infringement of the requirements laid down for the proper medical care of the indentured labourers would be reported to the government and not be covered up by pro-planter immigration officials. As Adamson puts it, the upshot of all these changes was that "the atmosphere was now charged with animosity. On the one side stood the planters and Alexander – on the other, the governor; the attorney general; Dr Grieve, the surgeon-general; and Dr A.D. Williams, the acting medical officer to the Immigration Department."[96] Kirke's position in all of this was as an obviously anti-Indian one, and this is significant in making his handling of the evidence in the case more comprehensible. By his own account, Asian Indians in colonial Guyana were not to be trusted: "[W]ith oriental imagery and metaphor, the coolie magnifies his wrongs until they seem almost unbearable by any one man, but which, when touched by the spear of truthful investigation, melt away like the baseless fabric of a dream."[97] His sweeping generalization was that "amongst nations with other morals and diverse religions, speaking the truth on all occasions is not considered incumbent or praiseworthy".[98] Despite this local climate that helped to explain the outcome of the case, it was Kirke's and Alexander's views that were accepted by the Colonial Office (and by the government in India), as the following section will show.

The Rulings of Charles Bruce and Governor Irving

After the submission of the differing reports of Alexander and Kirke, on the one hand, and Robert Grieve, on the other, the government secretary, Charles Bruce, tried to summarize and forward his recommendations to the governor for transmission to the Colonial Office. The lack of unity among the commissioners proved a sticking point, but Bruce opted to solve this problem of the conflicting positions of the three commissioners by emphasizing (curiously) that despite the differences in views, there were certain broad areas of agreement and urged the governor to focus on these, namely: (1) Maharani's death was the cause of "sexual connection" with one or more of the crew; (2) there was insufficient medical evidence to prove that "this connection was effected by rape or forcibly resisted" (this second summary point was in opposition to Grieve's view); (3) that while the captain seemed to have had a problem disciplining the crew and the surgeon had committed certain acts of indiscretion, "the treatment of the emigrants by the Surgeon-Superintendent and officers was excellent". On the whole, then, Bruce concluded, no one should be censured, fined or imprisoned, a view which again conflicted with Robert Grieve's conclusions and recommendations, bringing into question Bruce's view of what represented "areas of agreement".

After perusing the report of the Commission of Enquiry and Bruce's summary recommendations, Henry Irving, in his covering letter to the secretary of state for the colonies, concluded that "nothing more could have been done [certainly on his part] than has been done in the cause of justice". He further claimed: "The main value of the inquiry appears to me to consist in the light which it throws on the life of the Coolies on board and their relations with the officers and crew of the vessel."[99] This statement obviously would have coincided with his own view of problems in the system.

Reaction of the Colonial Office

As was customary, members of the Colonial Office were asked to respond to the governor's despatch and its enclosures. Most agreed that the evidence was inconclusive but recommended that the commissioner's report be accepted. Mr Gill's response was: "Not much reliance can be placed on the evidence elicited at this enquiry but we must accept the conclusion arrived at as to the cause of death of the Coolie Maharani."[100]

Another civil servant at the Colonial Office commented: "The evidence in the matter of Maharani's death seems inconclusive against any particular individual if not as regards the actual cause of death." At the same time, he recommended a relocation of the water closets used by the women to avoid the possibility of them being attacked.[101] Another member, in a scribbled remark on the Minute Paper, expressed the view that there was a strong possibility that Maharani had, indeed, been assaulted but, nevertheless, the report should be adopted. Still another member felt, like Dr Robert Grieve, that Hardwicke should be censured "as both he and the captain failed to maintain discipline on the ship".[102] There was only one bold response suggesting that the captain should be warned that if any similar complaints were made about a subsequent voyage, he would be investigated, and that both Grant and the surgeon-superintendent should be dismissed. But apart from this one bold statement, none seemed to have challenged fundamentally the general report and findings of the Commission of Enquiry nor seemed concerned that only two commissioners had signed the report. And, certainly, no one in the Colonial Office suggested that anyone should be held criminally responsible for Maharani's death or challenged Irving's view about the value of the detailed and prolonged investigation.

The Colonial Office's reaction obviously suited the planter class and its interests in London and was consistent with the post-slavery commitment to save the plantation system in the Caribbean. Furthermore, as both Adamson and Walter Rodney have so eloquently shown, the late 1880s represented a period of economic crisis for colonial Guyana, with sugar prices crashing in 1884 and with the colony feeling from 1884 to 1888 the delayed effects of the international depression of 1873–79. The volume of immigration had also been declining since 1884, within the context of the development of the gold industry that drew off African-Guyanese labourers from the estates. In addition, this was a period of increased militancy among plantation workers of both ethnicities, with some inter-ethnic solidarity being formed.[103] Whereas there were only five minor strikes among Indian estate workers in 1884, protests escalated thereafter. Indeed, there were thirty-one strikes and other cases of protest in 1886 and more were expected. Such militancy and complaints of poor conditions by Indians had been met with some measure of improvement in conditions, though Henry Irving pushed for even more reform. The limited reforms, in some people's eyes, did not stem the tide of protests, especially among seasoned Indian workers. In fact, the view, according to Rodney, was that newly arrived Indians were more malleable than seasoned workers, so that Guyanese planters favoured the continued import of fresh arrivals.[104] Within this socio-economic environment, plantation owners, already renewing their calls for increased Indian immigration in the late 1880s, wanted nothing to threaten the future of the scheme where the plantation labour force would be annually renewed by fresh, arguably more malleable, Indian indentured workers. Both the conduct of the enquiry and the outcome must be understood within this context.

CONCLUSION

DESPITE THE ELABORATE ENQUIRIES, the cause of Maharani's death still seems mysterious. That she was raped seems quite clear, although mystery surrounds the identification of the perpetrators. But how did she die? Did she die from violence associated with the act of rape? Rape, after all, is an act that combines sex and violence; that makes sex the weapon in an act of violence.[1] Hardwicke's report indicated that Maharani had complained of a pain in her arm, possibly associated with being violently held against her will. Others testified that she complained of pain in her belly. But were other acts of violence perpetrated on her body that were not revealed by the surgeon-superintendent? Evidence of physical injury was, obviously, required by Henry Kirke. At least one male emigrant seemed to have believed that violence had occurred, though he was never able to convince the commissioners. Was the cause of death related to a medical condition? Depression and shock to the nervous system because of the mental effect of rape on the victim, as one report suggested as the cause of death, might well have resulted from the incident, but this would not have been sufficient to kill a person. The most possible scenario was that as a result of the rape, a virulent infection such as streptococcus or gram negative bacterial infection was introduced into the vagina and from there, to the cervix and uterus. The post-mortem indicated "inflammation in or near the womb" – peritonitis. This could have lead to a toxic shock condition and, in the absence of antibiotics at that time, rapid death. The symptoms as given by the surgeon-superintendent did indicate that Maharani's condition deteriorated rapidly. The severe fever that Maharani developed was also consistent with the type of infection described. Such virulent bacteria could have been carried by an asymptomatic person in his nose, throat or on his hands.[2]

The question of who raped Maharani is equally problematic. Was Ipson made to take the blame to protect the captain, surgeon or other high-ranking white officials? Why was Oliver, a white British seaman, never subjected to the same degree of interrogation as Ipson? Was the answer racism and discrimination, factors that were obvious to those who dismissed the case? On the other hand, since Ipson was indeed a "coloured man", how was he so lucky to escape conviction (guilty or not) within the context of a post-slavery "justice" system riddled with racism? Any suggestion that a fair justice system existed in the nineteenth-century Caribbean must be taken with caution. David Trotman has noted that in the nineteenth-century Caribbean, there was a tendency for judges to believe the rape accusations of women against men of colour. He believes that this was because "in the minds of many whites, rape by an accused African or Indian man was quite believable given prevalent racist beliefs that darker peoples suffered from uncontrollable passions".[3] Brian Moore has also underscored the hypocrisy in nineteenth-century colonial Guyana where, despite the immoral behaviour of some whites towards Indian women, white elites continued to pose as the moral (as well as political) guardians of Caribbean society and to ascribe looser morals to non-Europeans.[4] Was the outcome the result of gender solidarity in a Victorian, patriarchal society that cut across ethnic lines? This would surely go against all the evidence that testifies to the discriminatory practices of elites against non-elites of all genders in the post-slavery Caribbean. Ipson might simply have benefited from the socio-economic context of the time, where the feared economic effects of a discontinuation of Indian immigration filled the planter class and its supporters with dread and where racism made the acceptance of evidence by the "subaltern" Indians unlikely.

Another pressing question is why was the charge of rape so easily dismissed and the victim made to seem promiscuous? The answer to this might lie in the social context of the nineteenth century when convictions in rape cases lagged behind acquittals, causing many rape incidents to go unreported because of the difficulty of securing convictions. Trotman notes that in post-slavery Trinidad, the acquittal rate for rape increased between 1870 and 1899. More specifically, between 1893 and 1899, 77 cases were tried of which 46 per cent ended in conviction and 24 per cent were thrown out.[5] That rape was treated as a capital crime in the Caribbean as in Europe was not in doubt.[6] And the definition was universal: "the imposition of intercourse by force; unlawful sexual intercourse with a female person without her consent".[7] But in the Caribbean, as in other parts of the world, the tendency was to blame women for any sexual abuse that they might have experienced unless they could prove beyond a doubt that they had cried out or made some attempt to resist the attacker. This was why eyewitness accounts that a struggle had ensued between Maharani and her attacker(s) was so crucial to the Commission of Enquiry. Some of the emigrants and seamen did try to present such evidence, but despite the evidence of William Lee and James Grant, who both testified that they had heard some sort of struggle or "scuffle" on the night Maharani claimed to have been raped, with Lee even having seen Ipson with his hand on Maharani's shoulder, and of Chitamun, who said he had see someone taking a woman like Maharani to the forecastle, the evidence did not convince two of the commissioners. The fact that Maharani did not survive to tell her own story further affected the case. The official report of the commissioners thus ruled that there was no evidence of a scuffle or that anybody had held Maharani to enable a crew member or crew members to commit such an assault.

Perhaps if the medical evidence had been more supportive of the crime, more effort would have been made to convict the accused. But the commissioners ruled further, relying heavily on the evidence of the surgeon-superintendent, that "even the appearance of the woman after death repudiated the idea that she had been criminally assaulted by any man". This, of course, was contrary to Dr Robert Grieve's professional opinion as a member of the Commission of Enquiry. They preferred to believe that if Maharani had been taken to the forecastle of the ship, this had occurred without her "struggling or attempting to cry out", and that while there, Robert Ipson and others of the crew "had connexion with her, if not with full at least with forced consent on her part, the latter being more probable from the previous modest retiring character of the woman", and the fact that she had gone to the toilet by herself and had not told anyone in authority about having been assaulted. Obviously (but curiously), "forced consent" was not equated with rape.

This was, indeed, a scandalous conclusion. Maharani's shyness or "retiring character" should have been used as further evidence that she could have been forced and that any hint of force or lack of her full consent should have been called rape. Commissioners Kirke and Alexander even found "medical evidence" to further their erroneous notion that what happened to Maharani was consensual. The medical evidence, they claimed, "leads to the inference that the cause of death was inflammatory action in or near the womb, which might have been caused by sexual excess or excitement". This "evidence" was interpreted as excitement to which Maharani not only contributed but also gave her consent or, one assumes from their attitude, enjoyed. Using the same evidence, Grieve's independent report had concluded that Maharani had been raped and that the cause of death was, in fact, inflammation of the womb caused by "sexual excess" – a euphemism for rape. Similar views had been expressed in similar circumstances, for example, in the case involving Dr Prince of the *Ravenscraig* and in the case involving the sailors on the *Canning*.

The ruling on the behaviour of the sailors towards Indian women on the *Canning* was that, at least in one case, prostitution had been involved. Even if this were true, that sailors were not supposed to be encouraging prostitution on board emigrant ships seems to have been overlooked.

As Haynes Smith also pointed out, the commissioners did not question the surgeon-superintendent's unusual behaviour of giving an order for Maharani's "private parts" to be examined when she was admitted to the hospital to be treated for a fever and a pain in her arm.[8] Had the rumours of her assault, which had gone around the ship even while Maharani was in hospital (and before Mohadaya and Moorti spoke to him), influenced the actions of the surgeon-superintendent? Grieve's examination of Hardwicke also makes it clear that he was either incompetent or lied about his post-mortem findings, and his diagnosis of death by shock to the nervous system was considered ludicrous. Nevertheless, the general conclusion was that, in view of the surgeon-superintendent's medical report, there was no sense in pursuing further the criminal aspect of the case.

It is obvious, then, that racist and sexist traditions of the society had their impact on the legal system in the Caribbean. Elite men who dominated the legal system were affected by the prevailing stereotypes and characterization of non-European women as people of loose character and questionable morals. Such stereotypes acted as major obstacles in proving rape and, in those cases that reached the courts, were a major argument of the defence. As Trotman writes, "The idea that all non-European women were inveterate liars, sexually promiscuous, and devoid of any 'womanly sense of shame' dominated the nineteenth century thought."[9] Similarly, Moore notes for nineteenth-century

Guyana that "Victorian prudes" erroneously characterized non-elite women as less than virtuous. A prevailing belief among some whites was that "it is rare to meet with a virtuous female after the age of fourteen among the lower classes" and that "among the mass of people . . . sensuality is rampant in both sexes, and the prostitution of the female sex commences at that age when children in a civilized country have hardly been detached from their mother's apron strings".[10] Thus, as in Britain, many rape cases in Caribbean courts in the nineteenth century required such stringent proof of absence of consent (especially if the medical evidence, as in Maharani's case, suggested that the woman was not a virgin), that the likelihood of acquittals was great. This was compounded by the low age of consent for Indian women which was between thirteen or fourteen to coincide with marriage regulations.

In the end, Maharani's voice, filtered through the voices of the women who reported her ordeal, was ignored, for in the social context of the time, it mattered who was speaking, whose story counted as "truth". The Commission of Enquiry accepted the evidence of the higher-ranking surgeon-superintendent and captain, and ruled that Maharani could not have been attacked as she had claimed without an alarm being raised, especially as the alleged incident had taken place on a moonlit night. They ignored the testimony of G.W. de la Mare, the first mate, who said that his own logbook indicated that the night in question was foggy, not moonlit. Apparently, the surgeon's claim, "I consider it impossible for the women to have been pulled out of the closet without being able to cry out and give an alarm [especially] as the nearest sirdar on watch was supposed to have been 20 feet away at the top of hatchway",[11] was more acceptable to the commissioners than de la Mare's logbook entry.

More women were to suffer sexual abuse on Indian emigrant ships in the years ahead, as emigration to the British-colonized Caribbean continued until 1917. It is possible that had an example been made of members of the crew and officers on the *Allanshaw*, others may have been deterred from sexually abusing women on subsequent voyages. On the contrary, complaints continued to be made that emigrant women were subject to abuses of one kind or another on ships bound for Guyana and other receiving territories. In 1885, the same year that the *Allanshaw* sailed, the ship's cook on the *Hereford* was said to have been "the cause of a great deal of anxiety and trouble to the Surgeon". The surgeon found the cook and the engineer of the ship using the Indian barber as interpreter to allow them to communicate with the women on board. The cook was also reported to have "pulled up a woman's clothes" as he passed along the deck. He was logged and fined for this offence. Eleven days later, another report was made that "a girl named Yeruh was going up the poop ladder when the ship's cook came behind her. She being afraid of him, as all the women are, he having several times interfered with them, in her efforts to get out of his way, slipped and fell." The cook tried to grab her to stop her fall and cut her thumb with his knife in the attempt. The surgeon deemed this an accident and did not fine the cook even though it was the cook's actions which led to the fall and subsequent wounding.[12]

Even Dr Hardwicke, who escaped censure for his actions in Maharani's case, was implicated in other cases after 1885. For example, he was accused of misconduct on the journey of the ship *Foyle* on which he was again surgeon-superintendent in 1886. The report of the immigration agent general indicated that Aladin, a male emigrant on the *Foyle*, complained on arrival in Guyana that Hardwicke had taken "indecent liberties" with his wife, Asserum.[13]

It seemed that Aladin had formed an alliance (a kind of "depot marriage") with Asserum in Calcutta. In fact, he claimed that she had been "given" to him by her mother. They proceeded to register this "marriage" before the magistrate, as required, and to live as a couple on the voyage. Predictably, after a more detailed enquiry, the immigration agent general claimed that Aladin could not prove that any sexual intercourse had taken place, for "all that Aladin could testify to was that on one occasion he saw Dr Hardwicke sitting in the Chart Room with Asserum on his lap and with his hands on her breasts". Chamela, a female emigrant on the same ship, corroborated this, though she added: "I never saw him doing anything except holding her breasts outside her clothes." Asserum herself denied that Hardwicke had molested her. She further stated that Aladin had not treated her well on the voyage and that she had never really slept with him and had no wish to live with him as his wife in Guyana or to be located on the same estate as he. Dr Hardwicke, in his defence, claimed, and the immigration agent general seemed to believe him, that he was only treating Asserum the way he treated all children. The fact that she was someone's wife, although only fifteen, did not seem to deter him.[14] The result of the enquiry was that Hardwicke was not penalized in any way, although the immigration agent general did concede that the manner in which he treated Asserum was "objectionable" and he should be warned not to behave in this way with a girl that age.

Thus, this case demonstrates that in the case of the treatment of women, "the other Middle Passage", to use Ron Ramdin's term, replicated some of the abuses on slave ships and will no doubt give more ammunition to those who contend that nineteenth-century labour migration was no more than "a new form of slavery". Of course, the transatlantic slave trade was unique in its severity.[15]

PART TWO

APPENDICES

Minutes of Evidence Taken before the
Commission of Enquiry in Colonial Guyana

APPENDIX 1

Surgeon-Superintendent Dr Edward A. Hardwicke

Day 1, Friday, 27 November 1885

Edward A. Hardwicke, sworn and examined:-

One day while sitting on the poop, I noticed the woman Maharani lying on the poop under a blanket. I was not aware at first who it was and took no notice of it, as this was not an unusual occurrence. After an hour or so I saw her still remaining there, and I heard her call out to one of the girls to bring her some water. I then asked one of the girls who it was and what was the matter. They told me it was Maharani and that she was sick. I got up and went over to her and uncovered her. I asked her what was the matter. At the same time I felt her pulse and she told me that she had hurt her arm by falling on it, and that it was very painful. I examined her arm and found nothing the matter with it, apparently, but she had a quick pulse; and on asking her she owned that she had fever. I sent her down to the Dispensary to get some liniment and Medicine. Shortly after I went on the main deck and asked the Baboo (chief Compounder) if he had seen Maharani. He said he had not seen her. Then I sent him down in the between decks to bring her up, and he gave her some medicine. That night she was allowed to sleep below; but next morning early it was reported to the Baboo that she had been crying all night. He then brought her, at 6 o'clock in the morning, and put her into the hospital. This was the 25th of September, and an entry was made in the Journal and Case Book. The entry in the Journal was made after that in the Case Book. Next morning, the 26th September, I found she had abdominal pain and tension. The symptoms persisted during the day. She was very reticent and would give no information, and I considered the case somewhat mysterious. I saw her next morning at a quarter to seven. She was much exhausted, pulse small, quick and thready. She died at 10.30 that morning. About 11 o'clock a girl named Mohadaya came to me and made some remarks about the character of deceased, saying what a good girl she was, and asked me if I knew what caused her death. On telling her "no", she began to relate to me that Maharani had told her that she had been criminally assaulted by two sailors at night time. I questioned her particularly as to the date, but could not arrive at it. She said that Maharani's statement had been that she was in the closet and a sailor pulled her out, and he and another criminally assaulted her in turns, the one holding her mouth with her Sarree while the other assaulted her. Maharani endeavoured to describe both men, the one as being a man rather tall and stout, and that he was accustomed to wear a red shirt and had Tattoo marks on his breast, and that he was the same man that had previously assaulted Juggessar's wife. I then asked Mohadaya if any one else had heard this story. She said "yes", that Maharani had also told Moorti. I told her then that I should have to take her evidence. I then called Moorti and I got a somewhat similar story from her. I then went down below to the Captain's cabin and reported it to him. After this I decided to hold a Post Mortem and an enquiry. At 2 p.m. I performed the Post Mortem in the presence of the two Compounders. The notes made by me at the time are correct. The opinion I formed was that death was caused principally from shock, as I did not think that the evidences of injury on the Post Mortem examination sufficient to account for death; but there was undoubted Metritis [inflammation of the womb].

There was no evidence of injury from recent assault on the private parts. I saw no external marks of violence on the body. I would not expect to find any marks if the assault had been committed six or seven days before.

The covering of the Uterus was congested. There was no general peritonitis. The Uterus was natural in shape and size. As far as I saw there was no sign of disease or injury to the inner surface. The Vagina was not inflamed. I did not see any laceration whatever in any part of it. I consider in the case of an assault on a small Coolie woman, that the shock might persist and be sufficiently great to cause death even five or six days after. The Uterus and Vagina were both small. By shock I mean nervous shock. In a European I would expect the shock to be severe at first and become less severe as time passed; but I ascribe the shock in this case, to a considerable extent to mental depression as the result of shame. I believe it possible that a full grown man could have had forcible connexion with the woman within a week and not have caused more serious injury than what I saw. I do not consider that the fact of two men assaulting her increased the liability to the production of external marks of violence; but rather the reverse. The brain was not examined.

Without the subsequent information I should not have arrived at the conclusion that death was caused by shock; but I should have considered it solely due to peritonitis, but I should not have considered the case satisfactory. I do not consider it satisfactory now.

I consider it impossible for the woman to have been pulled out of the closet without being able to cry out and give an alarm. The nearest sirdar on watch was supposed to be about 20 feet away at the top of the hatchway. I have sometimes found the sirdars absent, in cold weather particularly.

Women sometimes come up alone at night to the closets; but generally in couples or more. Maharani bore a very good character as a modest, retiring girl. I think she might have come up to the closet by herself at night. The closet is about 6 feet from the Hospital. There is an attendant at the Hospital all night. If any outcry had been made it would have been heard. There was a good moon at that time.

After she came into the Hospital she was attended by the female nurse. She made no complaint to the female nurse, but after she was admitted to Hospital I told the Baboo to get the nurse to examine her private parts. The Baboo told me she had done so and found nothing wrong. Assuming this to be correct, i.e. that the nurse examined her, I still believe that the two men might have assaulted her as described. My attention was never drawn to the woman until the day I named. She could not have escaped my notice for two or three days. She was always on the poop with the women.

The general behaviour of the crew towards the women was good. I had not more difficulty than usual in keeping them apart.

There was no other charge or complaint of indecent behaviour made against any of the crew or officers of the ship. We have been more particular this voyage than on others I have been on, in this respect. I was more particular this time as I saw suspicious signs at the beginning of the voyage and was afraid the men might go for the women. My suspicions were confined to a few – among others the man Ipson.

I held an enquiry on board into the case of Maharani. Ipson, the man suspected, was not present. He was not arrested or accused or examined medically. I had no power to do so. I took notes of evidence at the time and when I got to St. Helena I handed them over to the proper authorities. They decided it was not necessary to take any steps there. On arrival here I reported the case and the man Ipson was at once arrested. I did not accuse the man Ipson 1st because the evidence against him was slender and 2nd because I thought it better to leave it for the investigation of the authorities at St. Helena in the hope also that by doing so more evidence would be obtained.

II Conduct of the Captain, Officers and Crew

The conduct of the Captain during the voyage was entirely satisfactory. He did everything in his power to protect the Immigrants, to keep the men from the women and to assist me in every way. He consulted me in matters connected with the crew and I agree with the course he adopted.

I have no fault to find with the Officers or any suspicion of anything having taken place between them and the female passengers. They were always willing to assist me.

In regard to the crew, at the commencement of the voyage I had a suspicion that some of the men intended to go for the women. The general conduct of the crew was good, with exception of the few cases mentioned in my Journal. I consider the conduct of part of the crew to have been mutinous on one occasion, 15th October.

I have had more occasion to discuss the conduct of the crew with the Captain on this voyage than on previous voyages. I did not consider this crew as satisfactory as others I have travelled with. This unsatisfactory condition was connected both with the Coolies and the discipline of the ship. It consisted of continual small annoyances, which, as a rule, are not recorded in my Journal unless they affected the Coolies. I do not think the Immigrants suffered in comfort or in any other way from the unsatisfactory character of the crew. I ascribe this to the vigilance exercised by the Captain and Officers of the Ship in assisting me in my duties.

I do not consider it can be said that there was a mutiny on board during the voyage at any time. The crew consisted of 41 men; and six of them were guilty of mutinous or disorderly conduct on one occasion.

III Mortality

There were 11 deaths during the voyage ascribed by me to cerebro-spinal fever. I can only ascribe the outbreak to temperature. The temperatures and daily occurrences are all noted in my records. I can arrive at no definite opinion beyond this at present. The cases are detailed in the Case Book. The ventilation was as good as usual and the temperatures were never excessively high. The Stores were very good and the water also. There was heavy weather at the commencement of the voyage and much sea sickness. From the river, we entered almost at once with a gale, and this may possibly have had some connexion with the outbreak.

The Coolies embarked at Calcutta do not carry any private supplies on board. We used the same kind of grain all through the voyage, but different kinds of dholl which were used alternately all through the voyage. We had some of all the different Kinds left on arrival. I am aware as a medical man that isolated outbreaks of cerebro-spinal fever have been owing to fungoid growth in grain which might not be detected on inspection of the grain. Putting aside the cerebro-spinal outbreak and two accidental deaths the mortality was not high.

Signed: Edw. A. Hardwicke, L.R.C.P.

Surgeon-Superintendent, Emigration Service

APPENDIX 2

Captain Frederick C. Wilson

Day 1, Friday, 27 November 1885

F.C. Wilson duly sworn and examined:-

I am Captain of the ship *Allanshaw*. I knew a girl named Maharani. I know she died on 27th September, Latitude 35:24S. and Longitude 19:27E. about 150 miles from land. The first I heard about the case was from Dr. Hardwicke and that was on the day of her death. He told me he had heard from Mohadaya that she had been ravished by one of the crew. I did not take any steps at the time. I left it to the Surgeon. I knew that a man was suspected. I did nothing to him. I did not mention it to him. I consulted with the doctor and he considered it better to get up evidence first. I made an entry in the Log. It was alleged that the offence had been committed the Wednesday before she died. It was fine weather, light breeze and moonlight. A petty Officer is on the quarter deck all night and the officer in charge is on the poop. Coolie Sirdars are stationed at the Hatchways. The fore hatches are closed with grating; the main and after hatches have sirdars stationed at them. The petty Officer walks up and down on the upper deck between the closets and the break of the poop. The Officer on the poop could not see clear along the main deck. The sirdars are, I believe, relieved every three hours. The Baboo sees them posted. As a rule I go round the main deck about 10 o'clock or 11 to see that all is right. I have known the sirdars go down below to the foot of the ladder in cold weather. It was cold at that time to them. I noticed this girl as a very quiet modest girl. I think she would be the last one a man would have taken any liberty with. The distance from the closets to the main hatch would be about 20 feet. The distance between the Hospital and the closets would be about seven or eight feet. There is generally some one sleeping in Hospital. It is possible that two men could have seized the girl, thrown her down and ravished her without being heard. Any outcry must have been heard. If she had been suddenly seized and gagged there would have been no outcry. I never saw a woman coming up singly at night to the closet. They always come up in twos or threes. Such an Offence could not have been committed in the day time. I never suspected Ipson of having had anything to do with any other woman. I had no suspicion while Maharani was alive that any of the crew had anything to do with her.

II Crew

As far as the conduct of the majority of the crew is concerned I had no fault to find. The only two men I really had any trouble with were Smith and Ipson. On one occasion they behaved in a mutinous manner, viz. Smith, Ipson and four others. One of the Ship's boys whilst swinging a knife cut one of the Coolies. I called him aft and asked him why he was so careless and he told me a lie. He said he had been cutting a piece of wood and the Coolie ran against him. I told him to walk for two hours on the poop with a capstan bar over his shoulders. A short time afterwards six men came on the poop and enquired why I was punishing the boy. I ordered them to leave the poop without giving them any answer. I saw one of the men with a bar in his hand which he had taken from the boy and I ordered him to give it back to the boy. He did not do so and I repeated the order a second time. He asked me why I was punishing the boy and I put my hand on the bar to take it from him. He wrenched the bar from me and threw me on the deck. I jumped up and ordered him to leave the poop again. One of the other men picked up the bar with the intention of throwing it overboard. I put my hand on it and took it from him. Two other men came to me in a threatening manner and the 2nd mate stepped in between them and myself. I told them if they interfered with me I would shoot them, and ordered them off the poop. They left the poop using abusive language. I took no steps with regard to them as I should have had to put the whole six in irons and that would have shortened my crew. I logged them, and told them I should take proceedings against them in Demerara. I consider the four men were led away by Ipson and Smith. On arrival I brought charges against them and had them punished. The mutinous conduct referred to occurred after leaving St. Helena. I disagree with the remarks made by the doctor that the general character of the crew was unsatisfactory. This is my second voyage with Coolies.

There was nothing approaching a mutiny. The conduct of the Officers was good.

The general conduct of the crew on this voyage was better than last time and speaking generally I was quite satisfied.

With the exception of two men the conduct of the crew was quite satisfactory.

I have never experienced before, a voyage at the end of which such charges had to be made as in the case of this voyage.

The man David bears a good character. The boy Clintworth is the boy I punished and was intimate with the other men and was led away by them. O'Brien bears a fair character. I think the statements of these men in regard to Ipson can be believed.

I was not afraid of the crew during any part of the voyage from St. Helena. Two of the men refused to work one Saturday, because they said they had not received their rice and I issued fresh rations of rice to them though their allowance had been issued. I did not know whether they had received them. They did not go to work that day till 4 o'clock. The rice was issued at noon. I never punished any of these men. I only logged them. I consider my behaviour towards the crew was the most judicious under the circumstances, considering the large number of Immigrant passengers on board.

Signed: Fred.^{k} Wilson, Master
Ship *Allanshaw*

APPENDIX 3

William Urquhart (Sailmaker)

Day 2, Monday, 30 November 1885

William Urquhart, duly sworn and examined:-

I am sailmaker on board the Ship *Allanshaw*. I have been two voyages in the same ship with Capt. Wilson including this voyage. I heard of the death of Maharani on board. I had no night watch except for the last three weeks after the mutiny. I heard after her death that there had been a rape committed. I did not hear at any time who did it. It was kept quiet until we came here.

I do not think a woman could have been dragged out of the closet and ravished by two men if the Sirdars had been on the watch and doing their duty. The boatswain kept watch on the main deck between the main mast and mizzen mast. There is no one between the main and foremast. The watch on deck remain forward and are not allowed to come aft unless for duty. An outrage such as that described could hardly have taken place on a moonlight night without attracting the notice of the boatswain. If the boatswain was on the weather side it might have happened on the lee side.

Two of the watch could easily leave and go aft without being missed.

II Officers and Crew

On the voyage to Calcutta the crew behaved very well. Ipson and Smith were the only two men who caused a disturbance on the ship on the voyage from Calcutta. One day five or six men went on the poop, to take possession of the poop apparently, and take the hand spike from a boy who was being punished. I consider their conduct was mutinous. I was not on the poop. After this, double watch was kept and the Captain took extra precautions to prevent disturbance. I remember one day two sailors complained that they did not get their rice. I know nothing about their refusing to work. The crew were well treated by the Captain and Officers on the voyage.

Since I was on the watch I have seen women come up at night to the closet all by themselves, but generally they come up three or four at a time.

The extra precautions were taken perhaps because there was a bad feeling in the ship. Very likely this feeling may have been caused by keeping the men from the women. There were disturbances of one sort or another all the way from Calcutta, more than I am accustomed to see and I ascribe it all to the two men. After the doubling of the watch there was a petty officer on each side. I would not like to go through the same passage again. If I were told that the crew said they went among the women regularly I would not believe it. The crew have been told more frequently this time to keep from the women than on either of my other two voyages. There is more chance of white sailors being talked of if they went among the women than Lascars would be. One of my voyages was with Lascars.

The Captain and Officers did all they could to protect the Immigrants.

William Urquhart
Witness

APPENDIX 4

Mohadaya (Return Emigrant)

Day 2, Monday, 30 November 1885

Mohadaya, duly sworn and examined through Interpreter:-

I came in the ship with Maharani. I have been in the Colony before. I knew Maharani well. I did not sleep with her. I am married. My husband is in India. I know Moorti. She is married, but her husband was not with her. She slept near Maharani. I do not remember when Maharani became sick. One day she told me she had a pain in her hand. The doctor took her to the Hospital. I saw her in the Hospital. She did not call me, I went myself to see her. She said she was very sick, that two sailors had connexion with her and that she was ashamed to tell me. I asked her if she had any pain and she said she had a pain in her belly. This was on a Friday. She did not tell me on what day the men had connexion with her. She said two sailors dragged her from the closet and had connexion with her on the deck. She said it was at night time. She did not say how many days this was before. I did not ask her. She described one sailor as having a red shirt and tattoo marks on the breast. I did not hear of any other sailors having connexion with the women or see them talking to the women. Maharani told me not to tell and that when she got better she would tell the Baboo. She only complained of a little pain in her belly. She was not very sick. After she died, the same day, I was speaking with Moorti and we told the doctor.

Maharani was young and about my size. She did not tell me that she struggled with the men or cried out. She said that she could not cry out because the sailor put cloth in her mouth. She did not say the sailor hurt her very much. I never saw Maharani go up to the closet alone or any other woman. The women generally go in twos and threes.

II Officers and Crew

The Captain and Officers were all good. All the crew were good and did not disturb the Coolies. I do not know why the men beat the Captain. The Sirdars sometimes go below if it is cold.

Mohadaya
Witness

APPENDIX 5

Moorti (Return Emigrant)

Day 2, Monday, 30 November 1885

Moorti, duly sworn and examined through Interpreter:-

I came in the Ship *Allanshaw*. I knew Maharani. I went to see her one Friday evening. She was in Hospital. I asked her what was the matter. She said that two sailors dragged her from the closet and had connexion with her. She did not say the sailors hurt her. She did not say she had a pain in her belly. I did not ask her whether she cried out. She did not say anything to me about crying out. Maharani told me nothing more. I do not believe what she said. I did not hear of any sailors troubling any of the Coolie women. None of them asked me to go with them. I told the doctor all Maharani told me.

(Statement read to her).

That statement is true.

Moorti
Witness

APPENDIX 6

Golap (Nurse)

Day 2, Monday, 30 November 1885

Golap F., duly sworn and examined through Interpreter:-

I was nurse on board the Ship *Allanshaw*. I remember Maharani. She was sick in Hospital. The Baboo told me to rub oil on her belly. No one told me to examine her private parts and I did not do it. I never told the Baboo I had done so. I rubbed oil on her belly. Maharani did not tell me anything about the cause of her illness. I do not know what was the cause of death. There was a good deal of pain in the belly. I think she died from this. I never heard that any of the sailors had connexion with the women. I slept below. The women go up to the closet six or seven at a time. I never saw one alone go up. If I wanted to go up I would take five or six with me.

II Officers and Crew

The sailors were very good to the Coolies and did not knock them about. The Captain and Officers were good; and the doctor looked well after them. I know nothing about the Captain being knocked down by the sailors.

Golap
Witness

APPENDIX 7

James T. Grant (Assistant Compounder)

Day 2, Monday, 30 November 1885

James T. Grant, duly sworn and examined:-

I was Assistant Compounder on board the *Allanshaw* on her voyage from
Calcutta. I remember the woman Maharani. On the 25th September she was
admitted into the hospital. Before that, she was brought to the Baboo and was
given a liniment, as she complained of pain in her arm. She had no other
medicine. On the same evening at 6 p.m. I went in the Dispensary and the
Hospital Attendant Heerdayaram told me he had heard Maharani telling
Moorti in his presence that two sailors had laid hold of her some nights before
on her way from the closet. One had taken her "Kapra" and held her by the
mouth to prevent her making a noise, while the other lifted her away (he did
not say where) and that both in turn had connexion with her. One he described
Maharani said had a red shirt: the other was not described. I sat in the
Dispensary after he told me this, mixing some mixtures to take round with the
doctor at 8 o'clock. After I finished I went into our berth and told the Baboo
about it. We had a talk about it, and he said he did not believe it, for he tried
before to ascertain from her what was the matter with her and she never gave
any account. On the 26th at 12.30, to satisfy myself I sent for Moorti, took
her into hospital, stood behind the patient as she lay in the bunk so that she
could not see me, and told Moorti to question her as to what was the matter.
Moorti asked her, but at first received no reply. She kept on asking her and
Maharani got at once into a rage, denied having made any statement as to her
having been violated by the sailors and further she accused Moorti of having
spread a report that she had been having connexion with sailors and was ill in
hospital with gonorrhea in consequence. She also told Moorti that to satisfy
herself she could send for the female nurse and have her examined. She then

said that the only thing that was wrong with her was that she had had a fall on the poop a few days previous. Moorti then left the hospital in a rage telling her she was lying. I think Moorti believed the story. On the 27th she died about 10.30, after taking three half ounces of wine. After she died the doctor went on the poop and some Return Coolies began to tell him about the report as to her having been criminally assaulted, and he began to hold an enquiry at once. I gave evidence before the doctor and signed it.

(Evidence shown to him and signature acknowledged).

I told the doctor about the fall on deck. I do not know why he did not write it down.

I saw a good deal of Maharani while in Hospital. She did not look very low at first. She looked low. She spoke to me freely and did not appear like a woman very deeply ashamed. She did not scream from pain in her stomach. Her legs were not drawn up. There was no discharge. The nurse Golap examined her. The Baboo told her to examine her, and I heard her tell him she had done so. After the nurse had examined her, order was given to rub her with oil. By examining I mean looking at her privates to see if she had gonorrhea. I think the Baboo suspected she had had connexion with sailors and had got gonorrhea. I know nothing of the doctor having given the orders for her to be examined. I heard she had been crying a good deal on the night of the 24th. She was not crying when she came into hospital. Her intellect was quite clear. Before her death we could form no opinion as to the nature of the disease she was suffering from. I did not connect the story of the assault with the cause of her death. It was hard for me to believe the story, as she was one of the women who stayed in the after part of the ship and never had anything to say to the sailors. I have seen other women speaking to the sailors and have had them punished for it. I never knew of them having had any connexion with the sailors. I do not believe the sailors were telling the truth when they stated that they had connexion with the women. I cannot ascribe any motive for their telling this lie. I do not think that it could be true, because four sirdars were always on watch. I never knew the Sirdars go down below. I do not know what happened after I went to bed except by hearsay. Moorti's statement struck me at the time as being very extraordinary, very important and one that ought to have been thoroughly gone into. I thought I ought to have told the doctor, but the doctor was a man who had very little to say to people.

I reported the matter to the Baboo as my superior officer and thought I had done my duty, although it was a reported rape.

In cases of Gonorrhea I had made a report to the doctor who referred it to the Baboo to have the parties examined. I was present at the Post Mortem. There were no bruises about the privates. There was a little discharge. She was a fair sized woman about 17 or 18 years of age. She was a quiet girl and I heard nothing against her character. I have been three voyages with Coolies.

II Officers and Crew

The Captain, Officers and doctor behaved very well during the voyage. I could not say the crew were a bad crew except Ipson and Smith. I never heard of their troubling the Coolie women except in this case.

On the 15th October about 6 p.m. a boy was punished by the Captain for cutting a Coolie man, and the boy was called up and questioned about it and was then sent forward, on which the crew cheered. He was sent for by the boatswain and the mate followed also. The boy was taken to the poop and ordered to walk with a capstan bar. Six of the men, Ipson, Smith, Baynes and three others came aft to release him. One of them, Smith, took the bar from him, and one asked the Captain what he meant by punishing the boy. The Captain ordered them to give the bar back to the boy. They refused. He then took hold of the bar and in the struggle with the sailor he was thrown down. He got up at once, and the men began abusing him. He then ordered them off the poop. One of them came down at once, and the others remained till they pleased to go, and gave abuse to the Captain. After between five and eight minutes they left the poop. When they got on deck Ipson said to the Captain, doctor and officers, "There is not a man among the lot." The 2nd officer then rushed down and had a fight with him. The fight lasted about fifteen minutes. The Captain did not interfere. Very few Coolies were there. While the fight was over the crew were mustered and asked if any were in league with these men for mutiny. They all denied it. One of them turned to the doctor and said he was the cause of all this row on board the ship because he was always getting the men aft for the least thing that was done. Ipson had been before him twice before for interfering with the Coolies. The six men were taken to the cabin and the articles were read to them, and the Captain told them he would log them for mutiny. After they left the cabin the first mate said to the Captain that he would have had Ipson and another one put in irons. The Captain and doctor said it was rather late to put them in irons as it was getting near the end of the voyage. I think Ipson and Smith should have been put in irons before for being "cheeky" to the captain. Captains I have sailed with before would have had them in irons before. The conduct of these men was mutinous and I never saw the like before. There was a good deal of dissatisfaction and small complaints during the whole voyage. On two occasions there were complaints as to their food. They were very obedient to the Officers, but cheeky to the Captain. They were well treated by the Captain and I think their misconduct was owing to the Captain's leniency. Generally speaking the voyage was not satisfactory and I never saw the like before. Only one of the Coolies behaved badly. When they accused the doctor of being the cause of the trouble I cannot say whether they meant it or not, and do not know what cause they could have had for saying so.

The Coolies were carefully treated and attended to and everything done to promote their comfort by the Captain, Officers and doctor.

III Mortality

I recollect having a good deal of sickness coming down the Bay of Bengal. The weather was very hot and the sea rough causing a good deal of sea-sickness. Under these circumstances I would expect the delicate passengers to be most liable to disease. Those who died of cerebro-spinal disease were mostly robust young men. It always came on suddenly, with insensibility and some cases lasted only one or two hours, others two or three days. There were no spots. The food was good throughout the voyage. There is a man on board named Lee who stated in my presence and that of two other people, that he saw Ipson having connexion with a woman and she was groaning and crying. This was at the port water closet. He was coming from the wheel at 12 o'clock. His reason for not giving evidence was he did not want to be called as a witness.

Signed: Jas. Theo. Grant
30.11.85
Assistant Compounder
Ship *Allanshaw*

APPENDIX 8

Robert Ipson (Able Seaman)

Day 3, Wednesday, 2 December 1885

Robert Ipson, duly sworn and examined:-

I was an able bodied seaman on board the *Allanshaw*. I shipped at Calcutta. This was my first voyage in that ship. I was born at Santa Cruz. I served my time in the American navy. I heard there was a Coolie girl named Maharani who died on board. All I know about it is that I was in the forecastle one day eating dinner, and the man named Warner, who is always on the poop assisting the sailmaker, came to us in the forecastle and said, "Well, no matter we're a rough crowd, but I believe every one has the principle of a bloody man." I being the nearest to him asked him what the devil he meant, so he told me he heard the doctor, the Baboo and the Captain were speaking on the poop that there was a girl in the Hospital sick and they thought some of the sailors must have been getting foul of her. One of the fellows said, "it is all a bloody yarn, it is not true." We did not believe it, and after dinner we took no more notice of what he said and went on the forecastle head. This was while the girl was yet alive. While we were there the Head Topaz Sirdar came and spoke to Warner on the Starboard side. We were on the port side and we heard the Sirdar and Warner speaking about the girl, so we all went over to the starboard side and commenced speaking to the Topaz and Warner, and the Head Topaz Sirdar said "they say it is sailors, but he knew it was no sailors". He and all the Sirdars knew it was those aft, it was no one but the "mallah Sahib"; so he commenced to tell us about the Coolie Sirdars at the hatches being given tobacco to keep their mouths shut, for almost every dark night the Officers carry a woman in the sail locker or their rooms. That is all I know about the case – But there is a man named Lutchmun a Return Immigrant, who worked in the cabin all the voyage who told me, Bain and McGinnis that he knew that the mate used to keep company with this girl. He speaks English well. He also told me that the Steward had sent him to bring up a woman at night for him. I know the woman. She is in the Depot now – and he carried her to the Steward's cabin. He also said that the 2nd mate had sent him for a woman. I know this woman also. She is also in the Depot now. He pointed out the women to me. Lutchmun made the Statement about the mate having connexion with Maharani about a week before she died. About three weeks before we got to St. Helena, Lutchmun told me that the Captain and the doctor were making it up to charge the sailors with the death of Maharani. I did not know till the night before we arrived at Demerara that I was going to be charged with having caused her death. The Captain and Officers never mentioned it to me. Lutchmun said that the Captain said he would bring me up on this charge because I was a rough character on board. He said "never mind, call me as a witness and I will speak all I know of the Officers during the voyage."

I heard the Head Topaz Sirdar say that she had been "torn". Lutchmun told me an enquiry was being held. He was the sailors' friend. Nothing was said to me. My shirts were not looked at. I had about 6 red shirts and one white.

I never sailed with Coolies before. No sailor had connexion with Coolie women. They had not a chance. We were watched too close. The boatswain was on the quarter deck, the Sirdars at the hatches, and the mate and apprentices on each side of the poop.

Thos. David is in the Starboard watch. I had no conversation with him until we left St. Helena. What he said before the Magistrate is not true. I had chancres after leaving St. Helena. I had connexion with a woman at St. Helena. He (Thos. David) is not friendly to me because I would not allow him to kick Clintworth about the deck. The woman I had at St. Helena was a woman from shore. Clintworth was in my watch. I have no reason to think he would tell a lie. (Clintworth's statement read to him). That statement is not true. I know Maharani. I never spoke to her. I never had a chance. She was always at the mate's door or on the poop. I do not know a man named Emanuel Anderson – (Statement read). Now I know the man. He was in the other watch. His statement is not true. I know O'Brien. (Statement read). I deny this statement. I know John Anderson. (Statement read). I had a conversation with this man the night after she died about Maharani. He told me there was suspicion in regard to the sailors. I said why did they not take all the sailors aft and have them searched, as well as the Officers, because I had suspicion of the Officers and was certain none of the crew had anything to do with it. We were all willing to go. Every one in the forecastle had a suspicion of a man aft about Maharani. I myself have seen larking between the Officers and Coolie women, the Captain, the doctor, first mate, 3rd mate and Steward. I have seen extra diet given to the women by the Captain, doctor, mate and Steward, soft tack, butter, cheese, sugar and cooked food. I have also seen them get fresh water and soap to wash their clothes. This was done to about half a dozen fancy women. I don't know their names. Two of them are in Depot now. The Captain used to get out of his armchair and let one of them sit down in it. The engineer of the ship passed a remark that if he could write properly he would write a letter to the Emigration agent about the carrying on of the officers. (Mohadaya and Moorti produced and identified as the two women mentioned above). Mohadaya was the one the Captain gave his chair to. Moorti was the one the Steward had in his room. Mohadaya is the one the 2nd mate used to have. I have seen the Captain and the doctor shoving their hands between a woman's legs and asking "what is this?" and they used to carry a woman into the pilot house. Almost all the sailors have seen this while at the wheel at different times. One day I saw the Officers lying on the quarter deck and women sitting on them and sometimes they would be on the women; and then the women chased them round the deck with a pot of red paint to paint their faces. The same day I was brought ashore the carpenter told me the lot of us ought to speak about the carrying on of the Officers.

I know a man named Lee. He was in my watch. If he said he saw me having connexion with a woman near the water closet at night it would not be true. Lee and I are not good friends. He passed a remark to me one day that he would get me into trouble if could. I had put a bar of iron in his bunk for a pillow. All the watch heard him. Warner heard him. Erickson also.

I never had anything to do with the Coolie women. Maharani was looked on as the mate's woman by all the crew.

II Officers and Crew

I was not popular on board the ship, because I played practical jokes and challenged people to "lick it out" when crossed. One day I was standing by the carpenter's bench and a boy Clintworth said, "look. I can sling this knife open." I said, "look how you sling it for if you hit me I will break your neck." Without looking behind he swung it and it opened. At the same time a Coolie ran up behind him to go to the closet and it touched the end of his finger and scratched

it. I said "you see what you have done. You deserve a bloody good flogging."
The Coolie went aft and complained to the doctor and captain that his hand
was cut. The Captain called the boy who told him a lie. The boy came back
and said the Captain was going to punish him for nothing. The boy went on
the poop with a handspike and six of us went aft to tell the captain the true
story as to how the Coolie got cut. When we got aft Erickson went on the poop
first and asked the Captain what he was punishing the boy for. We were all on
the poop by this time, so the Captain in a threatening attitude told Erickson
to go off the poop at once before he had time to tell the story. Erickson went
down and then asked the Captain to come down and let him speak to him,
because he was not a dog. The Captain then went up to Smith. Smith had the
capstan bar. I don't know how he came by it. The Captain grabbed at the bar
at both ends and tried to wrench it out of Smith's hands. Smith would not let
go the bar, thinking the Captain was going to hit him with it. The Captain in
trying to wrench it from him fell down alongside the hen coop with the bar in
his hand. Smith did not fall. The Captain jumped up, looked at me and said,
"I will blow the lot of your brains out you black sod." I then said to him, "It
will be the last damned shoot you ever will make." He then ran towards Bain
with the bar and said he would poke his guts out. The bar was lowered and
pointed towards Bain. The Captain loosened his right hand from the bar and
caught hold of Bain by the collar. Bain put up his hands to pull away the
Captain's hands from him. The Captain dropped the capstan bar and said he
would punch something. I did not hear what. I did not interfere in this at all.
We all went down on the main deck after we were all told to go and I heard
the first and second mate passing a remark. I did not hear the remark. It was
something about a black scoundrel and I thought it applied to me. I turned
round and said to the 2nd mate, "There is not a damned man among you."
The 2nd mate took this as a challenge and came down off the poop and said,
"There is a bloody man among us and here is one." I had my back turned to
him and he hit me on the back of my neck. Some of the fellows then called
out to me, "Go it Bob; don't take it." I turned round then and hit the 2nd
mate and we had a good fight. It lasted about an hour. I got the best of it. The
Captain called all the six who went on the poop into the cabin and told us he
would log us. He read the Merchant Shipping Act to us; but not the entry in
the Log Book. I did not see him writing. The entry was not read to us till the
morning we arrived in port. We were not punished on board; we returned to
duty. I had nothing to do with the complaint about rice. Two men Smith and

Bain complained one day about their rice. All during the voyage there was grumbling about rations. We thought we were cheated out of our whack. We laid the blame between the Captain and the Steward. We could go and see our rations weighed; but one day I went and the Steward told me I was too late. We did not get enough; the quality was good.

We went aft to beg the boy off, as we wanted him to dance and sing.

There was not a good feeling between the Officers and men except in a few cases. There was always an "envy" feeling right through the voyage. The men always used to make game of the Officers. I am accustomed to make fun of the Officers when they come fooling around. I mean when they give unnecessary orders to tease the sailors. This was done on board the *Allanshaw*, and I think this was the cause of some of the bad feeling. The envy I spoke of had nothing to do with the woman. If the Officers spoke bad to the men, the men spoke bad to the Officers. The Captain never punished me or threatened to punish me in any way. I know I have frequently been logged as a turbulent scoundrel. I have nothing to say about the captain except that he does not know how to treat men as men, but as dogs. I saw no rows in the ship. As far as it goes I took it all in fun. I do not think a fight with the mate for an hour anything particular, nor the captain falling down in a struggle. I went to Calcutta as quartermaster in the Bayard. I shipped from Ceylon. I never was logged. I don't think any jealousy of women caused me to be disliked on board. There were no more fights between Officers and men.

When we went aft we had no intention of taking possession of the ship, or ever shewed such intention. The men did not think they could frighten the captain. By treating us like dogs I mean "hollering" at us, bullyragging us round the deck and treating us scornfully. I signed my articles at Ceylon to be discharged at Calcutta.

When the six men went on the poop we had nothing in our hands. Our manner was not boisterous. We allowed Erickson, the easiest man in the ship, to speak.

Signed: Robert Ipson

APPENDIX 9

John Smith (Able Seaman)

Day 3, Wednesday, 2 December 1885

John Smith, duly sworn and examined:-

I was an able seaman on board the *Allanshaw*. I shipped in Calcutta. I am an Englishman. I heard of a girl named Maharani dying on board ship. There was some talk about it. I did not hear any one spoken of in connexion with her death. I heard that it was said some of the sailors had connexion with her. I belonged to the port watch. I do not know of one sailor having had connexion with women on board the ship. I never heard the men talking about having the Coolie girls. I never heard of the Officers having anything to do with the Coolie women nor having any indecent play with them.

I heard Ipson and one other say that the mate played with Maharani. By playing I mean talking and laughing, nothing indecent.

There was a good deal of gossip in the forecastle at the time of Maharani's death and the men did not like it to be said that some of them had something to do with it. I heard it was only a yarn got up against the sailors. The men in the ship said that the blame should have been aft and not forward. This was after she was dead and buried.

I took my turn at the wheel with the rest. Some of the women used to be on the poop and some on the quarterdeck. I never saw or heard of any officers putting their hands between a woman's legs and rolling about with them on deck. I never saw women running after the officers with red paint. When the men said the blame should be aft, not forward, I think it was unjust. I never saw any undue familiarity between the officers and crew and the women. I never gave the woman's death a thought. I heard it was said the sailors were blamed for it, on account of some of them having had connexion with her. I do not believe this was the cause of death.

Dr Grieve: If any one said that there was great difficulty to keep the crew
              from the Coolie women or that the Officers larked with the
              women on the poop, would you believe it?

Answer: I would not believe there was any difficulty in keeping the crew
              from the women; nor that the officers larked with the Coolie
              women. I do not expect to go back with the Captain. I have to
              serve 4½ months in gaol.

II Officers and Crew

One day at the second dog watch I went aft with Ipson and four others on the
poop. Erickson asked the Captain what he was punishing the boy for. The
Captain ordered him off the poop and then made a rush towards me and told
me to go off the poop too. I had the capstan bar in my hand. I picked it off
the deck. The Captain got hold of it and tried to wrench it from me. He pulled
me away from the Chart house with it and I gave the bar a twitch which caused
the captain to fall on the poop. No blows passed between us. The captain then
went towards Bain with the Capstan bar. I do not know what happened then.
He rushed towards Bain. After this we all went off the poop and Ipson had a
row, a sort of a scramble with the 2nd mate; nothing very particular. We all
stood round and I said, "to it, Bob." It was not a regular fight. It was only
tumbling about and lasted about five minutes. The Captain then called all
hands aft and asked them whether they wanted to "mutinise". They said "no".
After this he took the six of us into the cabin, read out about mutiny on board
ship and assaulting the Officers, and then logged us. He did not read the entry
in the Log till we got to Demerara. I was not punished on board ship nor any
of the others. I never heard the men say the Captain was afraid of them. The
Captain and Officers treated us, as far as the working goes, the same as in any
other ship. One day Bain and I did not get any rice for dinner. I suppose the
Steward did not weigh enough out. I could have gone to see the food weighed;
but I never went and never saw any one else go. We refused to work until we
got our rice. I remained off work four hours. We got the rice at 4 o'clock. We
did not go to work till we got what we wanted. We were not punished for this.
We were never punished at all till we came to Demerara. When men refuse
duty they are generally put in irons at once. I knew I ran the risk. I was not
astonished at not being put in irons, as I thought the captain would give us the
rice when he found we had none. I never was ill-treated on board the ship. I

don't think we were treated as we ought to have been treated. They were so mean about the grub. We were never ill-treated in any other way. I was always spoken civilly to.

The boy was walking up and down the poop with the handspike when we went on the poop. I don't know who took it from him or how it got on the deck. I was on the poop at the time. I suppose the Captain thought I had taken it from the boy and perhaps he thought I was going to strike him with it. It would not astonish me to hear that the Captain was afraid of the crew. It was not a happy ship for me. Half the crew were all right and half weren't. I never was on a voyage where so many charges were brought at the end of it. I ascribe it all to spite, because I used to go laughing all round the deck. The Captain and Officers behaved all right to me. I don't know the cause of all the troubles on the voyage. The scramble between the 2nd mate and Ipson was a fight. The Captain and the mate did not stop it. Before I joined the *Allanshaw* I was paid off from the St. Mildred.

When I picked up the capstan bar my attitude towards the Captain was not a threatening one. I don't know why I picked it up. The reason why the captain rushed at me was because he was mad at us coming on the poop. I do not know why I went on the poop. I followed like a sheep.

Signed: John Smith

APPENDIX 10

James T. Grant (Recalled)

Day 3, Wednesday, 2 December 1885

James T. Grant, recalled:

I have told people outside that there was a little trouble on board the *Allanshaw*. When I said the voyage was not satisfactory I referred to the crew. I never heard that the mate was intimate with Maharani. I have seen the Officers laughing and talking with the women. I have seen the doctor take up food to the children. I know Lutchmun. He was employed as Steward's assistant and had an opportunity of hearing everything that passed. I have heard the women on deck saying that the Steward had a woman. I never heard this said of the mate. Some of the Coolie women and children used to get into the captain's chair when he left it. I never noticed any women treated differently to others. Mohadaya, Moorti and Mohadaya's mother were more on the poop than the others and were spoken to more than the others. Some of the Coolies said Mohadaya could get anything she wanted and they could not. She might get a little cloth sometimes. Others, about 8 or 9, did so as well. These were those mostly on the poop, I do not know why these people got these things. I heard some say she (Mohadaya) was mistress of the ship. I don't know why. Perhaps they were jealous. I never heard it said that she was kept by the Captain or the mate or second mate or Steward. I did not make any remark to any one outside that the Officers were too free with these women. I said the Return Immigrants were lively.

Sgd. Jas. Theo. Grant
Assistant Compounder
Ship *Allanshaw*

APPENDIX 11

G.W. de la Mare (Chief Officer)

Day 4, Friday, 4 December 1885

G. W. de la Mare, duly sworn and examined:-

I was first mate of the *Allanshaw* on her voyage from Calcutta. I was one voyage before in her. We shipped additional hands at Calcutta. Ipson and Smith were taken on there. Bain, Peterson and Sadderland were old hands and came from England. The first time I had to find fault with Ipson was when we were embarking the Coolies. He was looking down the hatches and I ordered him away. I had trouble several times with the five men now in gaol who were in my watch. I never saw the men talking to or interfering with the Coolie women. Once Ipson was logged for pushing against a Coolie woman and knocking her down. Another day he was logged for making a noise at the hospital door. He was logged again on 10th September for abusing the cook. I never had any complaint to make against the crew in regard to the women. I remember Maharani. She used generally to sit by my door or on the poop. My door opens on the main deck. The 2nd mate and I had the same cabin. There was no particular reason why Maharani should have sat at my door. She sat there the whole voyage till her death. Other women sat there with her. I remember the day this girl died. The first I heard of her death was a man pulling at the main brace called out "who split the Coolie?" This was during the starboard watch. I don't know who said this. No one made any answer. This was two days before she died. The next thing I heard was that she was in hospital and then that she was dead. There was a Postmortem. I heard her death was attributed to some one having had forcible connexion with her. No name was mentioned at the time. When this happened, that is, the night this was said to have happened, the night was foggy. (Official log says it was Wednesday night). I referred to my own log and found it was foggy. That night I had the watch from 8 to 12.

I think an assault such as that described in the log could have happened without being noticed. A sailor named Lee told me two days ago that he heard some scuffling near the water closet at 12 o'clock one night when he was leaving the wheel. The scuffling was with a woman. He did not mention any name. He said there was only one man, not two. (Extract from Log read as to the night of the 23rd, which was described as a fair night, little wind and a good moon. No noise was heard to cause a suspicion that anything was going wrong). That entry is correct. No steps were taken to enquire about the case till the Coolie women spoke about it. After that we all tried our utmost to find out all about it. I never heard anything said about it by the crew before we got into port. I knew Mohadaya and Moorti. I never had any conversation with them about the case. I don't think there is any truth in the assertion that the culprit should be looked for among the officers and not among the crew. I never saw anything pass among the Officers. I never saw any improper familiarity between the officers and the Coolie women. I never saw or heard of any indecent behaviour of the Officers towards the women, such as putting their hands between their legs. This is my second voyage with Coolies. I swear that I never saw any undue familiarity between the Captain, the doctor and officers and the Coolie women. Only the man at the wheel and the sailmaker were allowed on the poop. The women and children had free access to the poop. I myself never took any liberty with any woman. If any one said I did he said what was not true.

I take a solemn dying oath this moment that this woman Maharani never entered my cabin at all. I never heard this assertion until this morning when I had a conversation with Mr. Grant on the subject. I know Mohadaya. In regard to her being called Mistress of the ship I will tell you what familiarity I saw in that line. Mohadaya, her sister and her mother could always go on the poop and have their meals. I did not see others do it. I only saw these three. I can give no explanation of this. I know Moorti. She used to sit by my door with Maharani. I never saw her get her meals on the poop. The man at the wheel could always see what was going on. I know Lutchmun. He used to assist the Steward in the Cabin. I don't know his character. He was in a position to know more of what went on in the cabin than other men. He was never punished for anything. He was not known as a bad character on board. The sailmaker had an assistant named Warner. He worked on the poop. He was a pretty good man. He was never charged with anything. I know no reason why these men should tell lies about the Officers. Ipson was in my watch. I never saw Ipson and Lutchmun speaking together. I knew of Ipson being charged with having to do with Maharani about 4 or 5 days after her death. I heard the doctor and the Captain speaking about it when I was walking on the poop. Nothing was done to substantiate it. I never heard before my conversation with Grant that the crew said the blame should be laid aft. I don't know who the words "who split the 'Coolie' " were intended for. I reported it to the Captain. This was before the death of the woman. The log I keep is the ship's log. It is different from the official log. I keep the ship's log. It is now on board the ship. When Lee told me he saw scuffling I did not ask him anything about it. The *Allanshaw* sailed from London. I ordered Ipson away from the main Hatchway during the embarkation, because he had no business there. All that you have heard of familiarity between the Officers and women is false. I call it partiality for some women to have had their meals given to them on the poop. I am not as familiar with the names of the other Coolie women, as I am with these of Maharani, Mohadaya and Moorti.

I have seen no undue intimacy between the captain and these women at meal time. Breakfast was served out at 10 a.m. and dinner between 3 and 4 p.m. These women were Return Coolies, who are generally more decent than the others. They spoke English. There is nothing reprehensible in my opinion in these women being on the poop.

I cannot say these women were better looking than the others – they were better dressed. I cannot answer the question as to whether I would be surprised to hear that Mohadaya had been described as a woman who would meet a man halfway.

The entries in the Ship's log are made by the Officer of the watch and refer only to wind, weather speed, passing ships and they are copied from the log slate.

II Officers and Crew

After the insubordination of the 10th October nothing was done except logging the men after all hands being called aft. I saw a fight between Ipson and the 2nd mate. It was a stand-up fight. It lasted about five minutes. We separated them when we could manage it; but they were always going at one another. Ipson was logged several times. He was one of those guilty of insubordination on the 15th October and was suspected of having ravished a woman, but nothing was done to him except that the affair of Maharani was reported at St. Helena. We put an extra man on watch on the quarterdeck after the Maharani affair. I suggested to the Captain after the noise made by Ipson at the hospital door, to put him in irons. This was long before Maharani's death. I think he should have been put in irons, and then Smith and the others would have been more quiet. Strict discipline was kept on board. I do not think the Captain was unduly lenient. Once there was a complaint about rice by two men. This was on the 5th September. (Entry in log read). That entry is correct. That was the only time I heard any grumbling about food.

I have been at sea twelve years. I hold a Master's Certificate. I had no trouble myself with the crew. This was about an average voyage as far as discomforts go. The Captain and officers did all they could for the comfort of the Immigrants and for their protection. There were no complaints from the Coolies, men or women about the crew except what is entered in the Log. I think if the Captain had been more strict with the crew it would have been better.

The Captain did not tell me why he did not put Ipson in irons when I advised him to do so. I have formed no opinion as to the reason why he did not put him in irons. Taking the crew altogether they were a decent crew. I never was on a voyage before where so many charges were made at the end. I never was with such a big crew before. I can't tell why these should arise, whether they had anything to do with the food or not. I suspect it might have had something to do with the food. I did not hear the men grumble. I mentioned this about the food, because it is generally the food with sailors. I do not think the treatment received by Mohadaya would have led her to make a complaint. I never heard that the other Coolies complained of the exceptional treatment these three women received. It is not usual on board a ship for the 2nd mate and a sailor to have a fight. Mostly everything on board ship was done after consultation between the Captain, the doctor and myself; yet I cannot offer any explanation of why the men were not put in irons. I cannot say anything unless I see it in black and white. I know who gave evidence as to Maharani's death. It did not strike me as peculiar when I heard that the witnesses against Ipson in the Maharani affair were Mohadaya and Moorti. The sail locker is in the break of the poop, the opposite side to my cabin. I never saw any Coolie women going in there with Lutchmun. I have formed no opinion as to the cause of Maharani's death. I saw her about a week before her death. I was not aware that there was a lot of venereal on board. I never heard anything about it.

III Mortality

The people who were taken ill with the fever were taken suddenly with pain in the head and locked jaw. The weather was very hot and squally coming down the Bay. In the last voyage of the *Allanshaw* there were deaths from the same cause. I thought it was to be ascribed to the heat. There was no complaint as to the quality of the food. In my opinion the voyage of the *Allanshaw* was quite satisfactory in every respect.

I have seen other Coolie women and children go on the poop with their meals beside the three women named. The poop is reserved for the women and children. The door of the sail locker is not locked. When I suggested to the captain to put Ipson in irons he said, "There is no occasion. One must be careful when putting a man in irons. It must be for something." That is the only time I suggested that any of the crew should be put in irons.

The sail locker can be bolted inside after any one goes in. If I had been Captain I would have put Ipson in irons. I do not agree with the opinion of the Captain.

I am not surprised that so many charges have been laid against Ipson because he is a bad man. I never saw any woman or man with a woman go into the sail locker.

Signed: G.W. De La Mare
Late Chief Officer
Ship *Allanshaw*

APPENDIX 12

Alexander Bain (Able Seaman)

Day 4, Friday, 4 December 1885

Alexander Bain, duly sworn and examined:-

I was an able seaman on board the *Allanshaw*. I shipped in London. After we left Calcutta I was in the portwatch with the 1st mate. There were plenty of Coolies on board and a lot of Coolie women. I never saw any of the crew talking or laughing with the Coolie women. I never heard in the forecastle of any of them having had anything to do with them. A couple of times when I was at the wheel I have seen the doctor take one of the girls into the Chartroom. I cannot remember if it was the same girl each time. This was in the day time. I have seen the captain talking to them, but not playing with them. I have seen nobody else playing with them or talking to them. I know a man named Lutchmun. He was working in the cabin. I never saw Lutchmun with a Coolie girl or bringing Coolie girls in the cabins or on the poop. I don't know the name of the Steward. He is a coloured man. I never saw him bringing Coolie girls in the cabins or on the poop or talking to them. I remember the girl Maharani's death. A man came one day in the forecastle and said a woman was in the hospital and he thought some one had been with her. I heard this among the lot of us. I heard nothing more about her. I have seen her on the poop and sometimes at the break of the poop between the cabin door and mate's door.

I never heard it suggested as to who the man was that had been with this girl. I heard them say in the forecastle that they blamed them aft. They were thinking some one aft had something to do with her. By "them aft" was meant some of the officers. I never heard any of the sailors accused of this until we came into port and Ipson was arrested. Two or three other girls sat near the mate's door with Maharani. These girls were always together. One of the girls taken by the doctor into the Chartroom had a cut on her lip. (Mohadaya and

Moorti brought in). I know both these women. The little one (Moorti) was the one taken into the Chartroom. I was sometimes at the Wheel when the Coolies were eating their dinner and breakfast. I never saw any women and children taking their meals on the poop. I have seen Mohadaya taking her meals there, and I think her sister and mother with her. Sometimes there were six or eight or ten taking their meals on the poop. I never saw any women or children get food out of the cabin. If I heard that two of the sailors had seized Maharani, dragged her out of the watercloset, wrapped her head in a cloth and ravished her I would not believe it. I think it unlikely because they would have been seen or heard. I never heard any sailor say anything about having a Coolie girl, either that he had had one or would have one. We heard on a Sunday that she had died and then we heard that she was "split"; but no one was mentioned. Ipson never shewed his privates to me. I never heard anything about Ipson's privates. Two women came on board to the forecastle at St. Helena with baskets selling things. I don't know if any of the men had anything to do with them. Some of the crew went ashore.

The chartroom is a small wooden house on the poop. When the doctor took a girl in there they stayed about a couple of minutes. I never saw the doctor playing roughly with the women. I have never seen the doctor doing more than making fun with them, giving them cigars. By making fun I mean running round the poop. I have never seen him sitting with them. There were a good many women. Sometimes the poop was full of them. The two women Mohadaya and Moorti were most generally on the poop. That is how I knew them. I never heard the crew speaking of Mohadaya in the forecastle except as a fancy woman. I never heard anyone say who was the fancy man. I cannot say as to whether it would surprise me if I heard that the Captain was the fancy man. I never saw the Captain take more notice by speaking to her more than the others. I have seen the Captain and the doctor speaking to her more than the others. I have seen Mohadaya and Moorti playing the tom-tom on the poop. I could not see the break of the poop from the wheel. I never saw Lutchmun bringing women to the sail locker. I never heard anything in the forecastle about the sail locker. I never saw any of the Officers speaking to Maharani nor did I hear of it. I have no opinion as to the cause of Maharani's death I have not spoken to the mate since I left the ship. I saw him this morning but did not speak to him. I can tell nothing about Maharani's death at all. I never saw Ipson among the women. I never saw him talking to them. When Ipson was arrested we thought in the forecastle the Captain was down on him.

We thought the Captain was down on him because he was always fooling round the deck and was connected with the row about the boy.

I cannot see from the wheel into the Chartroom. The first time I saw the doctor take a girl in the Chartroom was in the forenoon. The doctor pulled her into the Chartroom. She came up on the poop alone. I did not see anyone else on the poop.

II Officers and Crew

I have been to sea about seven or eight years. I have been treated well enough, only they were mean about the grub. Sometimes we did not get enough to eat. One Saturday the rice came into the forecastle and Smith and I did not get our share, and I think there were a couple of others also who did not get their share. I did not get my rice for dinner. I got it between 5 and 6. I refused to work until I got it. I told the Captain I would not work until I got it. Five or six times we went aft about the meat which was a little short. We got the meal after we complained. We had no other complaints against the Captain and Officers. They did not tease us with extra work. The ship was much the same as other ships I have been in except in regard to food. The crew was a decent lot of fellows. I never saw a fight in the forecastle.

The time six of us went aft we went to see about the boy, to know what the captain was punishing him for. We went to beg him off. After we went below Ipson and the 2nd mate had a fight which lasted about eight minutes. When we went on the poop we had no intention to mutiny or to take over the command of the ship or interfere with the Captain. I do not know who started the idea of going on the poop. There were two or three of them. Erickson asked me if I was going aft. I said I would go with them. I never saw the Captain or Officers interfere with any of us. I don't think the captain was too easy as we were working all day.

I never refused before to work unless I got what I wanted. I did not think I would be put in irons for refusing to work till I got my grub. I have never been in a ship before where men went aft in this way or refused to work. It is the first time I have seen such things. I never saw men fight with officers before. I have seen the men fight among themselves. Ipson and the 2nd mate were not separated. I saw no one separate them; but the mate came and told them to knock off, and then the 2nd mate stopped. The crew and some of the Coolies stood round and watched the fight. The Captain was on the main deck. I think the doctor was at the cabin door. Ipson was treated on board the same as the rest of the crew, and Smith also. I don't think either the captain was frightened of the crew or the crew of the captain. I do not know if the reason we were not punished till we arrived in port was because the captain was afraid of us. I don't think there would have been any difference in the conduct of the officers or men if there had been no women on board. The boy was a pet among the crew and that is why we went aft to beg him off. I was in the same watch with Ipson. I don't know who was his chum. I never saw him shewing his privates nor did I hear of it; and do not think it a likely thing.

Signed: A. Bain

APPENDIX 13

William Lee (Able Seaman)

Day 4, Friday, 4 December 1885

William Lee, duly sworn and examined:-

I am a native of Montserrat and have been at sea nine years. I am an able seaman on board the *Allanshaw*. I joined her in London for the round voyage. I was in the port watch, the chief mate's. There were a great many Coolie women on board. I never knew of the crew having anything to do with the Coolie women except once. I was relieved from the wheel one evening at 12 o'clock and was coming forward, walking on the port side. On the fore part of the water closet, when I got opposite, I heard a bawling, very low and groaning. I stopped at the capstan and went up and heard the woman say "Salam, salam, he is too big." These were the words used. I don't know what she meant. I went up and saw this man Robert Ipson with his hands on her shoulder; it was the same woman who died. The woman was standing up and so was he, at the fore part of the water closet. I said to him, "if you follow these women you will get yourself in trouble". I said nothing more to him till next morning and I went to the forecastle, and took my coat off and went to our closet on the portside. I came back and went to my bunk and saw nothing more. I left him standing with the woman just as I found him. When I came back from the closet I found him in the forecastle. The woman was taken ill the next day. I did not see him doing anything to the woman. The woman died on Sunday. I did not tell the Captain or officers or the doctor what I had seen. Next morning after I had seen him with Maharani I told Ipson, "you are going to a very bad place, Demerara, to interfere with these people". He said, "damn her to Hell, she is big enough to bear it". I heard afterwards in the forecastle that two men had troubled this woman, but I saw only one man. I never heard any enquiry being made by the doctor and that is why I did not make any statement.

I never spoke a word about it until I told Grant sometime last week on shore. I remember Ipson being arrested. I knew that Inspector Wright came on board to make enquiries. I did not tell him, because I was then between decks. I came up when I was called. Mr. Wright called me into the cabin. I told him I knew nothing about it, because no one was called aft at the time and asked about it. I have been on other ships with Emigrants, and if any person troubled even a child all hands would be called aft and would be punished if proved to have been done on purpose. I told the Inspector I knew nothing about it because I did not want to get any one into trouble. I said to Grant, if all hands had been called aft at the time the doctor would not have got away so easily; because I did not think the doctor made sufficient enquiry at the time. If he had I would have spoken out. This is the nearest I have ever seen a man to one of the Coolie women on board the ship. I never heard any talk in the forecastle of any of the Officers having anything to do with the women. I never heard the officers accused of being the cause of the death of this woman.

I told Grant the same story I have told now. I never told Grant that I saw Ipson having connexion with the woman. If he had connexion with the woman under the circumstances mentioned it must have been with her consent. Ipson insulted the chief mate repeatedly and that is the reason I had nothing to do with him. He was a rough and unruly young man. Day before yesterday in the Depot I told the mate the story about Ipson. Last Sunday I told the captain about it. I told both the captain and mate that I saw Ipson standing with his hands on the woman's shoulders. I don't know if any one said that Maharani was the mate's woman. I never heard it. The Coolie women used to dance and play tom-tom on the poop. I never saw the Officers and doctor meddling with them. I heard on board ship about two days before arrival David and Anderson say Ipson had shewn his privates to them and they were mashed up – cut up.

II Officers and Crew

I had no complaint to make about grub except once about rice; but I got it with my tea afterwards. I did not refuse to work. The same day Smith did not get his rice and refused to work I did not get mine; but I did not refuse to work. I got my rice for my tea. All the crew said the captain was mean and I said the same thing myself and they did not like him. The men got the rations according to scale; but they were too little. It was not the Captain's fault.

After the death of Maharani, the watch was doubled. After nine years experience I think the discipline of the ship was good.

Signed: William Lee
Witness: C.M. King

APPENDIX 14

Walter R.S. Stokes (Third Officer)

Day 5, Saturday, 5 December 1885

Walter Reginald Stewart Stokes, duly sworn and examined:-

I am 3rd Officer of the Ship *Allanshaw* and was so on her voyage from Calcutta. I remember a Coolie girl named Maharani. I know nothing about her except seeing her at meal times. I heard that a sailor had connexion with her. I heard this before her death from the Coolies. I have the rations to attend to. The story was not brought to me, but I simply heard the Coolies talking among themselves. I heard that a man with a red shirt was accused, but no name was mentioned. I drew my own conclusions as to who it was. I took it to be this man Ipson. The next I heard of it was that she was dead. I saw the doctor have a Post Mortem on her. I was not present. I heard nothing more then, except that the captain could not come to any conclusion. I heard nothing more about the case until I came into harbour. I did not hear the result of the doctor's examination. I never saw any one troubling this woman or using familiarity with her in any way among either officers or men. I never saw any familiarity or indecent conduct towards any women on the part of either officers or men. I have been at sea not quite five years. This is my first trip with Coolies. In my capacity as 3rd Officer I had to do with the rations and had an opportunity of hearing things from the Coolies. I never heard any complaint about their treatment. They all seemed to be quite contented and satisfied. There was a complaint once about the grain.

I knew very nearly all the Coolies. I did not know her (Maharani) more than any others. I had no duties to take me on the poop. I am quite certain I heard the story about Maharani after her admission to hospital and before she died. I heard this from return Coolie. I don't know if it was a man or a woman. It might have been one of the women I saw outside the office this morning. I never heard of any familiarity between the Officers and women. When not serving rations I principally stopped in my room. I serve out the water, that is I fill the tanks. If any one said I was larking with the Coolie women it would not be true. I know nothing more about Maharani. When I was told the story about her I did not think it was possible on account of the watch kept. I never heard of any instance or statement about a sailor and the women.

The Captain took steps to find out as to the truth or otherwise of the story as to the cause of death of Maharani. He asked myself and others about it. The discipline on board the ship as far as the women and Coolies in general was concerned was good and strict.

II Officers and Crew

I remember Ipson. He was troublesome from the beginning of the voyage. I used to go round the hospital and between decks at 8 o'clock every evening with the doctor and Ipson used to cause annoyance by getting in front of the hospital door, making noises with his mouth and also throwing stuff, rice, dholl or anything he could get hold of into the hospital. He was reported for it, but he denied it. He was found out at last and I believe he was logged for it. I consider that logging was a sufficient punishment for that Offence. This was on the 23rd of August. I remember the occasion on which a boy cut a Coolie with his knife and was punished by being made to walk the poop with a capstan bar. Six men came aft on to the poop and one man, Erickson, asked to see the captain. The captain ordered them off the poop, and he (Erickson) went. The Captain ordered the others off, but they would not go. One of them, Smith, took the bar from the boy and refused to give it back when the captain ordered him. The captain made an attempt to wrest it from him, and in the struggle was thrown down and his head struck against the hen coop. The captain got up and ordered him off the poop again, but he would not go. Bain got possession of the bar and attempted to throw it overboard. The captain took it from him and gave it back to the boy. He ordered them off the poop again and they went, using very foul language. Then a fight took place between Ipson and the 2nd Officer. It lasted about 15 or 20 minutes. The fight came to an end of itself; they gave it up. The captain then fetched all hands aft and asked each man individually whether he intended mutiny. They all answered "no". The captain then took the six men to the cabin and read the clauses of the Merchant Shipping Act to them. I left the cabin then. The 2nd officer who was present told me that the captain told them he would punish them in Demerara. As far as the discipline of the ship is concerned everything was carried out as it ought to have been. Every precaution was taken for the protection of the Immigrants. I don't think the captain was too lenient. As to the cause of the disturbances I think Ipson came on board with the idea that he would do as he liked. I looked upon him as a troublesome character; a regular gaol bird. I don't think anything else should have been done after the affair on the poop than was done by the captain.

I am still an officer of the ship, serving under the captain. The first officer has left. I know he urged that Ipson should be put in irons. I do not agree with him in that opinion. I think he (the Captain) would have found himself in the wrong when he got to Demerara if he had put Ipson in irons. I did not think Ipson had done anything to render him justly liable to be put in irons. I have only sailed under one other Captain and have been at sea five years. During the time I was at sea I never saw behaviour like Ipson's. I believe Smith was more led on, than a bad character. I say the same of Bain. There was no complaint against Bain from London to Calcutta. I know nothing of these two, Smith and Bain, refusing to work on account of not getting their rice; now heard of it. I have nothing to say against any of the crew except Ipson.

I think that, as Ipson would have been in irons about two months, the captain had sufficient reason for not taking this course; and also after any experience of five years it is only in cases where life or property is in danger that such extreme measures are adopted.

I don't think that if Ipson had been more strictly dealt with at the beginning, there would have been less trouble during the voyage. I think that Ipson would have given the same trouble on any other ship. I think it quite satisfactory that there should be a charge of murder, theft and disobedience of orders and assaulting the Captain at the end of the voyage. I do not think it satisfactory that these things should have happened. When I said it was satisfactory, I meant that they should be punished for their acts.

I think it would have been more satisfactory if these things had been prevented, instead of punished afterwards. I don't think they could have been prevented.

I consider the charges against Ipson were well founded, and that they were not instituted through pique.

Ipson was charged the moment we arrived in Demerara and he has been in gaol on one charge or other ever since, viz. a month. I know he has never been able to make his own statement, for he has always been charged and never was a witness.

Signed: W.R.S. Stokes
3rd Officer
Ship *Allanshaw*

APPENDIX 15

August Makohl (Engineer)

Day 5, Saturday, 5 December 1885

August Makohl, duly sworn and examined:-

I was engineer on board the ship *Allanshaw* on her late voyage from Calcutta to Demerara. I told some of the people on board that if I could write English I would send a report to the Immigration Office of the behaviour of the people on board the vessel in regard to the Coolies. I was never allowed to come aft and was always chased. In other Coolie vessels I have always been allowed aft on the quarter deck. I have seen them people playing and skylarking with the girls, laughing and talking I mean. By "them people" I mean the people aft, the Officers and others except the Baboo. They were allowed to do this and we were not. I never saw them doing anything wrong. What I want to ask is why the Officers were allowed to do this and we were not. We signed articles not to do so, and the Officers being allowed to do so was leading us on. My opinion is that if we were not allowed to do it, the officers should not have been allowed. I never saw the doctor using any improper familiarity with any of the women. I could see along the quarter deck.

I came to make this remark because the others were talking about it and they saw more than I did, because they worked aft. They talked about a woman. They generally talked about women. I could swear as far as I know that none of the crew touched a woman; and I never heard any of them say that they had. I heard after the death of Maharani that four men had connexion with her, then afterwards I heard it was three, and last of all I heard it was one man who wore a red shirt. I did not believe it. Ipson spoke to me before he knew he was accused of it; and said he would be the first to bring up the man who did it if he knew who it was. He did not say that the blame should be among the Officers or that the sailors said so. He blamed nobody. The sailors talked a

126

good deal about being kept from going aft and had bad thoughts about it. This did not cause any bad feeling between the Officers and men. There was a talk that the captain was mean about the food. I do not agree with it. I got what I signed for. It was a comfortable ship. Ipson was in trouble because he was a rough childish man, fond of playing tricks and had no experience. I do not agree that he was a turbulent scoundrel. He used to come and talk to me. In my opinion the officers and crew were better on this occasion than on others when I have been with Coolies.

The reason I did not make any complaint to the Immigration authorities on arrival was because I was afraid it would get me into trouble with the Captain. I have come now and made my statement because I am forced to do so. The only complaint I have to make is that I was not allowed to go aft. If I had written or spoken before, that is all I would have said. The Coolies were well treated as far as I could see. I have been five voyages with Coolies.

What I meant when I spoke to Ipson about reporting the behaviour on board was, about the skylarking with the women.

Question by Chairman:	If you had written to the Immigration Authorities on arrival here what would you have complained of?
Answer:	I would have asked why we wasn't allowed to come aft on the quarter deck. We weren't allowed to talk with the women. We were always stopped not to do so; and the officers were doing it.

Signed: August Makohl
Engineer
The *Allanshaw*

APPENDIX 16

Joseph Warner (Able Seaman)

Day 5, Saturday, 5 December 1885

Joseph Warner, duly sworn and examined:-

I am a native of Antigua. I shipped on board the *Allanshaw* in Calcutta as an Able seaman. I know nothing mysterious about the conduct of the Captain, Officers or doctor in regard to the women. I only know that they were very Kindly treated and the women were always allowed to play their tom-toms and dance on the poop. I have seen the captain and the doctor giving them sweets. I mean confectionery. I never saw the Captain, doctor or any of the Officers use any improper familiarity with any woman on board that ship. I could not say so because it would be a falsehood. I was employed on the poop all the voyage. I was sailmaker's mate.

By improper familiarity I would mean playing with them; pulling them about, taking them into the Chartroom or sail locker or rolling about on the poop with them would in my opinion be improper familiarity. I never witnessed any of these things. I was daily on the poop. I never told any one I had seen these things. If any one said I did, it would be false. I have heard such things daily spoken of on board. This was a repeated topic of conversation among the sailors. I put this down to the strictness of the Officers and the jealous feeling of the men in consequence. By jealousy I mean that the men felt being Kept off the quarter deck. The Officers were very distant with the women. I have seen the 2nd Officer putting them out of the way. In regard to the death of Maharani I heard two old women who spoke a little English saying "bibi sick". I could not make it out till next day when I heard a theory that a woman had been badly treated by some men and was ill in consequence. I did not believe it and do not believe it now. I don't think Ipson was justly charged. I never saw anything between the men and the women. I think it impossible that Ipson could have been guilty, as he had no chance of getting at the women. I have left the Ship because I did not want to go home this winter. I took a free discharge.

II Officers and Crew

I did not like the discipline of the ship. I have been thirty two years at sea and have been in various Kinds of ships, but the first time in a Coolie ship. When I talk of the discipline I mean the discipline of an Emigrant ship and the strictness of it. We were not allowed to walk about freely. Lee was a disagreeable man and had growls with nearly every one. I could not say that I heard him threaten to get Ipson into trouble. They were not good friends. He (Lee) got on with the Officers better than Ipson. Ipson was a "reprobated" character.

I was daily on the poop and never saw the captain, the Officers or the doctor put their hands on the women's private parts between their legs and I don't believe it ever happened. Captain Wilson is a very strict man with his passengers and crew in regard to his whole duty. In regard to the men coming aft I blame the men. They were a set of blessed vagabonds. I refer to those six men who came on the poop.

Signed: Joseph Warner

APPENDIX 17

Captain F.C. Wilson (Recalled)

Day 6, Monday, 7 December 1885

F.C. Wilson, recalled.

I have never had sexual communication with any of the female Immigrants on board, especially Mohadaya, Moorti, Maharani, Parbutti and Sumoondury.

I never took any indecent liberty with any of the women, never put my hands between their legs, or tickled them. The most I have ever done was, if they were lying on the hen coop, to slap them on the bottom to make them get out of the way. I never saw the doctor take any Coolie woman into the Chartroom on the poop. I never saw any indecent behaviour on the part of any officers towards the women. I don't think Maharani sat in front of the mate's door more than any other women. The Coolie women are in the habit of going to the same place every day, even when they take their meals. The Engineer had no right aft, unless he came aft to receive orders. I spoke to him two or three times about it, and the 2nd mate checked him also. He messed in the halfdeck with the boatswain. The discipline on board Coolie Ships is more strict than on cargo ships. The crew have to be more watched.

The Coolies mentioned were not differently treated to the others except in regard to coming sometimes on the poop to get their food. Others sometimes got it there as well. The statement that the alleged assault on Maharani was reported to me before her death is false. If I had heard of it I would have taken steps to make enquiries and would have been too pleased to find it out. I knew the Engineer was not pleased at not being allowed to come aft. He wanted to know the reason why he was not allowed to do so. I did not know of any general complaint as to food, not more than on other voyages. I put down all the troubles of the voyage to the blackguard character of the two men Ipson and Smith, and the crew being so closely watched. I consider the conduct of the six men in coming on the poop was mutinous conduct. I cannot say for certain anything about syphilis, except that I heard of one or two cases on board in the early part of the voyage. I remember one man, one of the Immigrants, having chancres soon after starting. I did not hear much of syphilis being in the ship before we arrived. There was nothing in my behaviour or that of my officers towards the particular women named which I think could lead the men to believe that they were particular pets of ours.

They were cleaner than the others, were better behaved and spoke English and I heard their names called out often. I sometimes had to refer to them, as they spoke English to interpret for me and help to Keep order.

I always went round the main deck between 10 and 11, to see if all was right. I don't know if this is done by other Captains. I did it as an extra precaution.

Signed: Fred. C. Wilson

APPENDIX 18

Lutchmun (Return Emigrant)

Day 6, Monday, 7 December 1885

Lutchmun, duly sworn and examined:-

I am a Return Immigrant. I lived here five years. I went back to India in the Ganges last year. I came back in the *Allanshaw* this voyage. I was shipped as an Immigrant and was Hospital Assistant. After seven days I was made cabin boy. I know a man named Ipson, one of the crew. I knew all the crew. I did not talk to them. I knew them by seeing them on board. I know the Steward; but don't know his name. I know a girl named Maharani who died. I never saw any one play with Maharani. I never told any one that I saw some one playing with her. I never went down in the between decks and brought up women for the captain, officers or Steward. I never told Ipson that the mate had connexion with Maharani. I swear that. I know a girl named Mohadaya, a Return Coolie. I never saw any of the Officers or Captain or men playing with her. She was up on the poop and she used to skylark with the doctor, making some dance, beating tom-tom, and she used to put red paint on people, women and sirdars, sporting about. I never heard any of the sailors talking about the Officers having connexion with these girls. Three days before Maharani died I heard that somebody interfered with her on deck. I heard the Baboo say this. I went to look at her on the day she died; her mouth was swollen, her belly was swollen; she could not speak. Two or three hours after I heard that she was dead. I heard a sailor with a red shirt was accused. I did not talk much with the sailors. I had no time. They did not speak much to me. I did not tell the sailors that one of them was blamed for touching the girl. I never heard the sailors say who had done it. One night about three days before her death, Tuesday or Wednesday, I was between decks with a bad knee and a little after twelve, I heard a Coolie man come near where I was rubbing my leg with

132

turpentine and he told me some mischief was going on at the starboard side of water closet forward.

I asked him what sort of mischief. He told me about a Coolie girl, a short girl, three sailors (two white and one black) took the girl to fuck. She begged to get clear. A man named Chitamun told me this, that they took her to the forecastle and had connexion with one after the other, and that he watched them for three quarters of an hour. Chitamun went to the closet with a sick man and waited for him outside. Chitamun also said that Ramkhelawan a Sirdar at the after hatch came to him and asked him what was going on. Ramkhelawan said "there is a girl missed aft and come forward". He knocked at the forecastle door and no one answered. Chitamun called to the sick man in the closet "come, let us get away". Chitamun and the sick man came down and told me all this. The sick man's name was Baboolall. That is all I heard of it. I did not tell any one except the Steward. I told him after the girl died. I did not tell any of the Officers. Chitamun did not tell me who the girl was, or who the sailors were, except that one was a nigger – a Demerara nigger. He said the girl shouted and cried "bap-re-bap". I never spoke to Ramkhelawan or Baboolall about it. I was not asked, and therefore did not think it necessary to tell. I never heard Ipson's name mentioned in the matter until I came to Demerara. I never told Ipson that I had heard that he had ravished the girl.

I know the man Bain and all the sailors. They used to come every Friday to buy goods from the slop chest. I used to help the Steward, but I never spoke to them. If they said I had a great deal to say to them it would be a lie. I was no friend to the sailors. The money paid by them for what they buy is paid to the captain. The things they buy are tobacco, clothes, boots, etc. – nothing to eat. (Ipson's statement read to him). This statement in regard to me is all a lie. Half a dozen girls who kept themselves clean were allowed on the poop and there was plenty of dancing and playing and putting mess on the doctor and themselves and not on any of the Officers, but on some sirdars. I know the doctor has left the Colony. I have not spoken to any one about this since arrival. I have not mentioned it. No one asked me. I was at the door of the cabin when the enquiry was going on in regard to Maharani's death. I know that witnesses were being examined about it. Two or three were in together. They would not have me in the cabin. They put me out. The Captain spoke to me last Sunday when I was on board the *Allanshaw* about the Maharani case. I was in the cabin sitting down. Lee was there. I told the captain the same story I have told now, as Lee told him I knew something about it and he asked me what I knew.

When I said I did not speak to any one I meant on board ship. I have not been to Schoon Ord. Moorti is my wife. I was not married to her in India. On board ship I promised to keep her. Although I had a conversation with Moorti about the man with the red shirt I never told her what I knew. I am living with Moorti now. I never heard of any sailors having connexion with the women. There was a row and contention among the sailors all the passage, and they made a great noise aft. It was always about food not being sufficient. This was done very often. They used to get what they wanted after they complained. Four always came aft making a row. Ipson, Peter, a short stout man whose name I do not remember and Bain. When I spoke of a black man in connexion with Maharani's case I meant a black man like Lee. The sailors made more row in this ship than others I have been in. I have been in four or five ships.

When I say the doctor was skylarking with the girls I never saw him doing anything indecent. They were blackguard, rough and rude in their play, getting red paint, flour etc. and throwing on people. The captain said on Sunday that I would be called to give evidence as he would give my name in to the Agent General. The Engineer told me on Saturday night that Ipson wanted me. The Captain did not try to frighten me in any way; but told me I must tell everything I knew. Before the captain told me to tell all to the Commission, he knew what I was going to say.

When I said that six women were on the poop I mean they were always there. There were generally forty or fifty.

Signed: Lutchmun
Witness

APPENDIX 19

Heerdayaram (Hospital Attendant)

Day 6, Monday, 7 December 1885

Heerdayaram, duly sworn and examined:-

I was hospital attendant on board the *Allanshaw*. I worked under Mr. Grant. I remember when Maharani came to the Hospital. I was attending to her and the female nurse Golap also. When she went to the Hospital first she had fever and said her head was hurting her. I know a woman named Moorti. I remember her coming to the hospital to see Maharani. I remember Maharani making a statement to Moorti. I remember what she said. She, Moorti, went to the hospital at 6 o'clock on Friday night, and asked Maharani what was the matter with her. She said her belly hurt her. Moorti then asked Maharani why her belly hurt her. Maharani answered, "one night I came outside to go to the closet and one of the sailors caught hold of me in the closet took me up and carried me away." Moorti asked her then "where did he take you to?" Maharani said nothing. Moorti then asked her if she knew the sailor, and she said he wore a red shirt. Moorti then asked if she (Maharani) could point out the man, and Maharani shook her head. She did not say where the sailor took her to. She only mentioned one sailor. She told Mr. Grant this story at 7 o'clock the same night. I asked Maharani myself about this story and she would not say anything. I did not hear any other Coolies talking about this. I did not hear any of the officers speak about it, as I am always about the hospital. I never heard the sailors talking about it. I never heard any of them accused of having assaulted Maharani. I have never seen or heard of anything wrong between the sailors and women. I know Ramkhelawan. I never spoke to him about it. I know Lutchmun. He was butler. I never had any conversation with him on the subject. I don't believe it, because I did not see it with my eyes.

I saw Maharani when she came to Hospital. She said she had fever. I saw her face, but did not notice anything wrong with her mouth. At 6 o'clock on Friday night she complained of her belly to Moorti. On Saturday the big Baboo went to her. She was faint and did not take her food. She was groaning, but did not say anything. On Sunday Baboo and the doctor went and examined her belly and it was swollen. I do not know what she died of. She was very quiet during her illness and did not say much.

Golap was sent by the Baboo to examine Maharani's privates. She went and shut up the hospital door. Golap said nothing to me about the examination. The women's water closets were near the hospital. I did not sleep in the hospital. I left at 8 o'clock. I have seen one woman sometimes go to the closet by herself, but generally there were more.

There were three men with syphilis and one with gonorrhea. The first was one week after leaving Calcutta. It was a man with sores. His name was Mohungoo. The Baboo said he had come with it. The other two were long after. I know nothing about the women. I saw the people who got sick and died of fever. They used to come in with their heads hurting them. They could speak, but soon lost their senses. The Baboo put blisters behind their necks. They soon died, most in one or two days. There were no convulsions, no spots on the skin, no vomiting. They lay on the floor, but rolled. I can't say if there was much fever.

Signed: Heerdayaram
Witness

APPENDIX 20

William Clintworth (Cabin Boy)

Day 6, Monday, 7 December 1885

William Clintworth, duly sworn and examined:-

I know a man named Robert Ipson. One day he was chasing a Coolie man from the forecastle door. The Coolie man sat down about 10 yards from the forecastle door, and said to another Coolie "that is the man had connexion with the Coolie girl and that is why she died". One day Ipson was talking to me and O'Brien, he said, "last night I had a Coolie woman at the closets". Three or four days after he told me the same story. I did not hear of any other man having a Coolie woman. He first told me this three days before the woman died, and the 2nd time it was after she died. I did not tell anybody about this story. Nobody asked me about it. I am not sure whether he said it in earnest or was merely skylarking. Sometimes if Ipson had anything to eat that he did not want he would give it to me. This is the first sailing ship I have been in. I was pretty comfortable on board. One Saturday there was grumbling about the rice. There was no grumbling about anything else. I was sixteen years of age last July. I was in a Steamer one voyage.

I was in the same watch with Ipson, Bain and Smith. They were always together. They were all bad, but Ipson was the worst. He was never in his bunk at night. He was always walking the deck. He would be there three hours out of four. (Statement of O'Brien read). I was present when O'Brien made to the Captain the statement which has just been read. I do not know whether what Ipson is reported to have said was true or not. He was always swaggering about.

Signed: William F. Clintworth

APPENDIX 21

James T. Grant (Recalled)

Day 6, Monday, 7 December 1885

There were a few cases of syphilis at the beginning of the voyage. It began with a man. He came on board with it. I only know of two cases among the women. I have seen more cases of syphilis in other voyages. I attended to the dispensing of the medicines for the sailors with the Baboo. I do not know of Ipson having been treated for Chancres. At the beginning of the voyage there was a man named Jackson, boatswain, who had chancres. This was after the first Coolie man had been treated. I think the sore was on the first Coolie man when he came onboard. Jackson said he got his in Calcutta. None of the crew complained of getting the disease on board ship, and none of the Coolies complained of getting it from the sailors. I know Lutchmun. I never saw him speaking much to the sailors. I have seen him standing near Ipson and warned him. I never heard before that Maharani was taken to the forecastle and shut in. I don't know if it is likely. It might be. It is hard for me to say. I did not know that Moorti was married to Lutchmun. I know she is living with him now. I suppose he must have made some arrangement with her about this on board ship or in Calcutta. I knew before this enquiry was held that the men were going to report that the Officers and doctor had been skylarking with the women. I went ashore and to Schoon Ord. after the ship was inspected.

Signed: Jas. Theo. Grant
Assistant Compounder

APPENDIX 22

William Leslie (Steward)

Day 7, Tuesday, 8 December 1885

William Leslie, duly sworn and examined:-

I was Steward on board the *Allanshaw* on her voyage from Calcutta to Demerara. I lived in a cabin in the after part of the ship, in a passage leading into the saloon. I know Lutchmun. He was employed under me as cabin boy. He was always with me from the 7th day after leaving Calcutta, except four days when he was off duty with a bad knee. He always slept between decks with the other Immigrants. I remember when Maharani died. It was on a Sunday morning. It was at this time that Lutchmun had a bad knee. There was a good deal of talk about this girl. Lutchmun, on the day he returned to work, told me he had heard from some parties that they had seen the girl on deck forward somewhere. This was after Maharani's death. He said he heard some one had taken her to the forecastle. (Statement of Lutchmun read to him). This is what Lutchmun told me. When I heard this story from Lutchmun I did not tell anybody and I told Lutchmun that if the Captain or the doctor asked him about it he must tell, but if not, he need not say anything. I thought that this was right, as, if the story was true there were others in the forecastle who knew more about it. I heard nothing about this story from any one else. I heard no conversation between the Officers or sailors about it. I have nothing to do with them. I never interfered with any of the Coolie women. If any one said that I sent Lutchmun to bring women for me at night it would be a lie.

I know a girl named Mohadaya. I know Moorti; that is Lutchmun's wife. Lutchmun was not living with Moorti on board. I never had any immoral connexion with Mohadaya or Moorti. I never gave any food to the women from the cabin. I never have seen any of the Officers or doctor give anything at all to the Coolie women. I supply and attend to the Cabin table and would know if anything was taken away. I heard the doctor tell the Captain that some one had connexion with Maharani. This was either on Sunday morning or Monday morning. Except this story I heard from Lutchmun I never heard of any sailors having connexion with Coolie women. I very seldom went on the poop. Sometimes early in the morning I went there to get mutton which was hanging out and I have sometimes been on the poop during the day to hang clothes. I never saw any indecent behaviour on the part of the doctor towards the women nor did I hear of any. He was generally sitting in his chair or writing in the Chart room. I have been on a voyage with Coolies before from Mauritius to Calcutta. I have been at sea 22 years. There were not many complaints about food. Once or twice there were complaints about rice, that it was not enough. The *Allanshaw* was a very comfortable ship, only a disturbance made by Ipson. Beyond that there was nothing particular in the way of annoyance or disturbance. I refer to the disturbance about the boy and other petty disturbances made by him. This did not concern me and therefore I did not look after it. I have not the least idea of the cause of these petty disturbances.

I don't trouble my head about anything but my own business and I know very little of what goes on in the ship outside my cabin, and a good deal might occur in the way of dissatisfaction without my knowing it. I know there was an enquiry held in the cabin on Sunday evening and Monday after breakfast in regard to Maharani's death. The one on Monday was before I heard the story from Lutchmun. When Lutchmun's story was told to me I knew that an enquiry was being held. I did not consider it my duty to tell the Captain or the doctor anything about it. I have never said anything to the Captain about it, as it was all hearsay. The Captain until now has not asked me anything about it.

I came ashore by the captain's leave this morning. He told me that I was wanted here to give evidence, but did not say what it was about. I know Grant. I should think he was in a better position to know things in regard to the Coolies than I was, but I can't say in regard to the ship. I speak more to the officers than the men. I had nothing to do with the men, and did not speak to them unless they spoke to me. I know of Ipson from hearsay among the Officers. He was not a favourite and I don't think he should be from all I heard from the Officers. I believe the Officers more than Ipson. I know Mohadaya and Moorti. I saw them in the cabin when the enquiry was being held. I did not hear what they said. I heard on board the ship that Ipson was the man with the red shirt who was said to have been concerned in Maharani's death. I heard the story of Lutchmun as to two white men and one black man having been concerned in the assault on Maharani, yet when Ipson was charged with manslaughter I did not think it necessary to come forward and state what I have heard. I am still employed on board the *Allanshaw* with Captain Wilson.

At the time I heard this story as to Ipson and the girl I did not know that he or any other man was charged with a criminal Offence. I did not hear of such a charge till I got to Demerara. The sail locker is near my cabin. I have never seen any woman taken in there or in the cabin by any one either officers or men.

Signed: W.H. Leslie

APPENDIX 23

Ramkhelawan (Sirdar)

Day 8, Wednesday, 9 December 1885

Ramkhelawan, duly sworn and examined:-

I came as an Immigrant in the Ship *Allanshaw*. I was made a Sirdar on board. I was a Sirdar all the time except a short time when I was sick. From 5 to 8 o'clock I used to watch at the after hatch where the women came up. I remember a woman Maharani who died on board. I know a man named Lutchmun. I don't remember his having a bad leg. He used to sleep sometimes below and sometimes above. I know a man named Chitamun. I had no conversation with Chitamun and Lutchmun about Maharani a few days before her death. I don't remember going to look for a missing woman forward. I don't remember going to knock at the forecastle door. One night there was a sailor dressed as a woman and I asked Chitamun whether it was a man or a woman. Chitamun said to me "I saw some one going this way. I don't know whether it was a man or a woman". I saw this figure, a man or a woman, run forward and I went to see who it was. That is all I saw that night. I never told this to anybody. I did not hear any of the Coolies talking as to the cause of Maharani's death. I never heard it said that either an Officer or sailor did anything to this woman. I heard nothing of this at Schoon Ord.

I know the figure was a sailor, a little boy dressed in woman's clothes. I ran up to the boy and saw him. I did not hold him. I asked him "Who are you?" He laughed. I went to the forecastle. I don't know if it was customary for this boy to go about dressed in woman's clothes. That was the only time I saw him dressed in that manner. I don't remember whether this was before or after Maharani's death. This was about two months or two months and a half after we left Calcutta and was one night when I had a talk with Chitamun. That was the only night Chitamun said anything about any one near the closet.

142

This boy had on something like a Sarrie and a piece of cloth on his head. I would know the boy if I saw him. I don't know if it was a black boy or a white boy. At 8 o'clock there are no black boys or Coolie boys on deck.

Signed: Ramkhelawan
Witness

APPENDIX 24

Dr Finlayson (MD)

Day 8, Wednesday, 9 December 1885

Dr. Finlayson, duly sworn and examined:-

Compounder Grant came to my house one day. I do not remember the day. I had very little conversation with him about the ship. There were two remarks he made; one was about the death of Maharani, and the other was about the general conduct on the vessel. In regard to the first point, what he said was, as far as I can remember, much the same as the evidence given in the Sheriff's Office. As to the second point, he said there was a good deal of skylarking. He spoke of it as something unseemly and I understood him to refer to the men and women, the whole lot of them. That was my impression. The impression on my mind was that the discipline was not what it ought to have been. It did not convey any impression that an enquiry was necessary in regard to the skylarking. When Grant was summoned he came and shewed me the Summons. I don't know what day it was. I told him he had nothing to do but to tell the truth as to what he saw and what he heard. He gave me the impression that he was afraid to speak up, and I have that impression still that he had a fear of prejudicing his interests. It has come into my head that he has been threatened, and I told him that the impression he gave me was that he had something to say if he chose to say it. I have been a Medical man in the Colony since 1862. I mentioned these impressions about the skylarking to Dr. Grieve.

I did not consider his statement of sufficient importance to render it necessary for me to advise him in the matter.

The impression still left on my mind is that there was laxity of discipline on board.

The skylarking mentioned by Mr. Grant I understood to refer to men and officers all round.

I do not consider a captain would be doing his duty who allowed romping between the sexes.

Signed: Alex. Finlayson

APPENDIX 25

Chitamun (Passenger)

Day 8, Wednesday, 9 December 1885

Chitamun, duly sworn and examined through Interpreter:-

I was a passenger on board the *Allanshaw*. I remember a man named Baboolall being sick. I looked after him. I took him to the closets, sometimes twice in a night. I recollect something particular happening one night. This was about eleven weeks after we left Calcutta.

I remember a girl named Maharani who died on board. This happened two days before Maharani died. When Baboolall was in the closet I remained outside. I saw a sailor holding a Coolie woman's hand. He was carrying her in his arms. He took her into the place where the sailors live. I did not hear the woman calling out. She was not struggling. There was only one man. He was a sailor, the same man who beat the captain and who was handcuffed when the ship came into port. I know the man. I am quite certain as to the man. I was holding Baboolall's hand and Ramkhelawan Sirdar came up and said to me, "Chitamun, did you see a sailor carry a woman this side?" "You are a Sirdar, you are watching. I brought a sick man to the closet." Ramkhelawan went to the door and I went and took Baboolall down below. Ramkhelawan did not tell me anything afterwards. I have told all that I saw. I saw Ramkhelawan standing at the door listening when I went down. I know a man named Lutchmun. I told Lutchmun this story the same night. I never told any one else. I know that Maharani died. The woman the sailor was carrying was about the size and appearance of Maharani. I never heard any of the Coolies say that some one had troubled Maharani.

Signed: Chitamun
Witness

APPENDIX 26

James T. Grant (Third Deposition)

Day 9, Saturday, 12 December 1885

James T. Grant appeared at his own request and made the following statement:-

I was summoned to give evidence before the Commission appointed to enquire into the history of the voyage of the Ship *Allanshaw* and I wish to give a history of it now.

For a fortnight after we left Calcutta things went on quite nicely and the Immigrants began to get rather lively, having got over their sea-sickness. The single women were all allowed on the poop; also a few women with children who kept themselves clean. They used to be on the poop all day, and the doctor would be passing a little joke with them for the first week or so, and now and then give them a cigar or cigarette and so on. They continued on the poop and were allowed to take their meals either on the poop or on the deck. After a time the doctor objected to their being allowed to eat on the poop and told me to place a sirdar at the foot of the ladder at meal time to prevent their going up. The first one or two days no one went up, as I kept them all down. After those days he allowed certain women to take their meals on the poop. The sirdar was told to let them go up and he did so. When this happened the other women began to make remarks, saying why should they not be allowed also to go up. I don't believe the doctor heard these remarks, as they were not made in his presence. While these women were on the poop the doctor would pass jokes with them, put red paint on them (the kind used by them for their heads) and pulling them about. This seemed to me to be in joke. This went on every day, he keeping them amused and lively, except as to the red paint. The first remark I heard from the women was that these "Returns", Mohadaya especially, was mistress on board the ship. I took no notice of this. Later on it was said she could get what she wanted and the others couldn't. Sometimes when coming up from between decks or washing before dinner I heard a remark passed that Mohadaya was "locked up in the Chartroom so long today with the doctor". This was said a lot of times. I took no notice of these remarks. On the 13th September between 10 o'clock and 11 o'clock in the morning all the women on the poop began daubing each other with red lead used for painting the bulwarks. As I passed them I said, "who started this foolish game?" One said to me, "the doctor, who rubbed some on a woman's face". Then the women got some and rubbed it on the doctor's face. They then continued rubbing the paint in each other's faces, and on the sirdars, the 1st, 2nd, and 3rd Officers. Seeing this I took a cane in my hand and threatened that if any of them touched me I would strike them and they could then complain to the doctor. The 3rd Officer was standing near me and he was daubed by one of the women who seemed to be half crazy. He had a piece of wood in his hand and struck her with it on the face. I thought at first it had gone into her eye, but I found out afterwards that it had only marked her cheek. This red paint game lasted all day till 6 o'clock except meal time. About half past four the doctor told them to stop, but they took no notice. Whilst this game was going on, the sailors came amidships to see what was going on. I often heard remarks passed by the women of certain things they had seen done by other women on the poop. As it did not concern me I took no notice of it. One day about meal time, 9 o'clock, they were all sent below for breakfast. Mohadaya was the only one left on the poop. I went down in the between decks to arrange them in order, to come up for meals. When I came up I heard a report that Mohadaya had been locked up in the chartroom with the doctor. I thought nothing of it. After a while I became almost sick of continually hearing remarks passed by the women, that they had seen such and such things and the women weren't ashamed. After hearing these remarks I said it was all nonsense my being on board ship and knowing nothing of it, and it might create a row in the end. I said to myself, should it create a row in the end, I might be called to say what I know. So one day I was on deck, it happened to be my day for issuing rations to the women at the after hatch. I saw the chartroom door shut and another woman was standing outside by the door.

After a while the woman standing outside turned the nob and the door opened and Mohadaya came out. She glanced down on the deck, saw me and laughed. She then went more aft near the wheel. This is the first occasion I saw her. On another occasion between 5 and 6 in the evening I saw one of the chartroom doors open, the girls were around skylarking, trying to push each other in the chartroom; and all of a sudden I saw a hand stretched out, Moorti dragged in and the door shut. After a time the door opened and she came out. When she came out she came down off the poop immediately and stood at the after part of the after hatch and began crying. Some of the other women crowded round her and took her down in the between decks. After a few days Moorti had a quarrel with a woman and the woman I believe cursed her in her own language and told her that the doctor had had connexion with her; and she went and complained to the doctor. I believe he told her not to take any notice of it. One morning the doctor, the Chief Compounder and myself were going round the between decks when Phagoo, chief Topaz, came up and told the doctor that he was sitting forward near the sailors and overheard them speaking among themselves, that if any of sailors were to be taken charge of or accused of killing Maharani, they would report that the doctor did nothing all day but play with the women. He used the word "play", but the general term on board was skylark. The doctor said to him, they can do as they like, and that he did nothing and was afraid of nothing, and told him not to listen to what the sailors said.

I know that the women and children have a right to the use of the poop. The women allowed to take their meals on the poop were Mohadaya, her sister and mother, Chowry, Tetry and a few others. The women who made the remarks were those on the deck, not always the same women, and one who was on the poop.

Once a Coolie man was pushed down by a sailor near the water closet. I took the man to the captain and he took him forward. I went with him. The captain went to the break of the forecastle. There was a sailor washing his clothes. The captain asked him if he knew anything about the Coolie being pushed down and he said no. The Captain then went in the forecastle and told the Coolie man to follow. As soon as they went a few yards in, the Coolie was ordered out by the sailors who told the Captain the man had no right there – his place was on deck. The captain told the man to go out. The sailors said to the Captain that if he wanted them he must muster them on deck. He did this and the Coolie man pointed out the man who pushed him down. The Captain took him aft on the poop and after enquiry said he would log him. Before the man went to the poop Ipson, who was standing some way off the captain and 2nd officer when the captain asked the men whether they had ever seen any of the officers strike or illtreat the Coolies, said, "no, but we have seen them fooling around with the women". The 2nd officer said, "if you saw me fooling round with the women why did you not catch me. You can sit up during your watch below it won't be much trouble and then you can catch me. Can you prove it?" Ipson said, "Yes, I can prove it and others too without any trouble." This was the only occasion on which I heard any of the sailors make any accusation against the Officers about the women.

I did not see Mohadaya locked in the chartroom with the doctor on the day when I went below to arrange the people for their meals. On the day when I saw her come out of the chartroom I did not see any one else inside. It was a white hand that dragged Moorti into the Chartroom. I don't know whose it was; but from what I have learnt the doctor was the only one up there. The Captain was below, and the Officers were on deck. The doctor used the chartroom, and the captain, more especially the doctor. He used to read and write there.

When I say I was sick of hearing the remarks made by the women, the remarks were that Mohadaya and others were locked up in the chart room with the doctor. I never heard them say this was for an immoral purpose. If they had had anything disrespectful to say they would not have said it before me. I was sick of it because I heard of these women being shut up so often. The first person I spoke to about the Commission after getting my summons was the Rev'd. McFarlane, then to Dr. Finlayson, then afterwards to the Rev'd. May, then to my father, then to Mr. Spence, Manager of School Ord. and the head overseer on the Estate. I also showed the summons to the Captain and spoke to him about it, and also to the 1st, 2nd and 3rd officer – also to the Steward – also to Mr. Reis. I have shewn it to a good many – several others.

Dr. Grieve: Did you speak to any officer of the Immigration Department besides Mr. Reis after hearing of this enquiry?

Answer: After great hesitation, he said I might have done so.

Dr. Grieve: After hearing the names of the persons mentioned how do you account for the impression made on Dr. Finlayson that you had been threatened? (Question by Dr. Grieve).

Answer: I can't account for it.

Dr. Grieve: Have you been threatened or intimidated in regard to the evidence to be given on this enquiry, or has any inducement been held out to you to suppress the truth?

Answer: No.

Dr. Grieve:	Then how do you account for the evidence given today and the evidence you first gave?
Answer:	Because when I came here the 1st day I was asked questions about the death of Maharani and so forth and I never thought of volunteering any statements without being asked.
Dr. Grieve:	Have you no recollection of my asking you questions on these very points before?
Answer:	I have no recollection of it, except being asked my opinion as to why Mohadaya was called mistress of the ship.
Dr. Grieve:	Which is the true account? The account you gave us before or the statement made today?
Answer:	They are both true; only I did not like to enter into it more deeply than I was asked.
Dr. Grieve:	What made you come and volunteer the statement today?
Answer:	Because I was advised if I knew anything to come and tell it out. I was not advised before.
Dr. Grieve:	Did Dr. Finlayson not advise you?
Answer:	Yes, he told me not to be afraid, but to tell the truth. I said if I went and told everything I knew about the ship, I might come across the doctor again (I mean Dr. Hardwicke) and get into trouble. I am aware that the main responsibility in regard to the Coolies rests with the doctor; but I also am responsible. I would like to continue in the service as a Compounder.
Chairman:	Do you remember the name of the woman struck in the face by the Officer?
Answer:	Her name is Chunmonia. I did not report to the Surgeon that this woman had been assaulted, because he was standing at the break of the poop and I thought he could have seen it himself. According to my letter of instructions I ought to have reported it.

If a Compounder performed his duty faithfully on board these ships he would be at loggerheads with everybody on board. The doctor might order a certain quantity of rice and fish. It is very seldom that that quantity is correctly issued unless the Compounder stands by and checks it, for if he does not attend to it the 3rd Officer might cut down the quantity; and even when watching, if there is a pound or two short he would think it hard to open another bag. The 3rd Officer should have assisted me in the cleaning of the ship, but he did not do so this voyage. I complained to the Captain about it and he spoke to the 3rd Officer. That did not improve matters much as far as helping me. It was more than I could properly attend to.

Chairman: You considered it your duty to report to the Captain when you found the 3rd Officer was not assisting you to keep the ship clean, but you did not consider it your duty to report an assault committed by the same Officer in your presence?

Answer: I admit it was my duty, but I did not do it.

Mr. Clarke: What did you mean by the word "nonsense" when you said it was all nonsense etc. touching the remarks as to Mohadaya being locked up in the chartroom? Did you believe there was any truth in these reports?

Answer: I did not believe them because I wanted to see for myself. I applied the word "nonsense" to myself for being so foolish as not to go into the matter and find out for myself.

Mr. Clarke: Do you attach any indecent signification to the words skylarking and playing?

Answer: No. I imputed nothing immoral.

Mr. Clarke: Have you any reason to believe that during the voyage there was any immorality between the Surgeon, Captain and Officers of the Ship with the women?

Answer: (After much hesitation) I do not wish to form an opinion about other gentlemen.

Mr. Clarke: Has any threat or inducement been held out to you by any one connected with the ship in regard to your evidence?

Answer: No – none whatever.

There were some women not allowed on the poop. One in particular was driven off, Malida, because she had a quarrel with Mohadaya. Malida accused Mohadaya of being the doctor's wife, and the doctor on hearing this ordered her off the poop.

The Captain had not much to do with the Immigrants. He was kind to them; he did not play at all with them.

Chairman: You told us you spoke to Mr. Reis. What did you tell him?

Answer: I told him I had been summoned to attend this enquiry and that I had said a few words to Dr. Finlayson and it had got to the hearing of the Commission and that he had been summoned to state what I had said. I told him that what I had mentioned to Dr. Finlayson was about the disturbances on board and the games that were going on. I told him this, going to Albert Town. I met him on the road. He had very little to say. He said, "you must be particular; you have an English tongue; you have nothing to be afraid of." That is all that passed between Mr. Reis and myself as far as I remember. I remember the inspection of the ship after arrival. After finishing the inspection of the Coolies I remember walking with you round the between decks. After talking about Mr. Duncan's case, you asked me if there were any complaints on board ship and I said, "No, everything was all right." The same evening I went to Dr. Finlayson.

Chairman: Was there any other person in the Immigration Department to whom you spoke?

Answer: No, only to Mr. Reis outside.

Chairman: Have you any reason to believe that the Coolies did not get properly fed during the voyage?

Answer: They were well fed, with the exception of one day about grain. This was the only day they complained.

Chairman: Have you yourself had anything of an immoral character to do with any woman on board?

Answer: No. I kept myself away from them.

Dr. Grieve: Is it to your knowledge that all the Coolies and all who were connected with the Coolies had an opportunity of making a complaint to the Immigration Agent General at the inspection of the ship if they had wished to do so?

Answer: Yes.

Signed: Jas. Theo. Grant
Assistant Compounder
Ship *Allanshaw*
12.12.85

NOTES

Preface

1. Madhavi Kale, *Fragments of Empire* (Philadelphia: University of Pennsylvania Press, 1998), 5.
2. Gayatri Spivak, "Can the Subaltern Speak?", in *Colonial Discourse and Post-Colonial Theory: A Reader*, ed. Patrick Williams and Laura Chrisman (London: Harvester Wheatsheaf, 1993), 66–111.

Introduction

1. Lucille Mathurin, "A Historical Study of Women in Jamaica" (PhD diss., University of the West Indies, Mona, Jamaica, 1974); Lucille Mathurin Mair, *The Rebel Woman in the British West Indies during Slavery* (Kingston: Institute of Jamaica, 1975); Kamau Brathwaite, "Submerged Mothers", *Jamaica Journal* 9, nos. 2 and 3 (1975): 48–49; Kamau Brathwaite, *Women of the Caribbean during Slavery*, Elsa Goveia Memorial Lecture (Cave Hill, Barbados: Department of History, University of the West Indies, 1984); B.W. Higman, *Slave Society and Economy in Jamaica, 1807–1834* (Cambridge: Cambridge University Press,

1976); B.W. Higman, *Slave Populations of the British Caribbean, 1807–1834* (Baltimore: Johns Hopkins University Press, 1984); Bridget Brereton, "General Problems and Issues in Studying the History of Women", in *Gender in Caribbean Development*, ed. Patricia Mohammed and Catherine Shepherd (St Augustine, Trinidad: Women and Development Studies Project, University of the West Indies, 1988), 123–41; Bridget Brereton, "Text, Testimony and Gender: An Examination of Some Texts by Women on the English-Speaking Caribbean from the 1770s to the 1920s", in *Engendering History: Caribbean Women in Historical Perspective*, ed. Verene Shepherd, Bridget Brereton and Barbara Bailey (Kingston: Ian Randle Publishers, 1995), 63–93; Hilary McD. Beckles, *Afro-Caribbean Women and Resistance to Slavery in Barbados* (London: Karnak House, 1988); Hilary McD. Beckles, *Natural Rebels: A Social History of Enslaved Black Women in Barbados* (London: Zed, 1989); Hilary McD. Beckles, *Centering Woman: Gender Discourses in Caribbean Slavery* (Kingston: Ian Randle Publishers, 1999); Marietta Morrissey, *Slave Women in the New*

World: Gender Stratification in the New World (Lawrence: University of Kansas Press, 1989); Barbara Bush, *Slave Women in Caribbean Society, 1650–1838* (London: James Currey, 1990); Verene Shepherd, "Emancipation through Servitude?", *Bulletin of the Society for the Study of Labour History* 53, no. 3 (1988): 13–19; Verene Shepherd, ed. and comp., *Women in Caribbean History* (Kingston: Ian Randle Publishers, 1999); Verene Shepherd, Bridget Brereton and Barbara Bailey, eds., *Engendering History: Caribbean Women in Historical Perspective* (Kingston: Ian Randle Publishers, 1995).

2. Rhoda Reddock, *Women and Garment Production in Trinidad and Tobago, 1900–1960* (The Hague: Institute of Social Studies, 1984); Rhoda Reddock, "Indian Women and Indentureship in Trinidad and Tobago 1845–1917: Freedom Denied", *Caribbean Quarterly* 32 (1986): 27–47; Rhoda Reddock, *Women, Labour and Politics in Trinidad and Tobago: A History* (London: Zed Books, 1994); Rhoda Reddock, "Women and Slavery in the Caribbean: A Feminist Perspective", *Latin American Perspectives* 12, no. 1 (1995): 63–80; Linnette Vassell, comp., *Voices of Women* (Mona, Jamaica: Department of History, University of the West Indies, 1993); Linnette Vassell, "Women of the Masses", in *Engendering History: Caribbean Women in Historical Perspective*, ed. Verene Shepherd, Bridget Brereton and Barbara Bailey (Kingston: Ian Randle Publishers, 1995), 318–33; Patricia Mohammed, "A Social History of Post-Migrant Indians in Trinidad from 1917–1947: A Gender Perspective" (PhD diss., Institute of

Social Studies, The Hague, 1994); Patricia Mohammed, "Writing Gender into History", in *Engendering History: Caribbean Women in Historical Perspective*, ed. Verene Shepherd, Bridget Brereton and Barbara Bailey (Kingston: Ian Randle Publishers, 1995), 20–47; Patricia Mohammed and Catherine Shepherd, eds., *Gender in Caribbean Development* (St Augustine, Trinidad: Women and Development Studies Project, University of the West Indies, 1988).

3. Verene Shepherd, *Transients to Settlers: The Experience of Indians in Jamaica, 1845–1945* (Leeds and Warwick: Peepal Tree Press and University of Warwick, 1994); Rosemarijn Hoefte, "Female Indentured Labour in Suriname: For Better or Worse?", *Boletín de Estudios Latinoamericanos y del Caribe* 42 (1987): 55–70; Rosemarijn Hoefte, *In Place of Slavery: A Social History of British Indian and Javanese Laborers in Suriname* (Gainesville: University of Florida Press, 1998); Pieter Emmer, "The Great Escape: The Migration of Female Indentured Servants from British India into Suriname", in *Abolition and its Aftermath*, ed. D. Richardson (London: Frank Cass, 1985), 245–66; Walton Look Lai, *Indentured Labor, Caribbean Sugar: Chinese and Indian Migrants to the British West Indies* (Baltimore: Johns Hopkins University Press, 1993); K.O. Laurence, *Immigration into the West Indies in the Nineteenth Century* (Barbados: Caribbean Universities Press, 1971); K.O. Laurence, *A Question of Labour* (Kingston: Ian Randle Publishers, 1994).

4. David Galenson, "The Rise and Fall of Indentured Servitude: An Economic Analysis", *Journal of Economic*

History 44, no. 1 (1984): 1–26; David Northrup, *Indentured Labour in the Age of Imperialism, 1834–1922* (Cambridge: Cambridge University Press, 1995).

5. Emmer, "The Great Escape", 245–66.

6. Public Record Office (PRO), London, Colonial Office (CO) 571/3, Minute Paper 54685, "Notes on the Methods of Recruiting Emigrants in the Madras Presidency", 6 November 1915.

7. Joseph Beaumont, *The New Slavery: An Account of the Indian and Chinese Immigrants in British Guiana* (London: W. Ridgeway, 1871); Hugh Tinker, *A New System of Slavery: The Export of Indian Labourers Overseas* (London: Oxford University Press, 1974); Jeremy Poynting, "East Indian Women in the Caribbean: Experience and Voice", in *India in the Caribbean,* ed. David Dabydeen and Brinsley Samaroo (London: Hansib, 1987), 231–63; Jo Beall, "Women under Indenture in Colonial Natal", in *Essays on Indentured Indians in Natal,* ed. Surendra Bhana (Leeds: Peepal Tree Press, 1991), 89–115; Brij Lal, "Kunti's Cry: Indentured Women on Fiji Plantations", *Indian Economic and Social History Review* 22, no. 1 (1985): 55–72; Marina Carter, *Lakshmi's Legacy: The Testimonies of Indian Women in Nineteenth Century Mauritius* (Mauritius: Editions de l'Océan Indien, 1994); Moses Seenarine, "Indentured Women in Colonial Guyana", in *Sojourners to Settlers: Indian Migrants in the Caribbean and the Americas,* ed. Mahin Gosine and Dhanpaul Narine (New York: Windsor Press, 1999), 36–66.

8. David Trotman, "Women and Crime in late Nineteenth Century Trinidad", *Caribbean Quarterly* 30, nos. 3 and 4 (1984): 60–72.

9. Beall, "Women under Indenture", 89–115; Reddock, "Indian Women and Indentureship"; Poynting, "East Indian Women".

10. Madhavi Kale, *Fragments of Empire* (Philadelphia: University of Pennsylvania Press, 1998), 173. See also Woodville Marshall, *The Post-Slavery "Labour Problem" Revisited,* Elsa Goveia Memorial Lecture (Mona, Jamaica: Department of History, University of the West Indies, 1991); Douglas Hall, "The Flight from the Estates Reconsidered", *Journal of Caribbean History* 10 and 11 (1978): 7–24; and Thomas Holt, *The Problem of Freedom* (Baltimore: Johns Hopkins University Press, 1992).

11. See, for example, Alvin Thompson, "Historical Writing on Migration into the Commonwealth Caribbean: A Bibliographical Review of the Period *c.*1838–*c.*1938", *Immigrants and Minorities* 5, no. 2 (1986); Rishee S. Thakur, "East Indians in Caribbean Historiography", in *Indenture and Exile: The Indo-Caribbean Experience,* ed. Frank Birbalsingh (Toronto: Tsar Press, 1989), 207–17; and Brereton, "General Problems and Issues".

12. The title of these officials varied over time and space. While Jamaica was using the designation "protector of immigrants" by the late nineteenth century, Guyana retained "agent general of immigration".

13. Patricia Mohammed has been among those highlighting the myths surrounding this issue and seeking to clarify the representations about Indian women's sexuality, patriarchy, marriage and gender systems in India and the colonial Caribbean. See her "Writing Gender into History", 20–47. See especially p. 31.

14. *Among the Hindus and Creoles of British Guiana* (London, 1888), quoted in Poynting, "East Indian Women", 213.
15. James McNeil and Chimman Lal, *Report to the Government of India on the Condition of Indian Immigrants in Four British Colonies and Suriname, 1915* (London: HMSO, 1915). Grierson's report is discussed in Tinker's *A New System of Slavery*, 266–67.
16. Poynting, "East Indian Women", 215.
17. Reddock develops this in "Indian Women and Indentureship in Trinidad and Tobago".
18. See Thomas Atwood, *The History of the Island of Dominica* (London: J. Johnson, 1791). For critiques of such a perspective, see Beckles, *Centering Woman*, 26; Bush, *Slave Women*, 94–98; and Shepherd, *Women in Caribbean History*, chapter 3.
19. Beckles, *Centering Woman*, 23.
20. Edward Long, *History of Jamaica*, 3 vols. (London: T. Lowndes, 1774).
21. Orlando Patterson, *The Sociology of Slavery: An Analysis of the Origins, Development and Structure of Negro Slave Society in Jamaica* (London: McGibbon and Kee, 1967), 9, 108, 158–65, 167.
22. See B.W. Higman, "Household Structure and Fertility on Jamaican Slave Plantations: A Nineteenth Century Example", *Population Studies* 27, no. 3 (1973): 527–50, and "The Slave Populations of the British Caribbean: Some Nineteenth Century Variations", *Social History* 9, no. 18 (1976): 237–55.
23. For an edited version of Thomas Thistlewood's memoirs, see Douglas Hall, *In Miserable Slavery: Thomas Thistlewood in Jamaica, 1750–1786* (London: Macmillan, 1989).
24. Beckles, "Property Rights in Pleasure", in his *Centering Woman*, 22.
25. Ian McCalman, ed., *The Horrors of Slavery and other Writings by Robert Wedderburn* (Princeton: Markus Wiener, 1991).
26. Ibid., 46–47.
27. CO 384/160, Irving to Granville, Despatch no. 56, 1 March 1886 and enclosures.
28. Irving to Granville, 1 March 1885.
29. Several references are made to Ipson's black or "coloured" ethnicity. See, for example, an article titled "Outrage on the High Seas" which appeared in the *Daily Chronicle* of British Guiana, 7 November 1885, as well as his testimony and sections of the comments by Captain Wilson and Lutchmun. Elsewhere Ipson was described as a "clever yankee sailor" who had the US coat of arms tattooed on his arm, giving the impression that he was American (from the North). But Ipson said he was born in Santa Cruz (a name used for St Croix in the Danish Caribbean) and had spent some time in the American navy.
30. I thank Professor Brij Lal for this clarification and insight. I must also thank Professor Maureen Warner-Lewis for posing this question about the meaning of "Maharani" in follow-up discussions after the Social History Project's symposium on 15 April 2000 at the University of the West Indies, Mona, Jamaica. Her question sent me digging some more. But Professor Lal's view is that such a literal translation of this name should not be taken seriously.
31. CO 384/187, vol. 2, Report of the Protector of Immigrants, P.C. Cork, 2 February 1893, enc. in Jamaica Despatch no. 78, Governor Henry Blake to the Marquis of Ripon, 4 March 1893.

32. The names of the Indians were spelled
in various ways in the documents. For
example, Mohadaya appeared as
"Mahadaria" and "Mahadarie"; and
Moorti as "Murti" and "Moortee".
33. Enc. no. 2, CO 384/160, British
Guiana (BG) Despatch no. 56, Extracts from the Captain's Logbook, 9
September 1885.
34. Hardwicke to Edward Wingfield,
Under Secretary of State for the
Colonies, 28 April 1886.
35. Ibid.
36. Merry Wiesner, *Women and Gender in
Early Modern Europe* (Cambridge:
Cambridge University Press, 1993),
50.
37. See for example, Carter, *Lakshmi's Legacy;* Marina Carter, *Voices from Indenture: Experiences of Indian Migrants in
the British Empire* (London: Leicester
University Press, 1996); Marina Carter and James Ng Foong Kwong, *Forging the Rainbow: Labour Immigrants in
British Mauritius* (Mauritius: Alfran,
1997); Kumar Noor Mahabir, comp.,
*The Still Cry: Personal Accounts of East
Indians in Trinidad and Tobago during Indentureship, 1845–1917* (Tacarigua, Trinidad: Calaloux Publications, 1985); and Verene Shepherd,
"Poverty, Exploitation and Agency
among Indian Immigrant Settlers in
Jamaica: Some Evidence from Twentieth-Century Letters", *Journal of Caribbean Studies* (special issue, ed. Frank
Birbalsingh) 14, nos. 1 and 2 (1999–
2000): 93–116.
38. For her views on the use of testimonies and depositions, see Carter, *Lakshmi's Legacy;* Carter, *Voices of Indenture*; and Carter and Ng Foong
Kwong, *Forging the Rainbow.*

Chapter 1

1. K.O. Laurence, *Immigration into the
West Indies in the Nineteenth Century*
(Barbados: Caribbean Universities
Press, 1971); K.O. Laurence, *A Question of Labour* (Kingston: Ian Randle
Publishers, 1994); Hugh Tinker, *A
New System of Slavery: The Export of
Indian Labourers Overseas* (London:
Oxford University Press, 1974); Walton Look Lai, *Indentured Labor, Caribbean Sugar: Chinese and Indian Migrants to the British West Indies* (Baltimore: Johns Hopkins University
Press, 1993); Basdeo Mangru, *Benevolent Neutrality: Indian Government Policy and Labour Migration to British
Guiana 1854–1884* (London: Hansib,
1987).
2. Look Lai, *Indentured Labor,* 19.
3. Ibid. See also Laurence, *Immigration
into the West Indies,* and Verene Shepherd, *Transients to Settlers* (Leeds and
Warwick: Peepal Tree Press and University of Warwick, 1994).
4. Look Lai, *Indentured Labor,* 118.
5. See, for example, Alan Adamson,
*Sugar without Slaves: The Political
Economy of British Guiana* (New Haven: Yale University Press, 1972);
Veront Satchell, *From Plots to Plantations* (Kingston: Institute of Social and
Economic Research, University of the
West Indies, 1990); Sidney Mintz, "A
Note on the Definition of Peasant-
ries", *Journal of Peasant Studies* 1
(1973): 91–106; Michel Rolph Trouil-
lot, *Peasants and Capital: Dominica in
the World Economy* (Baltimore: Johns
Hopkins University Press, 1988); and
Jay Mandle, *The Plantation Economy:
Population and Economic Change in
Guyana, 1838–1960* (Philadelphia:
Temple University Press, 1973).

6. CO 386, Colonial Land and Emigration Commission, Letter Books, 1857–1866.

7. Ibid., vol. 99.

8. Rosemarijn Hoefte, *In Place of Slavery: A Social History of British Indian and Javanese Laborers in Suriname* (Gainesville: University of Florida Press, 1998), 31.

9. Mangru, *Benevolent Neutrality,* 96–97.

10. Joseph Beaumont, *The New Slavery* (London: W. Ridgeway, 1871) and Tinker, *A New System of Slavery.*

11. See for example, CO 571/5, Telegram from the Superintendent of the Widows' Home, Cawnpore, 29 January 1917. See also Verene Shepherd, ed. and comp., *Women in Caribbean History* (Kingston: Ian Randle Publishers, 1999), chapter 6.

12. CO 386/97, Colonial Land and Emigration Commission Correspondence, 1869–1874.

13. Verene Shepherd, *Emancipation and Immigration: A Pan Caribbean Overview* (Kingston: Alpha Boy's School Printery, 1999), 21.

14. CO 386/93, S. Walcott of the Colonial Land and Emigration Commission to R.G.N. Herbert of the Colonial Office, 14 October 1871.

15. See Brij Lal, *Girmitiyas: The Origins of the Fiji Indians* (Canberra: Australian National University, 1983), chapter 5; and Brij Lal, "Crossing the Kali Pani" (manuscript, 1999).

16. CO 384/144, BG Despatch no. 88, Governor Henry Irving to the Earl of Derby, 28 March 1888.

17. CO 384/161, Report of the Agent General of Immigration, enc. in BG Despatch no. 303, Irving to Secretary of State, Stanhope, 11 November 1886.

18. Mangru, *Benevolent Neutrality,* 97.

19. Laurence, *A Question of Labour.*

20. Look Lai, *Indentured Labor,* 33; Shepherd, *Transients,* 45–46

21. R.T. Smith, "Some Social Characteristics of Indian Immigrants to British Guiana", *Population Studies* 13, no. 1 (1959): 39. See also Look Lai, *Indentured Labor,* 35.

22. Tinker, *A New System of Slavery,* 137.

23. Brinsley Samaroo argues that there was greater tendency among British officials after the "Sepoy Mutiny" of 1857 to use the term "mutiny" to describe cases of unrest on emigrant ships; that, in any case, "revolt" was a more appropriate term than "mutiny". See Brinsley Samaroo, "The Caribbean Consequences of the Indian Revolt of 1857" (paper presented at the conference Asian Migration to the Americas, University of the West Indies, St Augustine, Trinidad, 11–17 August 2000).

24. CO 386/95, T.W.C. Murdoch of the Colonial Land and Emigration Commission to Frederic Rogers of the Colonial Office, 26 February 1863.

25. According to Professor Brij Lal, the name was obviously misspelled, "Parags" being more likely.

26. CO 384/187, vol. 2, Report of the Protector of Immigrants, P.C. Cork, 2 February 1893, enc. in Jamaica Despatch no. 78, Governor Henry Blake to the Marquis of Ripon, 4 March 1893.

27. CO 571/3, Minute Paper 54685, "Notes on the Methods of Recruiting Emigrants in the Madras Presidency", 26 November 1915.

28. Herbert Klein, *The Middle Passage: Comparative Studies in the Atlantic Slave Trade* (Princeton: Princeton University Press, 1978), 143–45.

29. See Ron Ramdin, *The Other Middle Passage: Journal of a Voyage from Calcutta to Trinidad, 1858* (London: Hansib, 1994), 22.
30. CO 387/2/LLY, Lloyds Register of Shipping, 1884.
31. Tinker, *A New System of Slavery,* 146.
32. Ramdin, *The Other Middle Passage,* 26.
33. Ibid., 123.
34. Alexander Falconbridge, *An Account of the Slave Trade on the Coast of Africa* (London: J. Phillips, 1788), 28.
35. Evidence given before the Police Magistrate, colonial Guyana, 13 November 1885, enc. no. 7 in Despatch no. 56.
36. Mangru, *Benevolent Neutrality,* 125.
37. CO 386/186, Report of the Agent General of Immigration, 3 January 1893, enc. in BG Despatch no. 9, Viscount Gormanston to the Marquis of Ripon, 10 January 1893.
38. CO 386/91, Colonial Land and Emigration Commission Letter Book, Murdoch to Rogers, 14 April 1858.
39. Enc. no. 3 in Despatch no. 56, Extracts from the Official Logbook of the Ship *Allanshaw,* 24 July 1885. See also the crew list, Maritime History Archive, Newfoundland, Canada.
40. Moses Seenarine, "Indentured Women in Colonial Guyana", in *Sojourners to Settlers: Indian Migrants in the Caribbean and the Americas,* ed. Mahin Gosine and Dhanpaul Narine (New York: Windsor Press, 1999), 56.
41. CO 386/95, Murdoch to Elliot, Colonial Land and Emigration Commission Correspondence, 31 October 1863.
42. CO 386/135, Walcott to Hunt Marriot, Colonial Land and Emigration Commission, 26 February 1863.
43. CO 384/169, Report of the Immigration Agent General, 5 January 1888, enc. in BG Despatch no. 15, Governor of British Guiana to Secretary of State Holland, 16 January 1888.
44. CO 384/169, Report of the Immigration Agent General, 26 November 1888, enc. in BG Despatch no. 398, Governor Bruce to Secretary of State Knutsford, 7 December 1888.
45. CO 384/160, enc. no. 7 in Despatch no. 56, Logbooks of Dr Hardwicke and Captain Wilson.
46. W. Jeffrey Bolster, *Black Jacks: African American Seamen in the Age of Sail* (Cambridge, Mass.: Harvard University Press, 1997), 2.
47. Ibid., 4.
48. Ibid.
49. Ibid., 69.
50. Ibid., 93.
51. Donald Wood, *Trinidad in Transition: The Years after Slavery* (New York: Oxford University Press), 138, quoted in Audra Diptee "Indian Men, Afro-Creole Women: Casting Doubt on Inter-Racial Sexual Relationships in the Late Nineteenth Century Caribbean" (typescript; forthcoming in *Immigrants and Minorities*), 6. Audra Diptee was kind enough to let me read her unpublished paper.
52. Tinker, *A New System of Slavery,* 157.
53. Captain's Logbook, enc. no. 7, Despatch no. 56.
54. Report of the Protector of Immigrants, Jamaica, 18 June 1891, enc. in Despatch no. 196, [?] Black, Administering the Government, to Knutsford, 22 June 1891.
55. CO 384/186, Report of the Agent General of Immigration, 10 February 1893, enc. in BG Despatch no. 35, Gormanston to Ripon, 21 February 1893.
56. Look Lai, *Indentured Labor,* and Laurence, *Immigration into the West Indies.*

57. CO 386/95–105, Correspondence/Letter Books, Colonial Land and Emigration Commission.
58. CO 386/95–105, Correspondence/Letter Books, Colonial Land and Emigration Commission.
59. CO 386/97, Murdoch to R.H. McCade, Colonial Land and Emigration Commission, 8 January 1873.
60. CO 386/135, vol. 2, S. Walcott of the Colonial Land and Emigration Commission to A. McGregor of the Colonial Office, 26 February 1861.
61. Ibid.
62. CO 386/93, Murdoch to Herbert, Colonial Land and Emigration Commission, 10 December 1874.
63. CO 384/144, BG Despatch no. 57, Irving to Derby, 20 February 1883.
64. CO 384/155, enc. in BG Despatch no. 40, Irving to Derby, 19 February 1885.
65. CO 384/155, Report of the Protector of Immigrants, 1885.

Chapter 2

1. Different witnesses gave different estimates of Maharani's age. Grant, who had seen her in the ship's hospital, estimated that she was seventeen or eighteen years old; the surgeon-superintendent's notes sometimes said sixteen, sometimes twenty. His evidence seems to indicate that he felt sixteen was more accurate. See *Daily Chronicle,* 28 November 1885.
2. Enc. no. 2, Extracts from the Medical History of the ship *Allanshaw,* in Despatch no. 56, Irving to Granville, 1 March 1886, CO 384/160.
3. CO 384/160, Hardwicke's evidence before the Commission of Enquiry, Day 1, 27 November 1885; Report of

the Commission of Enquiry, Enclosures and Minutes of Evidence, in BG Despatch no. 56, Irving to the Earl of Granville, 1 March 1886, ff. 1–2. See also *Daily Chronicle,* 28 November 1885.
4. Enc. no. 4, "Evidence taken in the case of Maharani No. 353 Female Kuli Emigrant on board the ship *Allanshaw* en route from Calcutta to Georgetown British Guiana", taken by Edward A. Hardwicke, Surgeon-Superintendent in charge, 27 September 1885.
5. CO 384/160, Despatch no. 56, enc. no. 3, extract from the ship's medical logbook, 27 September 1885. See also enc. no. 4, preamble to Hardwicke's investigation on the ship.
6. Ibid., f. 9.
7. *Daily Chronicle,* 7 November 1885.
8. Ibid., f. 10.
9. Ibid., f. 21.
10. CO 384/160, Mohadaya's evidence, ff. 36–38. This (like Moorti's below) was taken from the evidence in Guyana but used here because of its greater clarity and relevance.
11. Ibid., Moorti's evidence, f. 39.
12. Ibid., evidence of Mohadaya and Moorti, in enc. no. 4.
13. CO 384/160, enc. no. 4, Hardwicke's enquiry; ibid., Mohadaya's and Moorti's testimony.
14. Ship's logbook, 30 September 1885.
15. Ibid., evidence of Nathur, hospital topaz. "Babu" is a term used as a mark of respect to a high-ranking male Indian.
16. Ibid.
17. CO 384/160, Report of the Commission of Enquiry, ff. 12–13.

Chapter 3

1. Some of the documents say 8 October 1885.
2. Ship's logbook, October 1885, and Report of G.A. Banbury, Emigration Officer, St Helena, 8 October 1885, enc. no. 5 in Despatch no. 56. See also, enc. no. 6, J.C. [H]omagee, Law Officer of the Crown, St Helena to the Actg. Colonial Secretary, St Helena, Court House, St Helena, 9 October 1885.
3. See minute paper of 4/6/1886, L/PJ/6/176, India Office Records. See also *Daily Chronicle,* 7 November 1885. Published Report of Agent of Immigration, A.H. Alexander. Some reports say the journey was 106 days. CO 384/160, enc. no. 7, E.F. Wright, Inspector, Police Force to H. Kirke, Police Magistrate, 6 November 1885.
4. Ibid.
5. Kirke lived in colonial Guyana from 1872 to 1897. He was sheriff of Esse-quibo from 1887 to 1892. Previously, he had been a government emigration agent in India at the depot in Garden Reach. He claimed to have had great familiarity with and expertise in the working of the criminal law, having acted as judge of the Supreme Court for twelve different periods and three times as attorney general. According to him, "There is not a crime in the statute book with which I have not had to deal", but he does not list rape among them. Henry Kirke, *Twenty-Five Years in British Guiana* (1898; re-print, Westport, Conn.: Negro Universities Press, 1970), 291.
6. "Alleged Outrage on the High Seas", *Daily Chronicle,* 7 November 1885. See also *Royal Gazette,* 13 November 1885, 4.

7. Enc. no. 7 in Despatch no. 56, CO 384/160, evidence given before the Police Magistrate, Guyana, 14 November 1885.
8. Ibid., 18 November 1885.
9. Ibid., enc. no. 7.
10. *Daily Chronicle,* 7 November 1885; *Royal Gazette,* 13 November 1885, 4.
11. *Royal Gazette,* 18 November 1885, 3.
12. *Daily Chronicle,* 19 November 1885.
13. Ibid.
14. Ibid., 6 December 1885.
15. *Royal Gazette,* 9 November 1885, 4 and 18 November 1885, 3.
16. Enc. no. 7 in Despatch no. 56, CO 384/160, ff. 15–17.
17. This was about 150 to 200 miles from the Cape of Good Hope.
18. Ibid., Captain Wilson's evidence, f. 21. See also appendices 2 and 17.
19. Ibid., ff. 22–24.
20. Captain's logbook, f. 23. These coordinates placed the ship far south of the Equator. It would have been cold at this location.
21. Ibid., f. 24.
22. Evidence of Captain Wilson, f. 24.
23. Ibid., f. 28.
24. Urquhart's evidence, f. 31. See also appendix 3.
25. Minutes of Evidence before the Commission of Enquiry, ff. 39–40 and 163–68.
26. Ibid., James Grant's evidence, f. 43. See also appendices 7, 10, 26.
27. Hardwicke's evidence, f. 12 and appendix 1.
28. Golap's evidence, ff. 40–41. See also appendix 6.
29. Grant's evidence, ff. 46–47.
31. Ibid., f. 48.
32. Ibid., ff. 44–45.
33. Moorti's evidence, f. 40. See appendix 5.

34. This contradicts other statements that Ipson was African American.
35. The surgeon later admitted that Mohadaya did this but it was during an Indian festival – perhaps Holi?
36. Leslie's evidence, ff. 174–82. See appendix 22.
37. Lutchmun's evidence, ff. 153–62. See appendix 18.
38. Chitamun's evidence, ff. 192–93. See appendix 25.
39. Ibid., 193.
40. Ibid.
41. Ibid., ff. 193–94.
42. Ram's evidence, ff. 185–88. See also appendix 23.
43. Ibid., Lee's evidence, ff. 120–21. See also appendix 13.
44. Ibid., f. 121.
45. Ibid.
46. Ibid., f. 123.
47. Ibid.
48. Chetworth's (Clintworth's) evidence, ff. 169–71. See appendix 2.
49. Hardwicke to Edward Wingfield, Under Secretary of State for the Colonies, 28 April 1886.
50. William Urquhart's evidence, ff. 31–32; 34–35.
51. Ibid., ff. 31–32.
52. This is most likely St Croix.
53. This complicates his ethnicity even further. He may not, in fact, have been African-American, even though he served in the American navy.
54. Ipson's evidence, f. 58. See also appendix 8.
55. Ibid.
56. Ibid.
57. Ibid., f. 61.
58. Ibid., f. 63.
59. Grant (recalled), ff. 86–88. See appendix 10.
60. Dr Finlayson had been a medical doctor in colonial Guyana since 1862. He said that his impression after speaking with Grant was that he was hesitant to tell all for fear of prejudicing his interest in future voyages. He had urged Grant to tell all he knew. Folios 183–91. See appendix 24.
61. Grant's evidence, ff. 195–219.
62. Smith's deposition, ff. 77–85. See appendix 9.
63. Stokes's evidence on day 5, ff. 127–37. See appendix 14.
64. De la Mare's evidence, ff. 89–94. See appendix 11.
65. CO 384/160, BG Despatch 56, enc. no. 3, Extracts from the Official logbook of the *Allanshaw*, 29 August 1885.
66. Makohl's evidence, ff. 138–43. See appendix 15.
67. De la Mare's evidence, ff. 89–106. See appendix 11.
68. Ibid., ff. 90–91.
69. Alexander Bain's evidence, ff. 106–18. See appendix 12.
70. Ibid.
71. Ibid., ff. 106–18.
72. Warner's evidence, ff. 143–47. See appendix 16.
73. Ibid., ff. 148–52.
74. Hardwicke to Wingfield, 28 April 1886.
75. Summary of the Report of the Commissioners, Bruce to Irving, enc. in BG Despatch no. 56.
76. Ibid., f. 15.
77. Ibid.
78. Ibid.
79. CO 384/160, enc. in Despatch no. 56, f. 54.
80. Ibid., Remarks of Dr Robert Grieve's correspondence, 13 January 1886, f. 55.
81. Ibid., f. 55.
82. Ibid.
83. Ibid., f. 56.
84. Ibid., f. 57.
85. Ibid., f. 58.

86. See chapter 1 for a fuller discussion of this issue.
87. Dr Grieve's comments, f. 67.
88. Ibid., f. 63.
89. Ibid., ff. 59–60.
90. Ibid., f. 61.
91. Ibid., f. 64.
92. Ibid.
93. Ibid.
94. Ibid., f. 68.
95. Alan Adamson, *Sugar without Slaves: The Political Economy of British Guiana* (New Haven: Yale University Press, 1972), 150; CO 111/435, Irving to Granville, 25 June 1886.
96. Adamson, *Sugar without Slaves*, 151.
97. Kirke, *Twenty-Five Years in British Guiana*, 341.
98. Ibid., 233.
99. CO 384/160, Despatch no. 56, Irving to Granville, 1 March 1886.
100. CO 384/160, Minute Paper 4755, 8 April 1886.
101. Ibid.
102. Ibid.
103. Adamson, *Sugar without Slaves*, 146–59; Walter Rodney, *A History of the Guyanese Working People, 1881–1905* (Baltimore: Johns Hopkins University Press, 1981), 151–73.
104. Rodney, *A History*, 154–55.

Conclusion

1. Michael Kimmel, *The Gendered Society* (Oxford: Oxford University Press, 2000), 257.
2. Comments from Dr Kamla Dixon and Dr S. Wynter.
3. David Trotman, "Women and Crime in Late Nineteenth Century Trinidad", in *Caribbean Freedom*, ed. Hilary Beckles and Verene Shepherd (Kingston: Ian Randle Publishers, 1993), 254.
4. See Brian Moore, *Cultural Power, Resistance and Pluralism: Colonial Guyana 1838–1900* (Kingston: The Press, University of the West Indies, 1995), 36–42, 102–3.
5. Ibid.
6. For an extended discussion, see Georges Vigarello, *A History of Rape: Sexual Violence in France from the Sixteenth to the Twentieth Century* (Cambridge: Polity Press, 2001).
7. Ann Cahill, *Rethinking Rape* (Ithaca: Cornell University Press, 2001), 10–11.
8. W.F. Haynes Smith to the Governor, 17 February 1886.
9. Trotman, "Women and Crime", 254.
10. Moore, *Cultural Power*, 103.
11. CO 384/160, Report of the Commission of Enquiry, 1886.
12. CO 386/160, Irving to Stanley, 26 January 1886.
13. CO 386/161, Report of the Immigration Agent General, enc. in BG Despatch 303, Irving to Stanhope, 11 November 1886.
14. Interestingly enough, Asserum's age was misrepresented on the ship's list as eighteen; and this should have been known to the surgeon-superintendent.
15. See comparative discussion in David Eltis, *The Rise of African Slavery in the Americas* (Cambridge: Cambridge University Press, 2000), 117.

BIBLIOGRAPHY

PRIMARY SOURCES

Manuscript

Agreement and Account of Crew, *Allanshaw,* 1885–1886. Maritime History Archive, Memorial University of Newfoundland, Canada.

Agreement and Account of Crew, *Allanshaw,* 1884–1885. National Maritime Museum, Greenwich, United Kingdom.

British Library, India Office Records, L/PJ/6/176; L/PJ 816, 1886.

Public Record Office, London. Colonial Office (CO) Documents:

CO 111/435. Original Correspondence, 1886.

CO 318/422, 423. Files on Emigration to the Caribbean.

CO 384/114–129. Original Correspondence on Emigration, 1877–1880.

CO 384/135–192, 1881–1896. Emigration Despatches, West Indies.

CO 384/160. Report of the Commission of Enquiry Submitted to Governor Henry Irving, in British Guiana Despatch no. 56, Irving to the Rt. Hon. the Earl of Granville, 1 March 1886, with 8 enclosures.

CO 384/160. Minutes of Evidence, enc. in British Guiana Despatch No. 56, Irving to Granville, 1 March 1886.

CO 386/9. Colonial Land and Emigration Board, 1875–1878.

CO 386/88–136. Letter Books and Correspondence of the Colonial Land and Emigration Commission, 1851–1872.

CO 386/160, Irving to Stanley, 26 January 1886.

CO 386/161, Report of the Immigration Agent General.

CO 386/186, Report of the Agent General of Immigration, 3 January 1893.

CO 387/2/LLY. Lloyds Register of Shipping, 1884.

CO 571/2, 3 and 5. Correspondence on Emigration from India.

Printed

Newspapers and Gazettes

Jamaica Gazette, New Series and Supplements. 1870–1916.

Illustrated London News, 1881

Daily Chronicle (Guyana), 1885–1886

Royal Gazette (Guyana), 1885–1886

Argosy (Guyana), 1885–1886

Published Reports

1871. *Report of the Commissioners Appointed to Enquire into the Treatment of Immigrants in British Guiana, 1871.* British Parliamentary Papers (annual series), XX (C. 393).

1874. *Report by J. Geohagen on Emigration from India. 1874.* British Parliamentary Papers (annual series) XLVII (314).

1883. *Report on Colonial Emigration from the Bengal Presidency* (Grierson Report). Calcutta, 25 February 1883.

1910. *Report of the Committee on Emigration from India to the Crown Colonies and Protectorates* (Sanderson Commission). British Parliamentary Papers, XXVII (Cd.5192–94), 1910.

1915. *Report on the Conditions of Indian Immigrants in the Four British Colonies (Trinidad, British Guiana [Demerara], Jamaica and Fiji)* (McNeil and Lal Report). British Parliamentary Papers (annual series), XLVII (Cd. 7744), 1915.

SECONDARY SOURCES

Pre-1900

Atwood, Thomas. *The History of the Island of Dominica.* 1791. Reprint, London: Frank Cass, 1971.

Beaumont, Joseph. *The New Slavery: An Account of the Indian and Chinese Immigrants in British Guiana.* London: W. Ridgeway, 1871.

Canot, Captain Theodore. *Twenty Years an African Slaver.* New York: 1854.

Cochin, Augustin. *The Results of Emancipation.* Translated by Mary Booth. Boston: Walker, Wise and Co., 1863.

Falconbridge, Alexander. *An Account of the Slave Trade on the Coast of Africa.* London: J. Phillips, 1788.

Kirke, Henry. *Twenty-Five Years in British Guiana.* 1898. Reprint, Westport, Conn.: Negro Universities Press, 1970.

Long, Edward. *The History of Jamaica.* 3 vols. London: T. Lowndes, 1774.

Modern

Adamson, Alan. *Sugar without Slaves: The Political Economy of British Guiana.* New Haven: Yale University Press, 1972.

————. "The Reconstruction of Plantation Labour after Emancipation: The Case of British Guiana". In *Race and Slavery in the Western Hemisphere,* edited by S. Engerman and E. Genovese, 457–73. Princeton: Princeton University Press, 1975.

Afshar, Haleh, and Mary Maynard, eds. *The Dynamics of "Race" and Gender: Some Feminist Interventions.* London: Taylor and Francis, 1994.

Anderson, Bonnie, and Judith Zinsser. *A History of Their Own: Women in Europe from Pre-History to the Present.* Vol. 11. New York: Harper and Row, 1988.

Arora, G.S. *Indian Emigration.* New Delhi: Puja Publishers, 1991.

Barrow, Christine, ed. *Caribbean Portraits: Essays on Gender, Ideologies and Identities.* Kingston: Ian Randle Publishers, 1998.

Beall, Jo. "Women under Indenture in Colonial Natal". In *Essays on Indentured Indians in Natal,* edited by Surendra Bhana, 89–115. Leeds: Peepal Tree Press, 1991.

Beckles, Hilary McD. *Afro-Caribbean Women and Resistance to Slavery in Barbados.* London: Karnak House, 1988.

————. *Natural Rebels: A Social History of Enslaved Black Women in Barbados.* London: Zed, 1989.

————. *Centering Woman: Gender Discourses in Caribbean Slavery.* Kingston: Ian Randle Publishers, 1999.

Beckles, Hilary McD., and Verene Shepherd, eds. *Caribbean Freedom: Economy and Society from Emancipation to the Present.* Kingston: Ian Randle Publishers, 1993.

Birbalsingh, Frank, ed. *Indenture and Exile: The Indo-Caribbean Experience.* Toronto: Tsar Press, 1989.

Bolster, W. Jeffrey. *Black Jacks: African American Seamen in the Age of Sail.* Cambridge, Mass.: Harvard University Press, 1997.

Brathwaite, Kamau. "Submerged Mothers". *Jamaica Journal* 9, nos. 2 and 3 (1975): 48–49.

————. *Women of the Caribbean during Slavery.* Elsa Goveia Memorial Lecture. Cave Hill, Barbados: Department of History, University of the West Indies, 1984.

Brereton, Bridget. "General Problems and Issues in Studying the History of Women". In *Gender in Caribbean Development,* edited by Patricia Mohammed and Catherine Shepherd, 123–41. St Augustine, Trinidad: Women and Development Studies Project, University of the West Indies, 1988.

————. "Text, Testimony and Gender: An Examination of Some Texts by Women on the English-Speaking Caribbean from the 1770s to the 1920s". In *Engendering History: Caribbean Women in Historical Perspective*, edited by Verene Shepherd, Bridget Brereton and Barbara Bailey, 63–93. Kingston: Ian Randle Publishers, 1995.

Bush, Barbara. *Slave Women in Caribbean Society, 1650–1838.* London: James Currey, 1990.

Cahill, Ann J. *Rethinking Rape.* Ithaca: Cornell University Press, 2001.

Carter, Marina, and James Ng Foong Kwong. *Forging the Rainbow: Labour Immigrants in British Mauritius.* Mauritius: Alfran, 1997.

Carter, Marina. *Lakshmi's Legacy: The Testimonies of Indian Women in Nineteenth Century Mauritius.* Mauritius: Editions de l'Océan Indien, 1994.

————. *Voices from Indenture: Experiences of Indian Migrants in the British Empire.* London: Leicester University Press, 1996.

Chaturvedi, Vinayak, ed. *Mapping Subaltern Studies and the Postcolonial.* London: Verso Press, 2000.

Cottman, Michael H. *The Wreck of the Henrietta Marie: An African-American's Spiritual Journey to Uncover a Sunken Slave Ship's Past.* New York: Harmony Books, 1999.

Dabydeen, David, and Brinsley Samaroo, eds. *India in the Caribbean.* London: Hansib, 1987.

Dyhouse, Carol. *Feminism and the Family in England, 1880–1939.* Oxford: Blackwell, 1989.

Eisner, Gisela. *Jamaica 1830–1930: A Study in Economic Growth.* Manchester: Manchester University Press, 1961.

Eltis, David. *The Rise of African Slavery in the Americas.* Cambridge: Cambridge University Press, 2000.

Emmer, Pieter. "The Great Escape: The Migration of Female Indentured Servants from British India into Suriname". In *Abolition and its Aftermath,* edited by D. Richardson, 245–66. London: Frank Cass, 1985.

Ferguson, Moira. *Subject to Others: British Women Writers and Colonial Slavery, 1670–1834.* London: Routledge, 1992.

Galenson, David. "The Rise and Fall of Indentured Servitude: An Economic Analysis". *Journal of Economic History* 44, no. 1 (1984): 1–26.

Gates, Henry Louis, Jr., and William L. Andrews, eds. *Pioneers of the Black Atlantic: Five Slave Narratives from the Enlightenment, 1772–1815.* Washington, D.C.: Counterpoint, 1998.

Hall, Douglas. "The Flight from the Estates Reconsidered". *Journal of Caribbean History* 10 and 11 (1978): 7–24.

————. *In Miserable Slavery: Thomas Thistlewood in Jamaica, 1750–1786.* London: Macmillan, 1989.

Higgins, Lynn A., and Brenda R. Silver. *Rape and Representation.* New York: Columbia University Press, 1991.

Higman, Barry. "Household Structure and Fertility on Jamaican Slave Plantations: A Nineteenth Century Example". *Population Studies* 27, no. 3 (1973): 527–50.

————. "The Slave Populations of the British Caribbean: Some Nineteenth Century Variations". *Social History* 9, no. 18 (1976): 237–55.

————. *Slave Society and Economy in Jamaica, 1807–1834.* Cambridge: Cambridge University Press, 1976.

————. *Slave Populations of the British Caribbean, 1807–1834.* Baltimore: Johns Hopkins University Press, 1984.

Hoefte, Rosemarijn. "Female Indentured Labour in Suriname: For Better or Worse?". *Boletin de Estudios Latinoamericanos y del Caribe* 42 (1987): 55–70.

————. *In Place of Slavery: A Social History of British Indian and Javanese Laborers in Suriname.* Gainesville: University of Florida Press, 1998.

Holt, Thomas. *The Problem of Freedom.* Baltimore: Johns Hopkins University Press, 1992.

Jain, Shobita, and Rhoda Reddock, eds. *Women Plantation Workers: International Experiences.* New York: Berg, 1998.

Kale, Madhavi. *Fragments of Empire.* Philadelphia: University of Pennsylvania Press, 1998.

Kelly, Joan. *Women, History and Theory: The Essays of Joan Kelly.* Chicago: University of Chicago Press, 1984.

Kimmel, Michael. *The Gendered Society.* New York: Oxford University Press, 2000.

Klein, Herbert S. *The Middle Passage: Comparative Studies in the Atlantic Slave Trade.* Princeton: Princeton University Press, 1978.

Lal, Brij. *Girmitiyas: The Origins of the Fiji Indians.* Canberra: Australian National University/Asian and Pacific Studies, 1983.

————. "Kunti's Cry: Indentured Women on Fiji Plantations". *Indian Economic and Social History Review* 22, no. 1 (1985): 55–72.

Laslett, Peter. *The World We Have Lost – Further Explored.* London: Routledge, 1988.

Laurence, K.O. *Immigration into the West Indies in the Nineteenth Century.* Barbados: Caribbean Universities Press, 1971.

————. *A Question of Labour.* Kingston: Ian Randle Publishers, 1994.

Leo-Rhynie, Elsa, et al., eds., *Gender: A Caribbean Multi-Disciplinary Perspective.* Kingston: Ian Randle Publishers, 1997.

Look Lai, Walton. *Indentured Labor, Caribbean Sugar: Chinese and Indian Migrants to the British West Indies.* Baltimore: Johns Hopkins University Press, 1993.

Lorber, Judith, and Susan A. Farrel, eds. *The Social Construction of Gender.* London: Sage, 1991.

Mahabir, Kumar Noor, comp. *The Still Cry: Personal Accounts of East Indians in Trinidad and Tobago during Indentureship, 1845–1917.* Tacarigua, Trinidad: Calaloux Publications, 1985.

Mandle, Jay. *The Plantation Economy: Population and Economic Change in Guyana, 1838–1960.* Philadelphia: Temple University Press, 1973.

Mangru, Basdeo. *Benevolent Neutrality: Indian Government Policy and Labour Migration to British Guiana 1854–1884.* London: Hansib, 1987.

Marshall, Woodville. *The Post-Slavery "Labour Problem" Revisited.* Elsa Goveia Memorial Lecture. Mona, Jamaica: Department of History, University of the West Indies, 1991.

Mathurin Mair, Lucille. *The Rebel Woman in the British West Indies During Slavery.* Kingston: Institute of Jamaica, 1975.

McCalman, Ian, ed. *The Horrors of Slavery and Other Writings by Robert Wedderburn.* Princeton: Markus Wiener, 1991.

McDonald, John, and Ralph Shlomowitz. "Mortality on Chinese and Indian Voyages to the West Indies and South America 1847–1874". *Social and Economic Studies* 41, no. 2 (1992): 203–40.

Midgley, Clare, ed. *Gender and Imperialism.* Manchester: Manchester University Press, 1998.

Mintz, Sidney. "A Note on the Definition of Peasantries". *Journal of Peasant Studies* 1 (1973): 91–106.

Mohammed, Patricia. "Writing Gender into History". In *Engendering History: Caribbean Women in Historical Perspective,* edited by Verene Shepherd, Bridget Brereton and Barbara Bailey, 20–47. Kingston: Ian Randle Publishers, 1995.

Mohammed, Patricia, and Catherine Shepherd, eds. *Gender in Caribbean Development.* St Augustine, Trinidad: Women and Development Studies Project, University of the West Indies, 1988.

Moore, Brian. *Race, Power and Social Segmentation in a Colonial Society: Guyana after Slavery.* London: Gordon and Breach, 1987.

———. *Cultural Power, Resistance and Pluralism: Colonial Guyana, 1838–1900.* Kingston: The Press, University of the West Indies, 1995.

Morrissey, Marrietta. *Slave Women in the New World: Gender Stratification in the New World.* Lawrence: University of Kansas Press, 1989.

Nath, Dwarka. *A History of Indians in Guyana.* London: Thomas Nelson, 1950.

Nicholson, Linda. *Gender and History: The Limits of Social Theory in the Age of the Family.* New York: Columbia University Press, 1986.

Northrup, David. *Indentured Labour in the Age of Imperialism, 1834–1922.* Cambridge: Cambridge University Press, 1995.

Paiewonsky, Isidor. *Eyewitness Accounts of Slavery in the Danish West Indies, Also Graphic Tales of Other Slave Happenings on Ships and Plantations.* New York: Fordham University Press, 1989.

Patterson, Orlando. *The Sociology of Slavery: An Analysis of the Origins, Development and Structure of Negro Slave Society in Jamaica.* London: McGibbon and Kee, 1967.

Pool, Gail R., and Hira Singh. "Indentured Indian Women of the Empire: Between Colonial Oppression and the Brahmanical Tradition". *Plantation Society in the Americas* 6, no. 1 (Spring 1999): 1–46.

Poynting, Jeremy. "East Indian Women in the Caribbean: Experience and Voice". In *India in the Caribbean,* edited by David Dabydeen and Brinsley Samaroo, 231–63. London: Hansib, 1987.

Ramdin, Ron. *The Other Middle Passage: Journal of a Voyage from Calcutta to Trinidad, 1858.* London: Hansib, 1994.

Reddock, Rhoda. *Women and Garment Production in Trinidad and Tobago, 1900–1960.* The Hague: Institute of Social Studies, 1984.

———. "Indian Women and Indentureship in Trinidad and Tobago 1845–1917: Freedom Denied". *Caribbean Quarterly,* 32 (1986): 27–47.

———. *Women, Labour and Politics in Trinidad and Tobago: A History.* London: Zed Books, 1994.

———. "Women and Slavery in the Caribbean: A Feminist Perspective". *Latin American Perspectives* 12, no. 1 (1995): 63–80.

Robertson, Claire, and Martin Klein, eds. *Women and Slavery in Africa.* Madison: University of Wisconsin Press, 1983.

Rodney, Walter. *A History of the Guyanese Working People, 1881–1905.* Baltimore: Johns Hopkins University Press, 1981.

Satchell, Veront. *From Plots to Plantations.* Kingston: Institute of Social and Economic Research, University of the West Indies, 1990.

Scott, Joan W. *Gender and the Politics of History.* New York: Columbia University Press, 1988.

Seecharan, Clem. *Tiger in the Stars: The Anatomy of Indian Achievement in British Guiana, 1919–29.* London: Macmillan, 1997.

Seenarine, Moses. "Indentured Women in Colonial Guyana". In *Sojourners to Settlers: Indian Migrants in the Caribbean and the Americas,* edited by Mahin Gosine and Dhanpaul Narine, 36–66. New York: Windsor Press, 1999.

Shepherd, Verene."Emancipation through Servitude?" *Bulletin of the Society for the Study of Labour History* 53, no. 3 (1988): 13–19.

————. *Transients to Settlers: The Experience of Indians in Jamaica, 1845–1945.* Leeds and Warwick: Peepal Tree Press and University of Warwick, 1994.

————. "The Politics of Migration: Government Policy towards Indians in Jamaica, 1845–1945". In *Before and After 1865: Education, Politics and Regionalism in the Caribbean,* edited by Brian Moore and Swithin Wilmot, 177–89. Kingston: Ian Randle Publishers, 1998.

————. *Emancipation and Immigration: A Pan Caribbean Overview.* Kingston: Verene Shepherd, 1999.

————, ed. and comp. *Women in Caribbean History.* Kingston: Ian Randle Publishers, 1999.

————. "Poverty, Exploitation and Agency among Indian Immigrants and Settlers in Jamaica: Some Evidence from Twentieth-Century Letters". *Journal of Caribbean Studies* (special issue, edited by Frank Birbalsingh) 14, nos. 1 and 2 (1999–2000): 93–116.

Shepherd, Verene, Bridget Brereton, and Barbara Bailey, eds. *Engendering History: Caribbean Women in Historical Perspective.* Kingston: Ian Randle Publishers, 1995.

Smith, Raymond T. "Some Social Characteristics of Indian Immigrants to British Guiana". *Population Studies* 13, no. 1 (1959): 34–39.

Spivak, Gayatri C. "Can the Subaltern Speak?" In *Colonial Discourse and Post-Colonial Theory: A Reader,* edited by Patrick Williams and Laura Chrisman, 66–111. London: Harvester-Wheatsheaf, 1993.

Thakur, Rishee S. "East Indians in Caribbean Historiography". In *Indenture and Exile: The Indo-Caribbean Experience,* edited by F. Birbalsingh, 207–17. Toronto: Tsar Press, 1989.

Thompson, Alvin. "Historical Writing on Migration into the Commonwealth Caribbean: A Bibliographical Review of the Period *c.*1838–*c.*1938". *Immigrants and Minorities* 5, no. 2 (1986): 145–66.

Tinker, Hugh. *A New System of Slavery: The Export of Indian Labourers Overseas.* London: Oxford University Press, 1974.

Trotman, David. "Women and Crime in Late Nineteenth Century Trinidad". *Caribbean Quarterly* 30, nos. 3 and 4 (1984): 60–72.

Trouillot, Michel Rolph. *Peasants and Capital: Dominica in the World Economy.* Baltimore: Johns Hopkins University Press, 1988.

Vassell, Linnette, comp. *Voices of Women.* Mona, Jamaica: Department of History, University of the West Indies, 1993.

———. "Women of the Masses". In *Engendering History: Caribbean Women in Historical Perspective,* edited by Verene Shepherd, Bridget Brereton and Barbara Bailey, 318–33. Kingston: Ian Randle Publishers, 1995.

Vigarello, Georges. *A History of Rape: Sexual Violence in France from the Sixteenth to the Twentieth Century.* Cambridge: Polity Press, 2001.

Wiesner, Merry E. *Women and Gender in Early Modern Europe.* Cambridge: Cambridge University Press, 1993.

Unpublished Manuscripts, Papers and Theses

Diptee, Audra. "Indian Men, Afro-Creole Women: Casting Doubt on Inter-Racial Sexual Relationships in the Late Nineteenth Century Caribbean". Typescript. (Forthcoming in *Immigrants and Minorities.*)

Lal, Brij. "Crossing the Kali Pani". Manuscript, 1999.

Mathurin, Lucille. "A Historical Study of Women in Jamaica". PhD diss., University of the West Indies, Mona, Jamaica, 1974.

Mohammed, Patricia. "A Social History of Post-Migrant Indians in Trinidad from 1917–1947: A Gender Perspective". PhD diss., Institute of Social Studies, The Hague, 1994.

Samaroo, Brinsley. "The Caribbean Consequences of the Indian Revolt of 1857". Paper presented at the conference Asian Migrations to the Americas, University of the West Indies, St Augustine, Trinidad, 11–17 August 2000.

Shepherd, Verene, "Journey Interrupted: Maharani's Misery on the *Allanshaw* to Colonial Guyana". Paper presented to the Social History Symposium, University of the West Indies, Mona, Jamaica, April 2000.

———. "Daughter of Pargas: Investigating 'Criminal Assault' on Nineteenth Century Emigrant Ships to the Colonial Caribbean". Paper presented to the York/University of Warwick Post-Emancipation Conference, July 2000.

———. "Maharani's Misery: Narratives of a Passage from India". Paper presented to the conference Asian Migrations to the Americas, University of the West Indies, St Augustine, Trinidad, 11–17 August 2000.

INDEX

Adamson, Alan: analysis of reactions to Maharani's rape, 70–71

African-Caribbean: and the growth of Guyanese peasantry, 5

African women: comparison between treatment of Indian and, xviii–xix

Agreement for intending: example of form of, 37

Aladin: depot marriage of Asserum and, 79

Alexander, A.L.: and the inquiry into Maharani's rape and death, 47, 48, 64–66, 70–71

Allanshaw, xiii–xiv, xix; conduct of the crew on the, 96, 99; conduct of officers and Indian women on the, 62–63, 68–69, 85–86, 89, 91–92; emigrants on the, 33; incidents on the, 25–26; investigation, xxii–xxviii, 33–44, 45–73; mortality rates on the, 23, 24, 67–68, 86–87, 100; sexually transmitted diseases on the, 67–68, 136, 138

Alnwick Castle: sex ratio among Indian immigrants on the, 6

Anti-Slavery Society: and Indian immigration, 9

Asserum: depot marriage of Aladin and, 79

Atkins, Dr: marriage to Indian immigrant Janky, 30–31

Bain, Alexander: conduct of, 137; testimony of, 115–118

Bambury, G.A.: and the *Allanshaw* investigation, 45–47

Blacks: maritime occupation of, 26–27;

sexual abuse of Indian women by, 28, 29

Blundell: sex ratio among Indian immigrants on the, 6

British Guiana. *See* Guyana.

Bruce, Charles: recommendations on the Maharani inquiry, 71–72

Canning: prostitution on the, 77

Caribbean: Indian immigration into the, 4

Caste: issue in Indian immigration, 11

Class: myths re sexuality and, 78

Clintworth, William: relationship between Ipson and, 103; report of Ipson's rape of Maharani by, 137; testimony of, 137; testimony against Ipson by, 47, 56; Wilson on, 90

Chapman: complaints against surgeon-superintendent, 24

Chitamun: report of rape of Maharani by, 133, 142; testimony of, 55, 146; witness of Maharani's rape, 54

Colonial Office: reaction to the Maharani inquiry, 72–73

Commission of Enquiry (into Maharani's rape), 43–44, 48–73; findings, 64, 76, 78

Conduct of officers and crew: on the *Allanshaw,* 62–63, 68–69, 85–86, 89–90, 91–92, 94, 96, 99, 101–102, 103–105, 111

Cooks: on emigrant ships, 21

Crew (*Allanshaw*): de la Mare on the conduct of the, 113, 117–118, 120–121, 123–125, 130–131, 134